WHAT THE BEARS KNOW

WHAT THE BEARS KNOW

HOW I FOUND TRUTH AND MAGIC IN AMERICA'S MOST MISUNDERSTOOD CREATURES

STEVE SEARLES
AND CHRIS ERSKINE

PEGASUS BOOKS

NEW YORK LONDON

WHAT THE BEARS KNOW

Pegasus Books, Ltd.
148 West 37th Street, 13th Floor
New York, NY 10018

First Pegasus Books cloth edition October 2023

Interior design by Maria Fernandez

Library of Congress Cataloging-in-Publication Data is available.

ISBN: 978-1-63936-501-2

10 9 8 7 6 5 4 3 2

Printed in the United States of America
Distributed by Simon & Schuster
www.pegasusbooks.com

For our sons

CONTENTS

When the bears sleep, I sleep—right under the trees.
—Steve Searles, on his field study of black bears

🐾

It's hard to know if the bears are his spirit animal, or it's the other way around.
—Peter Alagona, environmental studies professor, UC Santa Barbara

🐾

Let Nature be your teacher.
—William Wordsworth

INTRODUCTION

In the late 1990s, the snow-globe village of Mammoth Lakes, California, hired hunter Steve Searles to shoot and kill sixteen troublesome bears. In the course of his preparations, the bears won Steve over, and he soon developed nonlethal tactics to keep them out of harm's way.

This memoir honors Steve's benchmark-setting work. But it salutes the bears as much as it does Steve, each bear offering a different lesson in such virtues as patience, dignity, and tenacity.

In time, Steve becomes a local folk hero, a reality TV star, and a nationally recognized expert in the humane treatment of animals. Don't tell Steve that. The gruff outdoorsman will quickly remind you the bears are the only heroes in this mountain hamlet five hours north of Los Angeles.

The most important life lessons come from them.

Experts say dogs can sense human sadness. To Steve, bears share an empathy that is even beyond that—almost a moral compass, an innate gentleness—that guides them in their encounters with man and beast.

Displaying the same adventurous spirit as Henry David Thoreau and John Muir, Steve Searles finds a fellowship with nature. Do bears understand things we don't? Are they dialed in to some greater mystical force, some sort of bear magic?

At first glance, this is simple stuff: the memoir of a reposeful naturalist, and the bears he saved from death row, and a template for how we can better live together in this shared world. You'll find this story to be not only a deep dive into one of the last wilderness areas in the American West, but also about the toll fear takes on all of us. And how fear leads to prejudice. And how knowledge is always better than bullets.

Close readers may find the timeline a little off. To tell the most compelling story possible, we adjusted some of the sequences. We took no liberties in the facts or the events themselves, just the relative order of them. Neither is this a textbook on the history of Mammoth's bears. It relies, almost wholly, on Steve's boots-on-the-ground experiences, as well as news clips, TV, and documentary projects and two years of extensive interviews I did with him. Together, I hope we captured the single-minded intensity, and the love, he has for his wildlife work.

Over the years, Steve also had to "put down" many animals that were injured by cars, ill, or wounded by hunters or other bears. There was never bloodlust involved. In fact, quite the opposite: Usually the mercy killings tore at his gut. In the course of his career, Steve believes he's probably euthanized more bears than any man on Earth, all necessary, all to put them out of their anguish.

This is some heavy stuff.

Forgive his language, for it is often colorful. Forgive his actions. Though necessary, they were often rough. Hence, the chronic silent battles Steve faced that often manifested themselves in anguish and even tears.

With total respect, I will tell you that Steve's a true weirdo, a real wack job, a total individual. I loved every minute of working with him, learning the way his keen mind works, his insights into worlds usually far beyond human comprehension.

Steve has a practical IQ that gets him through unique situations with bears. He always put this magnificent land and its inhabitants before himself. And, damn, is he ever entertaining. He is truly one of the most fascinating people I've ever met.

In the words of Jack Kerouac, who seems a kindred spirit, Steve runs "from one falling star to another."

This is his star-kissed life story. I hope you find it as layered and poignant as I do.

—Chris Erskine

CHAPTER ONE

BEARS, BEARS EVERYWHERE

Inch by inch, hour by hour, the flames are bearing down on us. We are a town under siege.

Through the same canyons that usually funnel wind, rain, and snow to Mammoth Lakes, comes a wall of fire unlike anything anyone has ever seen. Plush and super dry, the forest floor may as well be laced with lighter fluid.

The epic high winds feed a fire so hot it sterilizes entire swaths of wilderness. It is the potential apocalypse of all I hold dear—lakes, mountains, trees, animals, my house, my neighbors, my son.

My town, Mammoth Lakes, is almost a parable. Everything except locusts has hit the Sierra Nevada region since I moved here: floods, droughts, blizzards, avalanches, quakes, and, most destructive of all, this ferocious wildfire.

Thick, acrid ash falls during this 2020 fire. From this ornery orange sky, dregs of poison oak smear our faces, plug our tear ducts and noses. The next day, it's the manzanita that burns, a scruffy plant used in folk medicine. In short time, we become connoisseurs of our burning forests. We breathe it.

We eat it warm. It is as if someone has opened a giant urn. The ash isn't just wood ash and leaves; it is forest life, scorched.

We can feel it lumpy under our eyelids.

Nothing is surviving. Tree roots are burning underground. The nests of bald eagles, often reused for years, are scattered in this stinging ash fall, which includes the remains of tens of thousands of fleeing forest creatures.

How can I be so sure of this mass cremation? Because the mountain town of Mammoth Lakes, with its beltways of creeks and golf courses, its sprinkler systems and its pools, would have been their only escape route, their interstate out of the savage Creek Fire, as it is named. There is no Pixar parade of fleeing animals, though. They simply vanish, the deer running till their lungs explode, followed by bobcat, cougar, raccoons, porcupines, owls, skunks, moths, chipmunks, even the worms that churn and condition the soil.

The quivering aspen and the pines—lodgepole, Jeffrey, pinyon—all gone. The forest floor is wiped out—manzanita, buckwheat, bitterbrush, goldenrod, black oak, mule ear, and ferns. The nectar in the flowers, the wings of butterflies, sterilized and possibly gone for a generation or more, all the seeds cooked, along with hopes of a rapid and glorious recovery. We are witnessing the death of an ecosystem, an entire food chain falling on us now in an awful gray and black confetti.

By now, Americans know all about wildfires—we've been living with them and hearing of them for years. What makes the Creek Fire different, what raises the stakes, is that this is an especially magical piece of the planet, a carousel of national parks and wilderness areas. All appear at risk: the Ansel Adams Wilderness, the John Muir Wilderness, Yosemite National Park. The vaunted Pacific Crest Trail runs through Reds Meadow. Long-distance hikers heading to Canada will lay up for five or six days here, have a fling, play the flute, pound a burger, drink an ice-cold beer.

When outsiders ask me if the Sierra Nevada has ample wildlife, I wait a beat, then answer in my Sam Elliott growl: "It's Jurassic Park."

In essence, this is a sanctuary city for all manner of wildlife, a place that attracts and protects its forest creatures. After forty-four years up here, I've learned to read these woods. I can tell the time of year by the spots on the fawns wading a mountain creek. I can read the shadows, the sunlight, the chatter of the geese as if they are the pages of a kitchen calendar.

This is spectacular terrain, fierce and fragile, among the loveliest regions on Earth. The spirits of John Muir and Ansel Adams still roar through these tall granite canyons. Take particular note of the veritable wind tunnel that delivers rain, ocean winds, and—starting around Halloween—epic snows. By late December, we're the North Pole—so much snow that we hot-wax our shovels, as you would a set of skis. In winter, the air is especially fresh, as if it's just been born.

Indeed, this is California's Switzerland, well-muscled, almost brutally snowy. Come January, the icicles alone—big as tree trunks—could kill you. All winter long, they cleave off the roofs of cabins and hotels, another lethal reminder that winter up here is a form of war.

Most times, this tunnel of winds and wet storms is a superhighway of much-needed moisture and snow for Mammoth Lakes, a tourist town five hours north of Los Angeles. In winter, it coats the world-class ski runs and half-pipes where gold medalists such as Shaun White and Chloe Kim train. In summer, it feeds the crystalline rivers and lakes popular with fishermen. The hurricane-force winds, frequently topping one hundred miles per hour, ruffle these mountains a bit, adding movement to the painterly landscape and knocking loose the seeds that will be the next generation of pine trees, gusts that scatter the bees, the pollen, the fuzz of the wildflowers.

When the winds hit one hundred miles per hour in Florida, it's the lead story on CNN, the talk of Twitter. Here, no one says a thing. We go on with our lives and head out to the hardware store—just another day in this frosty paradise.

Mammoth Lakes is also a vital headwater. A snowflake that falls atop a black-diamond ski run might end up in someone's iced tea in Pasadena. It might come off the mountain on the tip of someone's snowboard, melt into a parking lot storm drain, feed a gushing creek on the way to reservoirs that flow into the canals that loop all the way to Southern California.

The Eastern Sierra is to drinking water what Wisconsin is to cheese. We are the kitchen faucet for millions of humans, dogs, cats, canaries, horses.

Obviously, this is a very abundant place, the glint of sun coming through those massive icicles, across a snowy tree branch, over the cross-country trails, the waterfalls, the *On Golden Pond*–caliber lakes filled with rainbow trout. Sometimes it feels almost greedy, this bounty, just miles away from the stubble of the relatively dormant desert. In Mammoth, this lush and popular pocket of the Eastern Sierra, we have too much of everything: water, snow, coyotes, tourists, cheeseburgers, putting greens, ski shops. Most notably, perhaps, bears.

The bears are where I come in.

Over three decades, I have been the bears' gruff camp director. As the town's wildlife specialist, reporting to the chief of police, I have been responsible for all the black bears that decided, among other things, that a schoolyard is a nice place for a nap. Or that a luxury hotel lobby is a convenient place to grab some calamari. Or that someone's Range Rover still smelled of the peanut butter sandwiches the kids left half-eaten under a seat. To a bear, that's bait. Hey, why not punch out a window and climb inside, tear up the seats, set off the air bags, gnaw the expensive leather on the steering wheel? Yum.

I was the one-man SWAT team that responded when any of that happened. If you dialed 9-1-1 and shouted *BEAR!*, I was the ponytailed first responder, roaring up in my white pickup and getting out with my trademark orange shotgun.

Known as the Bear Whisperer, I shooed and snarled at the five-hundred-pound trespassers, cowboy-cussed them, even shot them with nonlethal rubber balls to get them out of harm's way, off highways, and out of hot tubs and parking garages.

My career was crazy and remarkable. Somehow, I still have both arms, both legs. In fact, in all the years of crawling into bear dens to study their sleep habits, to watch them birth their babies, in all the years of confronting bears, nose to nose, in culverts and cabins, in trapezing lost cubs out of tall trees, I haven't suffered a single scratch.

Yet, in the late summer of 2020, this incredible life, this extraordinary stretch of bear magic, seems to have run its course.

Only the bears—the kings of the forest—manage to make it out of this firebox. In Mammoth Lakes, they begin showing up by the dozens, parched and frightened beyond measure. It is a California black bear's nature to do as little as possible, to conserve body mass. Bears are constant eaters, gorging themselves with seeds, wasp larvae, grasses—the occasional cheeseburger—to survive long winters snoozing in their dens.

So, the bears haven't panicked the way the other animals have, haven't run themselves to exhaustion. They stay only as far in front of the fire as absolutely necessary.

Now here they are, sooty and disoriented, the newcomers clashing with the bears that already reside here. It is as if two conventions have come to town, when we only have the space for one.

You and I, we use our noses to keep our glasses on, or to sniff an occasional IPA. The bears' noses are their sensory command centers. Their range can be measured in miles, their snouts thousands of times more powerful than ours. They use them to sniff out food, to anticipate changes in the weather and the seasons, to determine where the fresh water is, maybe a colony of bees, or where someone left some shrimp shells in the trash. They use them for romance; they use them to know when it's time to climb into their dens for five months when it snows.

In the normal course of my work, I might see eleven bears on a busy fall day, when they're preparing to go into their dens for winter. Now there are at least three dozen in our four-square-mile town. At least, that is how many I'm able to count. There could be twice as many here, the others hiding in the shadows, under decks, and behind the drapes of empty cabins. Generally, bears don't like the limelight. Like me, they prefer to exist in the margins.

With their snouts caked in fire ash, the fleeing bears are essentially blind. They can't source food, or sense enemies or territorial boundaries. Their lungs are parched, their kidneys starved for replenishment. At my urging, hundreds of residents leave five-gallon buckets of drinking water on their porches at night; the water is gone by morning. Inexplicably, at least to me, authorities are telling residents not to leave out water, saying animals will develop a dependency. Instead, they should rely on streams and lakes miles away.

I sit on my porch in the center of the village, at the cabin that has been my longtime home, and watch the bears' tragic migration. It probably hits me harder than most.

For I am this town's wildlife officer, known through countless encounters as the go-to guy when wildlife is in distress, particularly these misunderstood, quarter-ton outcasts.

I know very well that grizzly bears, shot to extinction in California, are alpha predators; they'll eat the tire off your truck. By comparison, all a California black bear wants to do is mow your lawn. They are the tie-dyed hippies of the bear kingdom.

Still, they get into more mischief than you'd hope. They learn faster than we do, good or bad—where to find free food and lodging, all the life basics, even where to find a fridge full of cold cuts and beer.

Since the late 1990s, I have chased them out of the grocery stores, the condos, the tourists' big SUVs. Bears have been in so many homes, often more than once, that I've lost count. Certain parts of town are almost a wildlife park. Everyone has my cell number (937-BEAR) in their phones.

Across the decades, I have tied myself financially and emotionally to these bears.

Now they need me more than ever. But my career has just come to a sudden, dramatic end. COVID has descended on Mammoth, just as it has on the rest of the world, triggering fear, confusion, and the kinds of heated debates that end friendships: During a pandemic, should a tourist town welcome outsiders, hoping the wilderness will be safe and restorative? Or should it hide and hunker down like everyone else?

There is a showdown over that, everyone panicky and in each other's faces, including me, a longtime resident with a few valid opinions.

As if all that isn't enough, the largest wildfire in California to date is now on the doorstep of my cherished little town, threatening to eat it whole, causing this mass migration of bears.

Now, you should know that I'm six-foot-five and noisy as a chainsaw, rough as ship rope. I'm gnarly, not easily spooked. I even look like a bear, more handsome than some, less than others.

I've thrived in this demanding region of lethal winters and fiery summers for almost half a century. I can fix anything, hammer together hotels, race a bike, chase a raccoon out from under your favorite pillow after he's shredded your couch while digging for stale popcorn.

Indeed, I've prepared my entire life for 9-1-1 moments like this one. Till now, I've always risen to the occasion, stood up against tough guys and rogue bears in near-impossible standoffs and on a popular reality show that reached the far corners of the planet.

Yet, here I am after the job loss, at a personal low point, so inconsolable I can barely breathe. The hopelessness of the situation is crushing me.

I am surrounded by these bears that have been my life's work. Bears, bears, everywhere, lost and in need.

To me, their ghostly presence is perhaps the most surreal element of all.

CHAPTER TWO

A GOPHER IN MY GLOVE

I grew up in Orange County, California, a land of pavement, palm trees, and toothy smiles, certainly a long way from the pine needles and waterfalls of Mammoth Lakes, a half day's drive to the north.

As a young boy, I am passed around like an old college couch. Everybody wants to get rid of me, nobody really has the time. If it weren't for the verbal and physical abuse, I wouldn't know adults even existed. A dozen times, they kick me out of the house.

The pattern rarely changes: Everyday conversations quickly turn to arguments, turn to rage. At Christmas, police are in the living room. There are court dates . . . drinking, late parties, cheating. When I am in elementary school, I come home to an empty house and don't see any adults till the bars close.

When I am seven, my stepdad decides to do me a favor and teach me how to swim. He tosses me like a load of towels into the pool. I splash frantically, trying to suck in some air, kick and thrash to the edge of the pool, where he stomps my fingers, crushing them. As I shriek, he laughs.

We are like that dysfunctional family in the TV show *Shameless*. Maybe worse.

In the fifth grade, fed up with me, my folks put me in a camper shell, where I use the stove to keep warm. I am ten or eleven. I am the punchline in the old quip: the beatings will continue until attitudes improve.

The family fridge is like a liquor cabinet, the freezer full of TV dinners. I'll go to Mom's apartment, open the fridge for a snack—nothing but booze.

As the weakest link, the slowest and youngest of the three kids, a misfit, a loser, an obligation they don't want, I am beaten with a belt, slapped around, thrown into walls.

In the sixties, of course, children are expected to be seen, not heard. My folks and stepfolks take that seriously. We aren't allowed to speak at the dinner table, yet when I am in fifth grade my mother lets us all drink and smoke cigarettes around the table at Thanksgiving.

My sister, Stephanie, and my brother, Michael, and I pack for a weekend visitation with my estranged dad, and he doesn't show up. We sit on the curb with our suitcases in the dark, waiting. Finally, our mom comes out and says, "Come on, let's go inside."

Michael, the middle child, is an all-star baseball player and an all-star kid. Straight-A student. At twelve, he gets up well before school and picks up litter and cigarette butts for petty cash in restaurant parking lots. Over time, my brother saves $120 to buy a Schwinn Varsity ten-speed, the sweetest ride at the time, so he can get a paper route for the *Orange County Register* and save money to buy a car.

Even my brother, a standout in math, a near-genius with numbers, can't escape judgment, the angry accusations, the domestic tensions, the hair-trigger rages. "Don't look at me like that, you little . . ." The moment he turns eighteen, my brother packs up and moves out at first light. "See ya, Steve," he says. "Sorry, I gotta get out of here."

Our childhoods in the land of endless summers were very dark.

My folks are heavy partiers, ne'er-do-wells on almost every level of domestic life. Between the two of them, there are five marriages before I turn fifteen. They seem in competition on this—three weddings for Dad, two for Mom. I bounce between them, living with every single couple more than once.

I look around, see the developmental differences between me and my siblings, me and my classmates. There are so many. I just lag. Even putting on shoes and socks is a struggle. I don't know my left from my right.

And no one is around to insist that I be happy with myself, because nobody wants to be around me. I am a latchkey kid, on my own, unreliable, a modern-day Huckleberry screwup.

If you tell me not to do something, I do it. At age eight or ten, I am smoking cigarettes, playing with matches, setting dumpsters on fire behind the strip mall.

I am a misfit, an eight ball, that square peg. By adolescence, I am smoking weed and drinking beer.

To punish me, they like to send me off to the barber to have my head shaved, which I'm forced to pay for myself. This is in the late sixties, when everyone has flowing, bitchin' Bee Gees hair. Not me. I am in none of the class pictures. When the teacher tells everyone to come in the next day ready for the class picture—in good clothes, hair combed—I'll be sure to ditch school.

When we change for PE, my junior high classmates see the belt marks on my back. Buddies head to the gym office and say, "Coach, you gotta help Searles."

While I'm still in elementary school, my mother takes me to a skin doctor for open sores on my hips, chest, and face. Turns out I have cystic acne, a terrible skin condition no doubt compounded by a lousy diet and stress. I live with that through my late teens—years of torment and teasing over this disfiguring disease.

In my late teens, I go on my own to specialists, who use me as one of the early test cases for Accutane, now a common and often successful acne treatment. Derived from vitamin A, it reduces the amount of oils released by the glands.

Every inch of my skin falls off, like a shedding snake, compounding my bad self-esteem.

My education is spotty. I blow off my homework. No one pushes me, checks in on me. I don't read well. I am a slow learner. "He never does anything the way he's supposed to," my teachers say.

Mom sees I'm not a good student and not fitting in. Frustrated at my progress, she encourages me to read by letting me borrow sex books, including the *Kama Sutra*. I read them cover to cover in elementary school.

There are few family dinners, no road trips, no projects with Dad.

Unsure of what to do with me, my real mom puts me in Little League, hoping to add some structure to my life. Maybe I could be a good athlete like my brother? Maybe there'll be one thing I am good at: Checkers? Auto shop? Let's start with baseball, a rite of passage for Orange County kids in the 1960s.

So, there I am, standing in the outfield, at that age when players are still more intrigued by butterflies than fly balls.

"Get the ball, you idiot!" the parents scream at me standing lock legged in the outfield.

"That Searles out there?" I hear the parents say. I already knew I don't fit in at school. Now I don't fit in in the dugout, the outfield, anywhere. My coaches are as disappointed in me as my parents.

"Yep, that's the Searles kid."

"What an idiot."

"His brother Mike was super good . . . a prodigy . . . an all-star."

"Well, he sure ain't Mike."

Thing is, when that ball is hit to me in the outfield, I could not care less. Life has already left me numb to nastiness and heckling. What do I care that a bunch of strangers are screaming at me? Adults are always screaming at me, or worse. I just tune it out, like I do with all the other stuff.

Besides, I have something better in my glove than a baseball. While standing around the scruffy outfield, waiting for something to happen, easily distracted, as I so often am, I discover a gopher hole; the place is infested, maybe fifty two-inch mounds the gophers have made.

I kick at it, the way kids do. The hole is about the size of a golf ball and freshly dug on the awful sunbaked field. The jittery little rodent pops his head out, then withdraws.

Hey, come here, buddy. It's all right. Come here . . .

With bits of dandelion and grass—a slobbery piece of Bazooka bubble gum—I manage to coax the little critter out of his hole and into my glove. It takes an inning or two, and there he is, in the pocket of my baseball glove, warm and safe.

Though I'm not much good with people, I seem to have a knack for critters. Every now and then, he peeks out at me, then withdraws.

"Searles, get the ball!!!" the parents scream.

Yeah. Sure. Screw you.

One day, my sister tells the family that it is a very special day: "Steve didn't cry today! Not once!"

Immediately, I start to cry. So much for streaks.

Because of all the dysfunction, normal adults become heroes to me—people who smile at me or feed me wholesome food stand out. My godfather, Larry Freeman, and his wife, Mickey, show us there can be another side to family life. We go to their house, and instead of over-sugared Kool-Aid, he and his wife serve us apple juice. Larry and Mickey are a loving, caring couple who will look after me my entire life. They are like rainbows to a kid who's seen nothing but darkness for as long as I can remember.

They don't necessarily fix the problem; they just give me hope.

Still, I am a square peg in a round world, nothing like anybody else. Freeform. Feral. My childhood is an era marked by adolescent trends and tastes. Free love. Rock 'n' roll. Cheap weed. Honda motorcycles. Bleachy, beachy blondes in cutoffs. My friends and I work part-time jobs, listen to Hendrix. Most days, we stand on the wet and chilly Pacific sand with boards tucked under our arms, squinting into the mist, trying to read the surf breaks.

At sixteen, another rare sign of someone believing in me: my folks send me off to spend the summer in Colorado with my dad's father. My grandpa, a gentle man and an avid outdoorsman, teaches me the trees, the plants, the stars, the animals. It is an outcast's dream—all this new territory to explore. No crowds of kids to mock me, no adults yelling at me, no unhealthy temptations—just a 14,000-foot mountain.

For the first time in my life, I feel at home.

Once back in Southern California, though, my life continues to be nothing but bad drama. I drop out of school in the tenth grade, make a few bucks buying and repairing old bikes, then selling them at the beach. We advertise by having girlfriends in bikinis ride them down the strand. The girls take off on two bikes, then return twenty minutes later on one bike, one girl riding on the handlebars and waving a wad of fresh cash.

By then, I've moved to Newport Beach, a splashy enclave on the coast, where some buddies and I manage to pool our money and afford an apartment. Back then, Newport is a regular place, full of middle-class folks, not the high-end weekend escape that it is today.

I surf, I rack up tons of parking tickets, meet a girl named Julie Cena, who manages to find a tolerable person behind my angry teen-boy persona.

She sits in the lifeguard tower in the late afternoon, when the guards have gone home. In the glow of late afternoon, she wags her tan legs while watching me surf. Some of the guys I surf with are starting to find their way a little. My buddy Chris, who runs the bike business with me, is learning to be a deepwater welder, an actual career that could lead to a sustainable and comfortable life.

Me, I still have a little problem with responsibility. I am content to sell the bikes, surf a lot, drink beer, have bottle-rocket wars, make Julie giggle. Amid all my troubles—or because of them—I've developed a knack for making people laugh.

At sixteen, I don't have any money or anyone to take care of me. I buy a tool belt and carpenter tools, scuff them up so they don't look new, and head off to construction sites to find work. I approach a supervisor. He says he has no work. Without budging, I say, "Sir, I'll work my ass off for free for one week, to prove myself. Just give me a chance." He gives me a stone-cold stare, then a smile. The foreman says he's never heard an offer like that and gives me a tryout. I wind up working for him for three years.

Suddenly, I'm almost twenty. Drifting. Aimless. Handy at fixing flats and most anything else, but too often a little stoned, selling weed on the side.

One day, a friend of Julie's mom offers us work at a condo complex up in Mammoth Lakes. "Where's that?" I ask. "Let's go!"

I have nothing to lose but my girlfriend. Besides, I still can't get my grandpa's Colorado mountains off my mind.

"Let's go," Julie says.

Before we leave Orange County, I want to make things right—an uncharacteristic need to clean up after myself. I drive down to the courthouse to pay my parking tickets, wait for hours without an appointment, finally stand before the judge as everyone is packing up for the day.

He says: "Who's this? What do you want? We're closed."

I tell the judge I want to pay off the thirty parking tickets before I leave town, though I am short on cash.

The judge laughs a little, looks at me quizzically. He isn't sure what to do with this kid with $1,200 in traffic fines, and finally decides that if I'll sweep the stairwells and stamp some files, he'll waive the outstanding tickets.

With a clean conscience, I load my truck, and Julie and I head off to the unseen little condo in a place I've never been.

All I know is it's up in the woods, at the base of a bunch of mountains. The drive up is kind of trippy, with Julie tight against me on the pickup's old-school bench seat, a houseplant next to her.

On my left, the jagged, frosted slopes of the Sierra Nevada range. We pass through these little nowhere towns, locked in time—Lone Pine, Independence, Big Pine—ringed by Native American reservations, jerky stores, bait-and-tackle shops. We pass Mount Whitney, at 14,505 feet the highest mountain in the contiguous United States and a busy hub for serious hikers.

With every passing mile, the mountain range grows more striking and thicker with snow. Off to my right, cactus and scrub. I am sure we'll leave that behind, but the desert seems to dog us the entire way up.

What kind of strange wonderland is this? What will I do? How will we support ourselves?

CHAPTER THREE

FINDING MY MAGIC MOUNTAIN

For me, the bears will come to represent the opposite of all that I faced as a child. When I start working with them, I realize I've pretty much already seen the worst that can happen to a person. Given my upbringing, it is really a miracle I didn't end up in real trouble, in a cult, or even dead.

But, as you'd expect, the transition from Orange County surfer dude to a respected wilderness expert hardly happens overnight. This three-hundred-mile move is a big jump for a kid who was merely playacting at being an adult. Obviously, I am still nothing like anybody else. I've grown up enough to realize I have to get my footing, establish a trade, or even get a temp job of some sort. I need to develop a circle of friends, some steady work habits, carve out a life in this rough and unfamiliar region.

More than anything, I learn that, at nineteen, I am on my own in the world.

I love this place immediately. This is God's country, simply breathtaking. When Julie and I arrive in 1978, Mammoth Lakes, California, isn't a city. It isn't a town. It is a village. Compared to the thriving ski mecca it is today, there is virtually nobody here.

Work crews with chainsaws have carved out a two-lane Main Street in a thick pine forest. Up on the ski hill, Dave McCoy, a visionary who boasts a big dose of mountain chutzpah, is still hand-lighting sticks of dynamite and dropping them down holes to crater out the bases for the massive lifts.

It is raw wilderness. Cowboy hats are common. Avalanches are everyday threats. There is no auto club. If you skid on a patch of glare ice and spin out into a ditch, you have no choice but to get out, cuss a couple of times, and just start pushing.

When I arrive in town with Julie and the houseplant—Julie in the middle, my hand on her leg—we find ourselves in a parking lot two miles from our rental. I see a big building and say to myself, "Wow, they have a huge jail here." It isn't the jail. It is the ski resort's Warming Hut No. 2, a grim four-story Soviet-style building with slotted windows. To me, it looks just like the Orange County Jail. What do I know of warming huts?

In those early days, pretty alpine architecture is not yet a thing. The emerging little ski village is spartan . . . utilitarian. Back then, mere survival is job one. The mountain is nothing like the world-class destination it will become. We are a drinking town with a skiing problem, yet the runs are epic, as the kids like to say. We ski in jeans. If you want to reach the best runs, such as Wipe Out, or the super-challenging Avi Chutes, you put your skis over your shoulder and start hiking.

I love this hill. I am home! Over time, tens of thousands of people will move here, decide it's too harsh for them, then leave. I never leave.

The autumn we arrive, Mammoth is already biting cold. In the heart of the village, eight thousand feet above sea level, temperatures often plunge into single digits by mid-October, whipped by sixty-mile-per-hour gusts through the passes. Not used to the freezing temps, and underdressed, I come down with pneumonia right away. It is humbling for this SoCal kid, more attuned to surfing than slip-sliding around an icy construction site. My first winter here, I wear snowmobile boots—terrible boots. I borrow this little twelve-inch electric chainsaw for firewood. It is like a kitchen appliance, a joke. Hardly an instant woodsman.

Fortunately, I am a strappy longhair with a chip on my shoulder, and I am eager to make a life up here. I almost kill myself pounding nails, working six full days a week, half days on Sundays. It is wholesome, hard work, amid the lodgepole, the fir, the heavy sap-filled pine cones *ka-booming* randomly off the roof of your car as you and your girl go off to dinner. *Wow, Christ, what was that?* I remember thinking.

At night, we dance on the bar, spit chewing tobacco on the floor at Rafters, a popular hangout on Old Mammoth Road in the heart of town. Today, visitors know Rafters as a stylish restaurant built around a two-story open fireplace. Back then, you half expected Wyatt Earp to blast through the door looking for a fugitive. Trust me, there are a few of those around. In those early days, everyone was fleeing something.

It is the Wild West with a contemporary twist: the decadence of the eighties.

A pal told me once, only half kidding: "Never lend your truck, your chainsaw, or your girlfriend to anybody in this town. They'll never be returned the same."

At night, it is not uncommon to buy blow from the bartender you are ordering your drink from. You see glass ashtrays, heavy as bricks: face up, that means they are for cigarettes. If they are face down, with a straw across the top, they are protecting small mounds of cocaine. Cocaine is becoming a very social drug, used by folks with jobs and decent clothes. It helps them the way caffeine does, offsetting the wooziness of the booze, a way to continue the night longer than it probably should go. We close the bars almost every night; you can't possibly do that without an accelerant.

If you are wise, you get to know the bouncers, who pass as a rough-and-tumble police force. There are no cops. Literally none. The town hasn't been incorporated, so the police department we have today hasn't yet been formed. At that point, I suppose the county has responsibility for us, but you rarely see the sheriff.

A family is a family is a family. Though flawed, this one is far better than the one I left behind in Orange County. The social scene is like a schoolyard. No one is "needy." We are restless souls, forming sloppy, rollicking friendships. Almost everyone is a little promiscuous. Roommates steal girlfriends; girlfriends steal roommates. Brothers steal their best friends' younger sisters. It is Animal House. On weekends, we party till we puke. No AIDS. No condoms. First base, second base, third base, score. Hardly hip or fashionable in any way. When we dress for a Saturday night out, we dress like you would to go hunting. Everyone wears plaid. Pendleton shirts. Gaiters over Levi's. Sorel Caribou boots; they weigh a ton, and your feet are always cold.

We get up in the morning, go to work. We never miss a day. Even the most hard-core punk-ass kids who live in Mammoth today wouldn't hold a candle to us. Nothing to brag about, of course. Decadence isn't admirable. But we are young and charging ahead.

Just as today, Mammoth Lakes women don't take any crap. They have to be gritty or they won't make it past January. Though outnumbered, the women are as fun-loving as the men. We look out for them. We won't let one be disrespected. If you hurt a woman, you'd better hope a sheriff's deputy shows up, because we'll rip you up way worse. Same with anyone of color. You don't dare slur them. For such an untamed place, there is an enlightened ethos, an unwritten code of conduct. We are all working and partying too hard, side by side, to bother with bullshit prejudice of any kind. Mammoth Lakes is a boom town, with blue-collar values, back in the days when that represented courage and fairness.

Despite the rough-hewn look of the place, it is a chill scene. There is enough of everything—jobs, adventure—for everyone. All bosses ask is that you show up on time, or earlier, and leave at the end of the day with a few more calluses on your hands. Fair enough.

The town is loaded with square pegs—rough country kids from California's Central Valley, city kids like me up looking for a break, Australians or Brits lured here after hearing too many Beach Boys songs. They've taken a wrong turn and ended up in a village with too much testosterone and no string bikinis. Instead, the women all wear flannel and could probably kick your ass in a ski race or a bar fight. The square pegs all found a place where they fit.

But there is lots of California sparkle, plenty of sun. Mammoth Lakes is noted for an abundance of clear days. Still, at times it snows great gobs—sixty feet some seasons. When it snows, there are no plows, because there is no municipal government to buy them and hire drivers. In winter, you ride your snowmobile straight to the bar. To buy weed, you head over to a beaten-down mobile home park called Walt's Ghetto, which has Christmas lights glowing all year long. Dingy, no pavement. Funky town. Mud.

Mammoth Lakes is a giant thrift store of pain and pleasure.

What a place for a drifty kid like me. That smell of pine, the forest floor, the lightness of the air at this elevation. In the mountains, the sun starts to dip below the horizon at three p.m., blocked by high ridges and snow-capped peaks. Dusk lasts four hours. At night, the Milky Way.

For some people happiness is the beach; for some people it's the jungle; for me it is these mountains. It smells like Evergreen, Colorado, my grandpa's house.

We are at the apex of the California wilderness; drop-dead gorgeous Yosemite is just over the ridge, walking distance in a day or two. When you exhale, it smells like pine needles.

Of course, my teachers were right: I never do anything the way you are supposed to, and here is one more example. I mean, everything seems on a whim, including finding this mountain mecca only because a friend of Julie's mom happens to know of an open condo. Yet, thank God for Julie getting me into the mountains, where I belong. It is a perfect fit for a feral, easily bored dude in search of new experiences and adventure.

One nasty blister at a time, I am helping build the bones of what will become one of the West's premier resorts, the go-to destination for Southern California skiers looking for a huge hill a half day away. In time, they will paper Mammoth Lakes in $100 bills, which will prove good for anyone who invests early and halfway wisely.

In the meantime, my coworkers and I have gas in our trucks and beer money in our Levi pockets. Jobs are plentiful, wages weak. We are paid piecemeal, not hourly. We are framers putting up stick walls. We frame the walls on a slab, stand them up, tie them off so they don't fall over, then go on to the next slab. If I really grind, I make a hundred bucks in a day. It comes to eleven cents for every square foot of what we build. All the work boots come to have salty white stains from me sweating through the leather.

The vacation condos can't go up fast enough. Labor comes from all over the world. Some of us are good with our hands; others just have strong backs. If you can work a circular saw, you have a better-paying gig. Carpenters are in such short supply that an all-female crew is hired to finish projects and clean up sites, an alpine version of Rosie the Riveters.

Rich-quick stories start to pop up. One local developer, Tom J. Dempsey, sells his station wagon to buy lumber for the first house he puts on the market. From there, he comes to build dozens of developments in Mammoth and across the West. His crown jewel: the 355-acre Snow Creek condo development, which is just starting up when we arrive in the late seventies.

He and ski guru Dave McCoy become local heroes . . . almost living legends. They create this town and the adjoining ski resort by charging ahead, figuring it out as they go—lionhearted men who learn the vagaries of this unforgiving climate and know when to take a risk.

I feed off that. I see in their success the possibility that I might make it as well, or at least not become the total screw-up everyone predicted.

I work my ass off for Tom Dempsey that first summer. On Sundays, the town is dead quiet, except for the sound of my lone hammer framing out houses by myself. I am nailing off roofs by hand. I just went gangbusters at it. I say to myself, "Dude, you only know one thing, so you better just do it and do it every single day."

In the summer, I build condos. In the winter, I find snow-related work. Looking for any in, I start a snow removal company with sixty employees with shovels and ice-breaking tools. I charge $7 an hour and pay my employees $6, pocketing the difference. I start the first work-furlough program in Mono County, hiring inmates who want to work, along with guards. I hire truckloads of Native Americans, Aussies, Kiwis. They crew by themselves; I never mix and match. They dig out the bus stops, clear roofs, shovel decks where residents can't open the doors anymore. I get a real estate map and start coloring in the ones I have accounts with. I see one that isn't colored in and visit the managers and owners, till I have the whole town colored in.

After a three-foot storm, we pull up to a development with several trucks and finish in an hour. Shoveling snow sucks. But we get after it. We are young; we are fit; we are tan; we are full of piss and vinegar. On the roofs, we have guys up there with ropes, crampons, and carabiners to keep us from flying off. Music blares.

Way over my head, not sophisticated, but I am getting it done. All this will later help me in my approach to business and working with the bears. I am methodical. I am creative. It amps my work ethic. It develops my style of problem solving.

I am building confidence; I want more. I have no credit. I come up with an idea: I spend months collecting credit card applications and mailing them off. Once I get twenty cards together, I put them in an accordion holder and head to a nearby real estate office. I tell them I want to buy a place. The guy looks at this crazy kid in front of him. I don't blink. He wants to know what kind of down payment I have. "Any sort of collateral?" he asks. I smile and pull out this accordion file full of cards. "I got these," I say. He laughs at me.

Well, somehow it works out, and I buy my own place; in fact, I like it so much I still own it. Now I have collateral, which I use to buy a rental property. It will take years, but I will accumulate seven multiunit properties, based on that initial credit-card semi-scam.

By this point, Julie has taken off for warmer pastures, and I am spending my spare time in the surrounding forests. I buy a shotgun and a .22 rifle cheap, install a gun rack in my truck's back window, and head off to hunt geese, ducks, and deer. I set out early, sometimes at three a.m., so early that the coffee freezes in my thermos.

We learn; we screw up. The glorious mysteries of the wilderness begin to reveal themselves. We move up the food chain as we hunt, quail and waterfowl and chucker, a bird that looks like a small chicken. It takes thousands of hours to master the bird calls, the proper camouflage, and all the techniques—the scat, the habitat. You get it wrong a hundred times before you get it right. People think of hunting as Elmer Fudd blasting away at things. Not the way we approach it. We learn every nuance of every animal. One time, at night, an owl knocks my hat off as I imitate its prey. "Screw this, I'm going home," I say.

Coyotes, as wily in real life as in the cartoons, sneak in and steal our duck decoys. You can get $100 for their pelts. I am a murdering bastard. We use the latest gizmos to mimic the mating sounds of our prey. My buddies and I will hunt for a few hours, then wipe the camouflage paint from our cheeks and foreheads and go work ten-hour construction shifts.

By then, coyotes are starting to be a problem all across California and other parts of the West. They constantly snatch dogs and cats out of backyards. The ever-present *yip-yip-yip* isn't coyotes celebrating moonlight kills, as is commonly believed. That would be like announcing over a PA that you have fresh meat. In truth, kills are done quietly. The yipping you often hear is a social indicator; the coyotes are either mating, or recruiting, or playfully challenging rival packs. Up here, we find that coyotes are better fed, less mangy, and stronger than their timid brethren on the outskirts of suburbs and cities.

In Mammoth Lakes, the coyotes are growing bolder and bolder. For decades, an old woman has fed the coyotes on Mammoth Mountain, the ski resort, and they've become acclimated and fearless. Generally, residents treat the coyotes like stray dogs, whistling at them, feeding them. Little by little, they've become more than mere pests. They are a danger.

The most troubling development: ski school instructors near chair 7 begin to pat down the kids before class to make sure they don't have candy in their pockets, because the coyotes have started to go after the candy as the children scream in terror.

In 1984, the cowboy town of Mammoth Lakes incorporates, and a couple of years later it boasts a police department, a city manager, and a full range of public services. My reputation as an avid and trusted outdoorsman has grown. One day, a representative for ski resort owner Dave McCoy comes to me.

"We want you to take out the coyotes that are terrorizing our guests," the rep explains.

"Consider it done," I say.

So, in exchange for a Yamaha snowmobile from the ski mountain, I am assigned to grim-reaper the coyotes, in a situation that, as always, is really caused by careless residents leaving their cat bowls and their garbage out everywhere.

LESSON NO. 1:
MOST WILDLIFE PROBLEMS AND ISSUES TURN OUT
TO BE CAUSED BY BAD OR CARELESS HUMAN BEHAVIOR.

After the ski mountain work goes well, the town manager asks me to assess the situation in the residential areas and take out any coyotes that are dangerous.

In a dense, increasingly popular tourist area, we have to be extra careful with public safety and shooting lanes. I enlist a partner in the project, a great buddy by the name of Kevin Peterson, an avid outdoorsman and one of the most capable guys I know. We spend months spotting where the coyotes lurk, then strategically and surgically planning the shots. I learn to imitate the sound of a dying rabbit to attract coyotes. The rabbits are mute their entire lives till they are killed, at which point they sound like screaming babies. Hungry coyotes race to that sound with bloodlust in their throats.

We work undercover—not as hunters, not as cops—so we won't alarm bystanders. *Boom! Boom!* The sound of a shotgun rings out between the canyons of ski hotels, breaking the night stillness. Everything about the town is new, everything is paved. The shot echoes loudly. As alarmed guests switch on hotel room lights, Kevin and I go quickly about our business. Often, bystanders have no idea what just happened. By identifying the alpha males who are at the heart of most incidents, we are able to keep bloodshed to a minimum.

Kevin and I are frequently amused by the low level of attention the gunfire draws—almost none. We speculate that visitors from L.A. are brave about such things. Or maybe the visitors think it is merely the World War II cannons the ski mountain uses to reduce the risk of avalanches, when crews fire shells preemptively into at-risk mountainsides, triggering the avalanches so they won't occur when skiers are around. In any case, few guests come to the windows when we pull the trigger and the shotgun rings out. Even fewer come out on their balconies to ask, "What the hell?"

One day, police chief Michael Donnelly tells me he wants to include our coyote kills in the police blotter of the local paper, along with the DUIs and stolen cars. I think that calling attention to what we are doing would be pretty stupid, and I tell him so. He insists, and from that point, in a line or two, the local papers print details of the kills: "1:30 in the morning on May 11, on Main Street, wildlife officer destroyed two coyotes."

Nuts, right? To me, it seems obviously wrong. We are just begging for a citizen backlash. Yet, there is no outcry. There are no "poor coyotes" letters to the editor. The consensus is, "Steve is doing the wet work, and we're going to support him." I even appear at city council meetings and explain the latest incidents.

Turns out, it is a genius maneuver by Donnelly. He uses the police blotter as an opinion poll, knowing that if residents don't approve, they'll speak up, at which point he'll change his policy. He knows that being transparent in our work is important, and far better than having some animal activist discover the coyote culling long after it is over. In that case, it would look like a cover-up, and we'd all be seen as cold-blooded assassins. It is a terrific example of the advantages to being transparent in situations like this.

Little by little, and with utmost care, we take out the coyotes. We still have the open garbage dumps in town, where everyone takes their trash. It is a major draw for the animals, a bait station. We use it as a safe kill zone. We also fill Folgers cans with bait and chain them to trees. I have mixed feelings. This is a wildlife problem created by man, with humans' sloppy waste management and poor behavior the root causes. At the same time, dogs and cats are disappearing, and we wonder, "Will a toddler be next?" That's how we justify it, as a public safety issue, pure and simple. As the packs grow, they became bolder. I know that the more you shoot, the more you have to shoot, because the animals start double-whelping—meaning they produce extra litters to make up for the ones that are lost.

Misunderstandings about wildlife have been rife for decades. From here to Montana, our national parks used to feature rental cabins with pails hung by the door, where visitors could put leftovers to feed the bears and other wildlife when they come around.

In Mammoth at this point, residents and visitors still feed the coyotes; they even whistle for them. That's a death sentence for the poor animals.

To test their mettle and their level of threat, I put a .357 Magnum in a McDonald's bag and rattle it. We never shoot the ones that run; they are no harm. The ones that approach, we blow them up. It is a horrible thing to have to do.

I tell my partner, Kevin, this situation is unacceptable. We can't let the town continue to feed animals to the point where someone has to put them down. I find myself increasingly furious: "This can't fucking go on. This can never happen again."

The culling of the coyotes takes months. I work with Kevin, and sometimes alone. I set up a camper van as a scouting point. In the chair 2 parking lot one night, I am parked next to a couple making out in the car as their twin girls play nearby in the snow. I stay because I know the coyotes are coming. The girls start squealing, from the cold, from the snow down their backs. That brings the coyotes fast, thinking it is a rabbit.

As the coyotes start coming, I step out of my camper van with a shotgun. The parents see me and start freaking out in a language I don't understand. They don't see four coyotes approaching their girls. Lord knows what might've happened.

Of the forty-three coyotes we kill, forty-two are males—more aggressive and the main culprits in rampant overbreeding.

At this stage, I am selling windows to builders and homeowners, and I have an encounter that perhaps foreshadows what the future holds.

After arriving for a bid in the nice part of town, I feel this vibration under my feet. I look down to see two bear cubs clawing at the drain grate I am standing on. *Oh shit.* Before the homeowner can even open the door, I dart inside. The owner looks a little confused. What a trip.

The town's bears are taking up where the coyotes left off. They are now everywhere.

Donnelly calls me into his office.

"Look, we've got a bigger problem than coyotes," the chief says. "Steve, we want you to kill sixteen bears."

There I am chasing almost every kind of critter with a gun. Must seem odd today, given how much I defend wildlife. Like much of my life, it makes no sense.

Here's the irony: when I was hunting for sport, I never shot a bear. I would get tags that allowed me to shoot one, but I never did.

Few Californians realize that hundreds of bears are taken by hunters each year in California, from early October till late December, one per hunter. Under state regulations, up to 1,700 bears can be hunted down, with sows with cubs, and cubs themselves, off limits. In 2021, the California Department of Fish and Wildlife reported, hunters "harvested" 1,266 wild bears.

You know, we like to rewrite history to meet our own needs. But without learning to hunt geese and deer, I never would have known enough about nature to save the bears. While hunting, I learn about the cycles of the seasons, how to read the wind, the scat, the changing skies. Those hunting trips are like my Eagle Scout badge, and later will help me when I am defending wildlife.

I'll repeat: until I needed to euthanize a bear injured by a car, a hunter, or another bear, I never shot a single bear.

But when I am hired by Mammoth Lakes to help cull their numbers, the local bears are out of control. I estimate that forty live in and around the village; other estimates reach as high as sixty.

The bears are under porches, in crowded parking lots, ducking through the automatic doors of hotels. In one incident, a 450-pound bear wanders through a school playground, sniffing out lunchboxes. In another, a mischievous cub bites a resident's hind end. Like the coyotes, and through no fault of their own, they become a significant public safety issue. The bears are fat and fearless, acclimated to humans and spoiled by easy access to restaurant leftovers and the dolts who toss them half-eaten sandwiches from cars.

Look, I get it: feeding bears (or coyotes or any animal) is fun. Unless you know better, why not? It's just a little treat. Hand-feeding a bear is one of the greatest kicks you could ever have. It can change your life, how you spend your money, how you'll vote. All of that—that joy and sense of adventure—is real. But it contributes mightily to bear overpopulation and skews their interactions with humans for the worse. They call it habituation. You feed your dog every day at four o'clock. If you forget, he'll be there by four fifteen to remind you. Same with wild animals.

Donnelly is looking for solutions and settles on me. In his eyes, the guy who helped cull over forty coyotes can also kill sixteen bears. But he could never have imagined the ripple effect his choice would have.

Novelist John Dos Passos once said: "People don't choose their careers; they are engulfed by them."

He may as well have been talking to me.

CHAPTER FOUR

THE THINGS I DON'T KNOW

My challenge: these hairy misfits, whose biology and habits are pretty much a mystery to me, running roughshod over the growing tourist town. Every week, another report of a break-in, a botched encounter, a bear hovering near our hospital. Meanwhile, the town is booming. Developers are building even more habitat and hideouts for them—decks, koi ponds, sheds, crawl spaces. New restaurants are popping up to serve the burgeoning tourist trade and dumping leftovers in unlocked dumpsters out back, a veritable smorgasbord. For the bears, each night is an all-you-can-eat feast.

I'm starting to wonder whether I should've taken this assignment. What do I know about bears, really? I know these mountains, the weather patterns, a bit about wildlife migration, how to load a gun. Sure, that's something. But I have no clue about how to take out sixteen beautiful but rambunctious bears.

Like many of us, the fact I don't know what I'm doing makes me more focused and determined. This was the most important task I'd ever been assigned.

When I come aboard, camping areas across the Sierra are having more and more issues. Rangers in nearby Yosemite have grown tired of bears barreling through campsites like NFL nose tackles, desperate for more marshmallows. They begin tagging the bears on the ear, as you would cattle.

The tagged bears are starting to show up in culverts around Mammoth Lakes. Have they been dumped there by Yosemite? Have they wandered over after being relocated nearby? Federal rangers deny any responsibility for the tagged bears, including the triple-taggers that have been busted three times. Yet, I have a hunch they are being left on our doorstep, like boxes of unwanted puppies.

Here you go. Good luck to you and Yogi.

Not the sweetest situation, obviously. You have this transplanted population of troublesome bears, foisted on a community unaccustomed to bears. Note that when I arrived in 1978, you rarely saw a bear—there just wasn't enough food. In fifteen years, the town has gone from no bears to being overrun. As a result, I am finding that there is no bear-proofing of garbage bins, no shutters on the rickety old summer cabins. It's lawless. The bears are bold, plentiful, and grossly overfed.

Enter me: a seat-of-the-pants "bear expert." As they say, I didn't know what I didn't know.

The animals clearly have the upper hand . . . bears that have no fear of people. A little spoiled, they are obese and accustomed to handouts. When they aren't eating, they are canoodling in our yards.

Day after day, I am discovering that black bears eat the most delicious morsel they can find and make it their mission to do so sometimes twenty-two hours a day to build bulk for the long, long sleep of winter. They are also lazy and prone to avoiding conflict.

Everything they do is guided by hunger pangs and this overwhelming urge to eat. A bear will take a half a Big Mac over a bush brimming with currants, just as you probably would. Man, is that greasy stuff good! There are more calories per bite, so it's far more efficient. For a bear, obesity is the goal. In these first few months, I learn that they are stomachs with feet.

In winter, everything is frozen, even the water supply. So the bears eat and drink in the warmer months, as much as they can. The cravings they develop for human food lead to car break-ins, stolen coolers, and some very frightened and unhappy campers.

I am also finding that this abundant human food leads to overpopulation. I learn that a fat male bear is a sexy bear, that the females are especially attracted to the bigger bears—Mother Nature's way of keeping the species strong and robust.

To my mind, the bears are being taught to misbehave. Often, residents feed their dogs outside, meaning that their food just sits there, baiting the bears. The restaurants and town dumps are other flash points. One T-bone or Twinkie at a time, the black bears of Mammoth Lakes develop a taste for human food, packed with flavor and calories, and certainly no match for the natural food they should be consuming.

At this point, I am still scared silly of the bears. On bear calls to cabins and cars, we bring a half dozen cops along, everyone carrying an AR-15 or a shotgun. Multiple agencies show up—sheriff, police, and highway patrol respond to a bear snoozing in a crawl space under a house, a ridiculous show of force for the sort of situation we are still learning to assess and deal with.

They've certainly earned my respect. In a short time, I realize that the bears are very, very smart. When a bear licks leftovers he finds in the trash, he's getting traces of human saliva. That apple core he picks out of your trash—he loves that. He can tell if you used mouthwash that morning, snuck a candy bar, or kissed the baby. The apple core gives him more information than a two-sided business card. You're having a conversation with the animal: "Here's what I like, here's how I live," and every Thursday—trash day—he learns a little more.

Brilliantly, he just connects the dots. It's part of his sophisticated olfactory radar. I begin to ponder how confused he would be if I put a bullet in his head, after years of humans wooing him with leftovers. I mean, he thought everyone loved him.

Eventually, the department gets me a uniform and a badge. I wear the badge on my belt, as a detective does. For me, it represents safety and respectability. I am a lawman, with shoot-to-kill privileges over sixteen outlaw bears. "Hey, Chief, I won't screw up," I tell Donnelly one day. "Yes, you will," he says. "When you do, come see me. We'll figure it out."

Not a bad buy-in from your boss, not a bad all-in-this-together approach. Donnelly is a good guy, even if he is as clueless about this entire situation as I am.

As with the coyotes I culled—methodically and patiently—I map out the bear dens, their turf, their proximity to public places. If a bear has been seen loitering around the post office or supermarket, I'll put a red check by his name. He will be the first to go. I figure that, as with the coyotes, I will target the alpha males first—the breeders, the aggressors, the troublemakers. I want to shoot the biggest, baddest bears. Surgical as a sniper, I plan on taking out the problem bears and leaving the peaceniks alone.

I am a methodical man. When I do something new—learn chess or take up golf—I always go into it full-on, make it an obsession. That's just the way I'm wired, which proves incredibly helpful when you have your work cut out for you. I have so much to learn. I learn a little, then pick up a little more. Like the bears, I connect the dots.

There isn't anything I won't try. Fanatical? Too weak a word for me at this point. To understand them, I even decide to crawl into their dens. Takes me a while to find the courage to cross the threshold, but I do it. The first time I try, I fear they will rip my spleen out. Merely finding a den is tricky, let along summoning the nerve to poke my head inside.

Hello?

I begin to look forward to snowy mornings when their tracks give me an indication of where they are. Before dawn, I dress in the dark and rush out to find their fresh tracks. Once I find the paw prints, I backtrack to their dens, where they have made mats of duff from the forest floor. There is always scat. Seeing the tracks leading away from the den, with no return tracks, I know the bear is still out, so I duck safely inside. I find some of these dens right on my own street, in the heart of town.

I'm lanky like Lincoln, made of pipe cleaners. I'm also relatively light on my feet; I can walk more quietly than anyone you know. When there's no snow, I have no way of knowing whether a bear is inside a den or not. Often, when I creep up to the den, not making a sound, I peek in to find the bear is staring right in my face. Oops. This happens over and over. If a bear happens to be home when I climb inside, I never surprise it. They always know I am coming. I am on their home turf, looking right into their dark and puzzled eyes.

My heart pounds. When I catch my breath, I try to soothe them, calm us both. I talk in a monotone: "Hi, buddy. Hi, buddy. It's OK." Eventually, they relax and fart and grunt and settle down.

By now, I am really getting into it. I crawl on my belly into their snow-covered dens and hook up microphones and tiny cameras to capture their sleeping habits in winter. If they knock one loose—son of a bitch!—I shimmy back in on my belly to fix it.

Scary stuff. I mean, even if you're the friendliest guy on your block, if some idiot barges into your house on his belly in the middle of the night to set up surveillance gear, you're not going to be real happy about it. If a sow has a cub with her, the risks are even higher.

I never said I am anything close to normal. Somehow, I go unscratched.

I study the bears from near and far, make notes, take photos, identify them as you would a fugitive. I carry a three-ring binder where I keep their mugshots, write down their physical traits, their habits, their encounters, their names (usually based on physical attributes). I take a side photo, a face shot. It takes a long time.

One novel development: to shoo bears away, to keep them out of harm's way, I begin to zap them with firecrackers. I also ping them with rubber bullets, as I experiment with nonlethal alternatives to shooting them. Real early, a lightbulb comes on: "Don't just scare them. Teach them to behave."

To roust one from a public space, I'll toss a Black Cat firecracker at his feet, or use pepper balls to make a point. I spray-paint their butts and color-code my charts so that I can identify the various bears later. Stupid stuff. I am figuring out this life-and-death situation as I go, with an emphasis on *life*. Some of it is inspired by TV segments I've seen of police using beanbags and water cannons on protesters. *Why not bears?* I think.

I work seven days a week. I keep ridiculous amounts of notes. When I shot the coyotes earlier, I kept the spent shells, attached them to the incident report, documented the whys and wheres of the kill. My boss, Donnelly, didn't care. He trusted me. Yet, I still feel a need to justify the town's faith in me. I want residents to know I'm not a reckless hothead hunter. As always, I am desperate for respect, despite my gruff shit-kicker shell.

Out in the field, I am trying all kinds of crazy stunts. An electrician buddy, Paul Rowan, helps set up a power pole in the middle of the main dump, and I put in super-bright floodlights with a motion detector. Does that keep the wildlife away from all that harmful and greasy food? No. All the strong lights do is turn the dumps into drive-in theaters. Residents hear of it, pull up in their cars, and treat it like the movies. It becomes a popular hangout for teens. The lights are a beacon for the animals and an entertainment option for humans . . . a free wild-animal park.

Way to go, Steve.

The king of trial-and-error tactics, I install a peregrine falcon decoy atop one of the light poles. I hope the sight of the falcon will drive off the ravens and other birds afraid of the famously aggressive peregrines. What I failed to realize is that the peregrine falcon isn't a natural predator in the area.

Instead of being scared away, the birds use it as a latrine. Coated in guano, the fake bird quickly resembles an avian version of Frosty the Snowman.

I am trying, but I am dumb as a doorknob about this stuff. I have to rip out the lights, take down the decoy falcon.

When they're feeding at the dumps, I am extra wary and afraid of the bears. You should never approach an animal while he's eating, even your beloved dog. I decide that I need a safe vantage point. So I core out an old disabled International Harvester Scout, a precursor to today's SUVs. Since the old engine doesn't run, I tow the vehicle to sites around town and use it as a fortress from which to observe the various creatures, mostly the bears.

In the meantime, my experiments with the fireworks are awkward, but they work. My tool kit is growing. I am using the type of pyrotechnics they use during prison riots—so loud they set off alarms in nearby cars. The bears are slowly falling in line. I am reinstilling their natural fear of humans, which we have trained out of them.

In trailing them, I find that the bears often use the town's five-foot drainage culverts as their own subway system through town, as a way to avoid people and cars and all the commotion. I walk hunched over through the big pipes with two guns and extra ammo. I dread coming around a corner and surprising a bear, my snout to his snout. I use a crowbar to open manhole covers at the junction of this system of culverts, sort of the trapdoor entry points. Almost every time I lift a manhole cover, there is a bear. If I want to drop down through a manhole, I pop the heavy lid with a crowbar, then park my truck right over the open hole, so city workers won't come along and replace the lid, trapping me.

Bears are largely nocturnal, so much of my work takes places after dark. Night after night, I find the bears and other animals enjoying a fine feast, dining on pizza, sampling the salmon with capers and dill, or the steak and mushrooms in brandy sauce, all of it from local restaurants and residential kitchens. Chances are some of it is still a little warm.

The conventional wisdom is that bears eat anything and everything. They eat constantly, that's true. But they are actually picky eaters. The restaurants with the high-priced seafood, the crusty sourdoughs, the lamb in coconut milk and peppercorns, prove irresistible to them.

Oddly, the voracious bears, guided by their powerful sense of smell, only eat the very best.

CHAPTER FIVE

THIS MOMENT CHANGES EVERYTHING

By now, my work is getting pretty personal. I watch the way the bears feed, how they pick a lover, the wild abandon in how they mate. I chase them up a tree so that I can determine the gender. When they have their fill of food, climb a tree, and flop down on a branch, I curl up in the pine needles under the tree. When the bears sleep, I sleep—right under the trees.

I'm out in the field every night. I set up my stakeouts, hour after hour, week after week. I settle back to watch this nightly floor show at the town dumps, the creatures gathering mostly peaceably for their government cheese. Late one night, about four a.m., a local restaurant owner pulls up with a big barrel of barbecue bones, dumps them on the ground, and pulls away. The animals pounce on them, fresh from the grill.

Moments later, the animals all dart into the dark woods, leaving this fresh feast behind. The larger bears are the last to go, turning an ear to the woods, a nose to the winds, before scattering as well, unaccustomed to being chased off by anything.

Their quick exit spooks me. I look down to be sure my shotgun is still at my side. I palm the handle of my sidearm. I am pondering the question "What has set off their radar systems so quickly?" when out of the forest comes the biggest black bear I've ever seen, pushing 650 pounds, and with the swagger of a heavyweight champion. He saunters to the dump, where he has his pick of the food, in no hurry and completely without fear.

Entranced, I immediately dub this titan of the forest Big.

For the next hours, Big's courage and commanding entrance impress me. I start to wonder, in a rare but critical aha moment: can I somehow become the biggest, baddest bear? By earning their respect, could I lead these mostly genial creatures out of town without spilling an ounce of their blood? Can we live together? Could we coexist?

From Big, I quickly realize that these bears have a pecking order. Though they display a courtesy to each other and are independent thinkers, they usually defer to the biggest bear. I decide to climb atop that pecking order, to appoint myself the baddest bear in town.

Only a young person could come up with such a wacked-out, outlandish idea. I mean, what a lordly concept, that I could somehow subordinate and outsmart these creatures in their environment, on their home turf. It is almost a vignette you'd read in the Bible, how the young man tries to train the bears, only to find the bears are actually training him.

But I know one thing for sure: if I am tough enough and wise enough, I shouldn't have to shoot anything, a bloody and brutal endgame that by now I am totally dreading.

I find that Big reminds me of the best cops I've ever seen. The truly tough cops, the ones who can really take care of themselves, have a super-power: their body language. When they wade in to break up a fight, they don't ever raise a fist. They barely raise their voices. They command respect just by their movement, which reflects the muscle of their experience. It isn't necessarily a matter of heft or bulk or swagger. It isn't boastful. It is professionalism and self-confidence.

So it is with Big.

I go back to see Donnelly, sit down in the chief's office, and tell him about my latest discovery. I explain how Big had commanded the pecking order. Taking a lesson from nature, I ask for Donnelly's blessing to try more novel tactics—rubber bullets, pyrotechnics, even coercion—to teach the bears to fear and respect me so that I can flush them out of danger and keep our town safe.

Donnelly says that is fine by him. Far as he is concerned, I can dance with the bears, put them in tutus, or in Broadway shows, as long as sixteen of the misfits go away. I'm sure he's thinking, *Steve will still have to kill them. What does it matter how he treats them up till that point?* Sure, mess around with them all you want, he says.

My thinking: I can avoid a bloodbath, and a public relations debacle for this town, by teaching the bears where they can go, how they can behave. I can find no literature to support this. It isn't based on any scientific journal. It is a feeling in my gut, based on my initial research: sleeping on the forest floor, seeing how the bears behave and avoid conflict. I see how they back down in the presence of a superior. I also fear that killing these bears would be a crisis management disaster for a town that prides itself on its wilderness aura, a town with carved statues of bears on nearly every porch.

Also, when it comes to wildlife management, the more you shoot, the more you have to shoot. Killing a creature causes an environmental sink—an abundance of food—that draws in even more bears. They can smell for miles and know when a habitat becomes available. If you kill one, here come two more.

So, there I am with my pecking order, me and the bears that I am liking more and more. As with the confident cops entering a bar fight, I need to teach the bears that I am the one not to cross.

The police dispatcher sends me out on every bear call, day and night, 24/7. I learn to read the room the moment I arrive, assess the mess, figure out where the immediate danger is, zero in on the culprit and the escape routes. Are bystanders too close? That is my first "read." I give the crowd a chance to finish taking their selfies, then move them back, without panicking the humans or the bears.

I fail, I learn, I fail, I learn some more. With Donnelly's blessing, I am slowly building an arsenal of fireworks, capture poles, welding gloves (to handle cubs), and a real live-ammo orange shotgun I use to keep people from overreacting. I'm a slow study. Yet, I learn that when I turn up on scene carrying a standard shotgun, a safeguard in case things go south, bystanders freak out. It supercharges the situation. Instead of being the heroic first responder, I am the wildlife SWAT team. Understandably, they are alarmed by the gun and afraid of what I might do with it. It heightens the tension in unappealing ways.

Among the background stories I pick up about black bears: their population has been steadily growing in California since the grizzly was hunted to extinction in 1928. A grizzly bear is a ruthless and notorious predator. All a black bear wants to do is share his sandwich. People often mix up the two. In fact, of the eight species of bears worldwide, black bears are the storybook bears—relatively affable and plump in the butt, with easygoing dispositions.

Until hunted out of existence, the grizzly gave black bears fits. Everything about them was outsized in comparison to the black bear: their jaws, teeth, claws, muscle mass; the alpha temperament. Grizzlies eat everything—you, me, your dog—as opposed to black bears, which, without humans leaving out camp coolers or leaving restaurant dumpsters unlocked, are primarily herbivores that graze on vegetation and the occasional decaying animal.

"Black bears are not particularly interested in flesh . . . they have been seen in the fields eating string beans," writer John McPhee notes.

Grizzlies can't climb trees, and the ability of the black bear to scrape and claw its way to safety—nearly as quick as a squirrel—was probably an evolutionary parlor trick the black bears used to escape the ruthless grizzlies.

Now, can they escape me? Can I, the man hired to hunt them, save them instead?

Can Big be my muse?

A WORD FROM CHRIS ERSKINE:

As you can see, Steve was raised by bears—who have taught him more than any parent or schoolteacher in his young life—and at this point is about to elope with a bunch of bears. He is a forceful personality, a big presence—entertaining, crude, somewhat frayed—all the traits you find in super-successful people. He also has a backwoods charisma, a roguish charm.

Did I mention brilliant? He'll try to wiggle out of that one, get me to change it. But I won't.

Honestly, I'll bet Steve was a defiant kid. Children who aren't loved usually are. So, how do they right themselves, how do they carry on?

Well, you're about to find out.

Steve is a different dude, in all the good ways. As his sidekick in this project, as his hostage/co-conspirator, we could not be more different. We're roughly the same age, that's about it. Politically, there is some overlap. (We both know BS when we see it, and there is so much of that lately.) We both look forward to a candidate who might bring everyone together. (We may have better luck with a bear.)

I remember when he first pitched writing this book together. I'd come to town to do a story for the Los Angeles Times, *like so many reporters in the past. We're in his truck, his Mambo Cadillac, the rattling vehicle he drives to death every year. There are stained foam coffee cups scattered everywhere, a strangely orange shotgun at his side, and we're bouncing along a country road. He's dropping f-bombs left and right, loud to louder—it's almost an aria. I figure the jiggling shotgun is gonna go off at any time, take off the roof of the truck, maybe my forehead too. If that doesn't get me, his smog of cigarette smoke certainly will.*

Then there are these wild bears he's talking about. At any moment, we could be stopping to deal with a ravenous five-hundred-pound nightmare.

I mean, who would ever spend two years around a difficult dude like this? "We're both damaged goods," I once warned him. "Isn't everybody?" he replied. I worried that we'd probably end up killing each other. Or, he'd kill me. He's the one with the guns. I don't like guns. I'm not even comfortable around garden tools.

To me, a story merely needs to be entertaining, that's all. If it has deeper, cautionary meaning—stands as some parable—all the better. But that's not my wheelhouse. My wheelhouse is "Let's go have ice cream and watch weird people walk by." I've made a career of that.

Yet, here we are, hammering out Steve's entertaining and enlightening life story. It is an honor to have worked on this memoir with him.

Know the concept of multiple intelligences, the belief that one standardized IQ test or SAT can't measure an individual's true intellect?

Indeed, I believe that there are alternative ways of thinking—often off the charts—that lead to major breakthroughs in fields such as science and human behavior. Steve comes at things in a different way than the rest of us. His mind has a different set of vectors. This alternative thinking is behind much of Steve's success—and his frustrations. It's the core of his uncommon sense of empathy and his ability to "get" animals, whether it's dogs or cats, horses or bears. I often wonder what would have happened if Steve had not gotten that assignment to cull those bears—both to the bears of Mammoth Lakes, and to Steve.

CHAPTER SIX

MY DEAR DEBS

A t this point, I'm still a part-time hourly worker, making the paltry sum of $10,000 a year for my wildlife work. I am exhausted. I'm not sure I can sustain a life like this. I am all alone out there, with bears I still only half understand. Fortunately, at that point in my life, I also add the best asset of all: Deborah Cogel—my wife, my life. Or, as I always call her, Debs.

By now you know I'm a tad unconventional, with some obsessive tendencies, maybe wired emotionally more like the bears than like other human beings. Heck, I'm even extra hairy like they are.

Well, I'm stubborn like them too. As evidence: over the course of a year, I ask Deborah Cogel out sixty times before she agrees to a first date.

Debs is fresh from New Zealand, with beautiful skin and blond hair. I meet her at a Mammoth Lakes kegger in 1988. By then, I've already been in town a decade. I find her irresistible. She shares my traditional values and is an amazing cook. I know she is the One.

Me? I am everything she never wanted.

My dating profile would look something like this: "Gruff mountain man, full of rough and rusty edges, profane to the point where it is almost a form of poetry, with a distinctive rhythm, couplets, imagery, and all sorts of anger and back-of-the-throat guttural qualities you don't find in most modern poetry. I like puppies, kind-hearted people, and long walks on the beach."

So, despite the long streak of rejections, I keep asking her out. She could've slammed me in the forehead with a shovel, and I wouldn't have taken the hint. Went on for months. Please? No. Please? No . . .

I bring over my work crew—I have the burgeoning snow removal company by then—and we dig her VW van out from a heavy snow. Picture this: we physically lift the van up and remove the snow underneath her assigned parking spot, then ten of us carry it back into its place—with my business card on the windshield. I do this several times. Please, please, please? She never calls. At what point does desperation turn attractive? Almost never.

I'm either a hopeless romantic or a goof who can't take a hundred hints. I spend thousands of dollars at the restaurant where she works, the Cask 'n Cleaver, in hopes of winning her over. Debs is restless like me, and she runs off to Alaska for a while. When she returns, I dial it back a bit and offer to make her a simple home-cooked meal, fully realizing it is just another in a chain of Hail Mary pleas.

She says yes.

One minor hitch: I don't cook. What now? My dream girl, the woman I've been pursuing for so long, and a great cook in her own right, finally agrees to a homemade dinner from a man who can't fry water. Fortunately, a couple of friends are professional caterers, and they help me prepare some pheasant I'd shot, bake it, and put it under the proverbial glass with a nice sauce, then they scram.

I am thrilled. I've actually pulled off an elegant dinner. Looks like something you'd see at the Ritz. Candlelight. Wine. Soft music. I even wash the dog. Debs smiles at the sight of it all, scoots her chair in, takes one bite, and chomps down on a shotgun pellet still in the bird.

Must not have been too bad, because she stays the night and every night after that for three decades.

I'm probably not the forever type that women dream about. My first love is the outdoors. My other passions are trucks and dogs and snowmobiles. My friends will confirm that I'm a total guy's guy. Probably not even fully domesticated. Not even certain I've had all my shots.

Of course, the next probable step for a guy like that? Marriage. After my childhood, I am deeply hesitant about getting married and particularly about having children. I am convinced that I have bad blood in me, that I might be violent the way my father was. Freaks the hell out of me. I feel guilty for things that haven't even happened.

I manage to overcome my fears and doubts, and the wedding date is set. It's three weeks out, and people are planning to fly in from all over. I start to have doubts again, telling sweet, patient Debs, "I don't want to do it." She says, "Fine. No problem. It'll be just fine."

I visit my best friend, a very troubled Vietnam vet, to explain: "I don't want to get married. I had a horrible upbringing, and I'm going to hurt my wife. I'm afraid I might end up hurting my child."

He argues that even a failed marriage can be a success. "We consider someone married three times to be a three-time loser," he notes. "Maybe that's actually a three-time winner . . . someone who has had the love of three people and shared lots of wonderful times."

He has turned a dishonor into a blessing, just the sort of creative thinking and sense of hope that I admire in others.

Having stepped back from the ledge, I go to my lawyer, who will perform the ceremony, to tell her I want a marriage pact for ten years, at which point we can renew.

OK, my attorney says with a smile. I run it by Debs. She's fine with it too. In my mind, this ten-year "lease agreement" will prevent the complacency that dooms so many long-term relationships. After ten years, if we're both still happy and content, we can re-up.

Several of our friends are so appalled by this novel marital arrangement they refuse to attend the wedding. To me, it provides a safety valve for a very challenging commitment.

I'm in again. When I arrive at our outdoor wedding, my friends all stand and applaud. They are that amazed I actually showed up. On that day, and for almost thirty years after, Debs becomes my co-conspirator, my lover, my sidekick, and my soulmate.

I don't gush over her out of obligation. I do it out of gratitude and the realization that I would not have had a fraction of my success, or any success at all, without her.

Everything that I have achieved, professionally and personally, I owe to my wife. With her support, I am able to respond at all hours to 9-1-1 wildlife calls, as well as other public safety calls where my outdoors expertise might come in handy. (For the record, we go on to "re-up" our marriage at the ten- and twenty-year marks.)

Doesn't matter if it is Christmas Eve or her birthday, I am on call pretty much 24/7. There is no assistant wildlife specialist. There is only me.

Before I get into bears full-time, I have been building houses. I come home bone-tired and walk out of my dirty clothes. The next morning, they are washed and folded. As I say, she is an amazing cook. Each day, cookies or cakes or pies or breads fill the kitchen. The windows steam. It smells like a house in a Hallmark movie.

At dinner, she typically gives me and our son, Tyler, a few choices. "Stroganoff? Steak? That chicken parm you like? Or do you maybe want pasta?" If Tyler and I each request something different, she happily makes both. For Debs, cooking is medicine. Doesn't matter who comes to our house, whether they are famous or whether they are poor, the first thing she does is feed them.

Remember my rocky childhood? Mom had nothing in the fridge but booze, and my stepmom thought hotdogs and beans were gourmet fare? By fussing over me like this, Debs makes me feel loved like no one ever before. I know it sounds traditional and dated, but I'd never experienced that sense of devotion and security.

Obviously a traditional home supporting a very untraditional job. But a good home. Flowers on the sill in summer. Stew on the stove when it snows.

I develop a presence around town, attend city council meetings just out of curiosity, get to know people. I take a 50 percent stake in a company called Country Glass, so I start doing window supply work seven days a week. I work till I drop, applying the same techniques, connections, and people skills I'd used in my snow-removal business—bidding windows, tub enclosures, sliding doors.

I'm insistent that I will never have children, and have strong beliefs that most parents just aren't prepared for the financial strain of it. I'm fond of ticking off a list of prerequisites to being a parent, such as $10,000 in savings, $10,000 in checking, a home, a reliable car. Debs and I finally decide we have enough boxes checked. I think Debs became pregnant that same night.

We suffer major heartache over a bad pregnancy that ends early when the baby's heart doesn't develop properly. Our second attempt turns out very well. After Tyler is born, we take him everywhere, including Grateful Dead concerts. As he grows, I teach him to fix cars, ride quads . . . all that twangy, blue-collar mountain stuff. He holds the flashlight for me during father-son projects. Snowmobiles are my other love, and I ride almost every day in winter. For years, from the time he's a wee lad, I spend entire winter afternoons towing him and his pals up hills on his snowboard, to otherwise inaccessible runs, on pristine snow, weaving through the trees. The boys have whistles on lanyards that they blow when they reach the bottom, at which point the dads ride down the hill to start the tow service all over again. We let him be a kid, in all the outdoorsy ways kids used to be kids. Kids are supposed to drink from garden hoses. They're supposed to skin their knees.

To a fault, I offer him these things because they are all I have to give. I am an avid outdoorsman. Never been to the theater. Can't help with trig homework. My skill sets are what I have, and I worry they aren't enough. Go-karts, mountain bikes, three-wheelers . . . I do the best I can with what I have. Science lessons happen when I take Tyler and his buddies hunting for scorpions with a black light. In the dark, the arachnids glow. No, the boys are never stung; a scorpion's deadliness is mostly a screenwriter's exaggeration. But the boys get an appreciation for the wonders of nature. It's what I know.

Mammoth isn't like most places. Physical education in a mountain town isn't dodgeball and rope climbing. It's on the ski mountain itself—snowboarding and skiing. It's all outdoors, much like our life is.

At this point, my hobby is still hunting, and I take it seriously. My buddies and I build coffin-like duck blinds so watertight that we can float them across the lake to their destination, where we dig them into the ground, like invisible forts. When we come back for the next hunt, we find that the hydraulics of the soil has popped them out of the ground like champagne corks. Oops. But we were into it. You might detest hunters and hunting. But to do it right, to shoot the animal in places that don't prolong the suffering, to tread lightly in the forest, is an art. A good hunter is an advocate of the wilderness. Seems counterintuitive, probably, but I know it firsthand.

In short, I am hardly a typical suburban soccer dad. I am a mountain-man dad. I attend all Tyler's games, though, every baseball, soccer, and football game, in the bleachers, cheering. In high school, Tyler plays offense and defense on the football team, frequently in single-digit temperatures, when his durag freezes under his helmet. The weather is so raw, opponents not accustomed to the mountain weather bleed just from the cold.

At Christmas, we craft the unofficial town tree. We build it out of plastic pipe in the driveway, number all the pieces, take it apart and tow it by snowmobile up to the top of what we called Broncs Hill, where we piece it back together and zip-tie all the lights on it. We place the thirty-foot tree atop a big boulder, attach a generator. Nothing fancy. The star atop the tree is a one-hundred-watt mechanic's light. The entire town marvels over this sudden holiday attraction, not realizing how rickety and jerry-rigged it all is.

Aglow on Christmas Eve, it quickly becomes a town tradition, bigger and better every year. My cronies laugh at me, then begin to pitch in to help. No permits. When we are done with the setup—plug in the lights, start the generator—we put our feet up on the snowmobile, lean back, and look down at the rat race far below, the line of headlights coming up to Mammoth for the holidays. We ride back down in an hour. When the Honda generator runs out, we run up more gas the next day. No one in Mammoth knows who is doing this. The tree just shows up on Christmas Eve and burns through the week. That's small-town living. Simple. No fuss. A humble tribute to the place we love.

In your wildest dreams, can you imagine being raised by me? As you can see, everything is done to an extreme. That becomes Tyler's normal. Everything is pumped up, heightened, whether it is working on cars or being dragged up a mountain by a snowmobile.

I play catch with Tyler for hours and hours. As a kid, I never got the chance to play catch with an adult male. No dad, no uncle, no boyfriend ever took the time to toss the ball. I am determined to give him the attention I missed. We even play catch in airports while waiting for our flights.

As he gets older, he seems unaffected by my growing status. There are film crews in the yard, satellite trucks. He glances at them, grabs his skateboard, and rides off, just another ten-year-old going off to hang with his buds. I'm almost 100 percent certain he won't mention that the *Today* show set up camp in his front yard.

If he spots a bear on the porch, he hardly looks up from his Game Boy. He just yells from the couch: "Dad, your bear's here!" That is just his norm.

I am raising my son to be a better man than me, just as I worked to be a better man than my own father. I think that's normal for boys and men. Dads seed the clouds with their sons' dreams. We hit the ground running every day, in hopes of giving them a better, more contented life. Sure, smash the patriarchy, shake things up. But never undervalue the role and worth of a devoted father. As a neglected son, I can tell you the importance of that firsthand.

As I look in vain to fill the emotional voids created in my own childhood, I am determined to raise a son who can be certain each day of at least one thing: his dad's devotion.

Tyler has always had zero embarrassment, zero ego. Everybody in the schools he attends, all of his teachers and peers, knows me and Debs and what we are about. Sometimes I am a local hero in the paper, sometimes the center of some storm. Tyler never buys into either extreme. To him, I am just a dad.

And Debs is the backbone of the entire operation.

The saintly, cheerful, devoted, amazing woman, wife, and mom. You think you have problems with the in-laws? She has married into a family of actual bears. And I am as married to them, and my work, as I am to her.

On many mornings, I get up early, pour a cup of coffee, pull on a fresh pair of Levi's, my white tennies, a flannel shirt, the entire L.L.Bean catalogue of woolly mountain-man clothes and head over to chat with my newest pal, a bear named Center Street.

I mean, what woman wants to wake up next to someone who does that each day?

Center Street is my other dependent, a bear who lives a block or two from my house. I dub him Center Street, since that's the road in the heart of Mammoth where he lives, sixty yards from the main drag, so close you can see the motor homes passing by. He is a very calm bear, living in the middle of a budding world-class ski town, behind the Shell station and a satellite location for the popular Schat's Bakery.

Big guy. Lives in a tree. Speaks mostly in grunts and moos. Every day, he and I chat.

That's right, we literally converse. Center Street inadvertently is becoming my bear language instructor. It is Beginner Bear, the introductory course.

One on one. Just the two of us. What a waste of time, right? No. Because I figure that if I can unlock the code of their various outbursts—the clacks, grunts, and huffs—then maybe I can work more effectively with the bears in tricky situations. From the noises they make, I might respond more appropriately, rather than just guessing at their moods or intentions.

So, every morning, a coffee mug in hand, I wander over for another language lesson. I moo. Center Street moos back. A mimic and a goof, the bear is far more tolerant of humans than he should be. We are tight that way.

"I'm not so keen on humans either," I tell him one day. "At least some of them."

He lies along his branch. I lie down flat on my back, looking up—clacking, mooing, grunting. There is a daycare center nearby. I spot a line of fifteen young children coming through the woods, a teacher on each end, kind of towing them along. They don't flinch, not the kids or the teachers. This is becoming the new normal. It's a beautiful thing. In the moment, a Glock on my hip, I recognize the yin and yang of this: a giant wild animal, a smattering of innocents. Can we really all coexist in this magical way? Is it really this simple?

I am highly sensitive to the pluses and minuses. At the very least, I figure I can turn the children into my ambassadors. They could grow up knowing the beauty of the animals, not the dangers.

I give a bear class to fourth graders every year and mimic Center Street's sounds for the students. The kids seem charmed by it. Will this help them to grow up to have a better understanding of wildlife? Will they grow up thinking that humans could talk to bears?

The moment Center Street sees me approach, he starts talking. It is like a Rosetta Stone language program in bear speak. He says something; I say something. Turns out, he is the biggest chatterbox of my career. He is a gnarly wild bear who needs to get something off his chest. No other bear in my career vocalizes like Center Street. Some bears don't respond at all—just like some people.

After an hour, I get up off the ground, brush the sticky pine needles from my flannel jacket and jeans, and wander back to the house for some breakfast with Debs.

Just another little quirk—a sideshow, really—for one of the oddest jobs in America, performed by one of the oddest creatures (and husbands) ever to wander the earth.

Me.

CHAPTER SEVEN

A BEAR NAMED HEMORRHOID

L ife isn't ceremonial. It's mucky and hard, and I'm flummoxed by it much of the time, just like pretty much everyone else. Imagine how bears process their hard turns: the loss of a cub, the suffering, the hunger, the mixed messages, and life's puzzling ups and downs.

Coming before my hiring as wildlife officer, a bear by the name of Hemorrhoid has a huge impact on how I will approach my work. He casts a spotlight on the vigilante mobs the lumbering creatures often face primarily for just acting like the bears they are, voracious and not so good with boundaries . . . puzzled, confused, doing the best they can in difficult situations.

Anthropomorphizing—there's a $600 word. I've been criticized for giving human traits to bears for so long that I waffle on the importance of it. Note that I never name them Betty or Bob. Don't care much for calling one B107 either, which is what many experts prefer. Sounds to me like an isotope, or a jukebox selection. At the very least, tagging one B107 relegates them to something less important than humans, rather than the big, beefy, beautiful creatures that they are.

We give our pets human names. We name constellations and mountain ranges. Why not bears? Wasn't numbering people something they did in the death camps, to make their mistreatment more tolerable? To take away not just their humanity but their essence as living, breathing, thinking, and feeling beings?

So, in my own work, the bears are never Suzie or Amir. I always name them for their physical attributes, or missing parts, such as One Ear, a bear who likes to fight so much that it has cost him some critical parts.

And in this particular case we have Hemorrhoid, so named because he is so big and determined, he will flip over these giant dumpsters so he can walk right in. That is an enormous pain in the ass for the guys who have to tip them back upright the next morning. Hence, Hemorrhoid, king of the dumpsters.

Now, Hemorrhoid's favorite playground is the Lakes Basin. This photogenic spot, with lakes, creeks, and campsites, makes all the postcards, all the Instagram posts, all the chamber of commerce brochures. The series of high-elevation mountain lakes, five minutes from town, glow an iridescent blue. The Sierra breezes keep them a little choppy, so the water glimmers. Their granite shells cradle the lakes, collecting very little algae or bottom muck. You could wash your baby in these lakes. You could use them to make soup.

As you might expect, these lakes attract the bears. The bears march through the shallows, scarfing dead fish or stealing stringers of trout that anglers tie to branches along the shoreline. Once you've had a stringer full of fresh rainbow trout, you'll never forget it, especially if you're a bear. In the ursine kingdom, it's what passes for high-end sushi. Like you or me, if they have a good meal, a bear will typically return to the sure-thing place rather than take a chance on somewhere else. They become regulars.

Therefore, the lakes are prime bear habitat. I learn to wade along with the bears, warning anglers to hide their coolers, bring in their stringers of fish, and step back out of the way until the bear passes and goes on to easier targets. Most folks understand the situation. "Here comes the crazy bear guy with Winnie the Pooh," they say.

Remember, bears are garbage disposals with insatiable appetites, feeding constantly to gain fat for winter. Dubbed hyperphagia, these stretches of relentless eating lead to all sorts of confrontations.

We might call it stress eating. For the bears, it's a way of life. It distorts their every impulse. Mash together your own human needs for sex, water, and food, and that'll give you an idea of how a bear feels about a half-eaten chicken wing.

Well, some bears prefer a nice beer now and then too. So it is with Hemorrhoid, who was born near the very lake where this all happens.

Let me set the scene: perfect mountain lakes, a sold-out campground, people sleeping in tents and Winnebagos, fishing, swimming, making s'mores. You know how good s'mores smell when you crisp the marshmallow a little too much, let it burn black? Think what that does to a ravenous bear, whose powerful schnoz could smell a can of baked beans on the far side of the moon.

Hemorrhoid causes problems for weeks at the Lake Mary Store, a marina with a convenience shop. Strong as a truck, he tips over heavy dumpsters to reach food and fish scraps.

He comes several times a week, always at night, opening the giant walk-in cooler that is easily accessible just outside the front door of the store, placed there so that supply truck drivers can restock it easily. The male bear is so beefy, so strong, from everyone feeding him. We haven't yet been able to bear-proof the dumpsters, or prod visitors to stop the handouts. The bear comes in, opens the door, crushes a six-pack, and sucks down the contents. Whoosh, whoosh, whoosh, he pounds down the beers, steals some eggs, some bacon. Now, not only is he a pain in the ass, he is also a little buzzed on a sixer of Bud Light.

I hear about the bear at the marina. The owner of the store is getting angrier and angrier, and you can understand why. The bear has damaged the big cooler door, and at this point he appears unstoppable.

One morning, I spot the Department of Fish and Game rep at the Shell station at the center of town.

I say, "Hey, I heard what's going on up at the lake. I know it's going to be a problem. My name's Steve Searles. Maybe I can help."

Unimpressed, he drives away.

So I say, "Well, great to meet you."

That same night, Debs and I end up going up to Lake Mary to see some of her fellow New Zealanders staying at the campground. A mom, a dad, their three daughters, and a couple of friends. The beer is flowing, and I'm entertaining them with every scary bear story I know as the campfire flickers and the surrounding areas darken. I put the flashlight under my chin to heighten the drama. Every story is tragic; I tell no nice bear stories. The kids and adults are loving it. Nearby, just beyond the curtain of fire, a coyote howls.

Before they go to bed, the campers all grab sticks to defend themselves in case a bear comes into their tents; that's how freaked out they are by my bear stories. They are terrified.

So they don't get any sleep, the kids are having nightmares . . . crying. "Thanks, Uncle Steve! Good job with those bear stories you told." Debs and I drive home.

Oddly, and unknown to anyone, 150 yards away, the owner of the store and his sons are working on a scary drama of their own. Quietly, they've obtained what we call a depredation permit, which gives the permit holder the right to legally gun down particularly troublesome bears. In the dark of night, the very same night in which I've told my bear stories, they take a $5 rotisserie chicken and use it as bait in front of the walk-in cooler.

They head back to their cars, grab their guns, and wait.

By this point, the campground is super quiet. The hunters fall asleep, and while they're sleeping, Hemorrhoid gets the munchies and decides to drop in for a beer and some chicken. Who doesn't like chicken?

Hemorrhoid is a noisy eater, unfortunately. The first to hear him is the store owner, who suddenly wakes up and—still groggy—fires the first round, breaking the stillness. The quietest quiet you can imagine, a summer lake in the middle of the night, erupts in gunfire. He's using a .270-caliber deer rifle, with some pretty good pop. And the lake is ringed by granite walls, virtually an echo chamber. The old man starts shooting, and the boys jolt awake and start shooting. Pretty soon everybody's shooting. They get out of their cars and shoot some more. Sounds like Beirut during the height of the civil war.

The visitors in their tents are waking. *Holy shit, what's happening here?* They can't tell their nightmares from reality. They look out into the darkness—that's no help. They can't see the bear walking slowly—and bleeding—over to the boat ramp, three hunters blasting away at him, sounding like more than the seventeen rounds they are using because of all the reverb. All they can do is hear it.

The hunters are scared, the campers are alarmed. Just the sound of gunfire juices the adrenalin, makes you breathe a little too hard. As the campers overhear this massacre, the store owner comes over to the boat launch ramp, looks down at the bear, and fires the last bullet into him, putting his lights out at the water's edge.

Killing the bear turns out to be devastating to the store owner—he'd known this bear since he was a cub. It is especially devastating to all the campers, who have overheard what I feel is a totally unnecessary death—a murder. In their minds, what they've just heard won't stop.

It is the dumbest, most militant, most poorly thought-out solution to a manageable problem. There's so much rock and water up there, a ricochet might've killed someone. It is not a good scene by any standard; a bullet out of a deer rifle can even skip off water and pierce a tent or aluminum camper in a heartbeat.

As soon as the smoke clears, a tow truck comes in to winch the bear's carcass to take it away, a final indignity to this messed-up night.

It's almost dawn now, soft light seeping over the mountains. The campers, still in their PJs, all pack up and check out—who needs this? Some of them drive down to my house, tell me what they saw, about the gunfire and the blood. I go flying in my truck to the Fish and Game compound down the 395, where they have an evidence locker. On the bear's depredation tag, attached to the carcass, it says, "Cause of death: Lead poisoning." Like some sort of joke. I was incensed and sad.

Talk about a senseless incident that gives me direction and purpose. Talk about a situation that propels my need to develop nonlethal ways to solve this type of problem.

Hemorrhoid provides that. This bloodbath has a huge effect on my future bear work, while knowing in the back of my mind how much worse it could've been had one of those children been hit by a zigzagging shot. The gruesome ending is also a reality check on the cultural hurdles I will face as the town's wildlife officer. The trigger-happy locals are inclined to shoot first and ask questions later.

I mean, everything dies. Some of these bears needlessly lose their lives, and it makes a difference. It's an anomaly, but their plight helps save other bears.

So it is with poor Hemorrhoid, the insatiable, Bud-drinking bear who is hunted down like a common killer.

CHAPTER EIGHT

WHY BEARS SLEEP UPSIDE DOWN

I 'm not training poodles. I'm training 450-pound delinquents.

Results are almost immediate, though; the bear problem changes just like that. Over time, the bears have lost their natural fear of humans. I prod them to remember what is in their DNA. I am trying everything—gas-powered cannons, cherry bombs. I am just experimenting. My fear becomes their fear. When I ram a dumpster to chase a bear out, then lay on the horn and yell at them, I am instilling respect. The next time I see the bear, the next night, he takes off running the moment he spots me. I can see it in his eyes, the way he turns back to make note of me as he flees: *That guy's crazy!* To be their protector, and to save them from being shot, I can't be their pal. This is tough love with fireworks. I am just getting them to remember what's been built into them for thousands of years—fear humans. Or else.

Each day, I take a crash course in bear behavior. I am learning their eating patterns, when and where they sleep. It's not theoretical. It's a hands-on masterclass. Early on, I realize I can never know everything about these bears. The challenge of that inspires me, appeals to my fickle nature. I've found something that I won't lose interest in. I know I have a lifetime of learning ahead.

People call me an expert on bears, but no one is ever an expert. It'd be like naming every star in the Milky Way.

Still, I am absorbing every little nugget I can, every ray of light. I learn their regimens, their guilty pleasures.

In watching them day and night, I learn how bears use their paws the way a safecracker might. They are able to open surprisingly delicate and tiny things—locks, linchpins, pieces of wire. They have no opposable thumbs, of course, but other than that they have us beat. Their fingers are much stronger. An inch and a half of claw shows, with another inch and a half recessed into their paws, a marvel of engineering that allows them to scamper up trees, something we already know that their cousin, the grizzly, is incapable of doing.

Bears, I am learning, have stinky yet extraordinary coats, with long guard hairs, three-inch strands on their sides and backs. There is under hair as well, like a set of thermal skivvies, protecting a thick, leathery skin. Like chaps, their heavy skin shields them from winter and the harsh realities of life in the wilderness, even bug bites and bee stings.

Beneath that, these bears have a generous sheathing of blubber— a 1.5-inch-thick slab of creamy fat that stores reserves of energy, then a layer of muscle three times that of a strong man. Knowing their anatomy is critical if you need to shoot bears without causing them undue suffering, either as a hunter or a wildlife officer who has to occasionally put down an injured bear.

Some parts of a bear's body are essentially bulletproof. Often, hunters skinning a bear will find a bullet from years before, a sign of the bear's toughness and pain threshold. Shooting a bear in the rear haunches is almost useless, like throwing rocks at a tank.

I find bears to be smarter than dogs. Living in the wild, they have to be more savvy. They have to figure out weather, droughts, seasons, food shortages. Over time, I learn the life cycle of bears. A bear's age is similar to a dog's. By age three, they are usually breeding. By fifteen, they are senior citizens.

For colors, I notice lots of variations. Though they're called black bears, in California I discover that they are rarely black. This leads to much confusion on black bears versus grizzlies.

Bears back East are black as Bibles. In California, where the sun is relentless and would sap a feeding bear of strength and fluids, bears dress in reds, mochas, burgundies, and lighter tans that are often described as cinnamon. Some are blond, such as a bear I dub Blondie, who, as you'll learn later, is a very troubled bear, a break-in artist, a mourning mother who faced a tragic ending.

Something in Blondie went haywire. But as I am learning, there seem to be no serial killer bears—no Jeffrey Dahmer bears. In fact, black bears never eat people. Some bears are troublesome, slow learners, stubborn, fierce. But I am finding no evidence of psychotic bears. In general, they are not as mental as many humans. Honestly, there are more people out there who eat people than there are black bears that eat people.

They have, as every bear expert will attest, a very sophisticated system of telemetry, with the GPS capabilities of a high-end German sedan. That's why, when wildlife officials invariably try to relocate a bear, sometimes a hundred miles away, the bear will come out of the cage, shake off the tranquilizer and the sense of dislocation and confusion, turn his nose up to read the winds, sight the angle of the sun, and follow the apple harvests as he slowly makes his way back to his soft pine needle daybed. Home at last. We all know the feeling. This remarkable return is probably the product of all the bear's skill sets, but a sense of telemetry is certainly at the center of it.

Millions used to be spent on relocation, till experts realized how futile it usually is.

It isn't that the bears need to get back among their friends, or the bustle of the town. They just want their own pillow. In fact, I am finding that bears have no real need for fellowship, the way we humans do.

Similarly, I find that the bears have great strength, matched with quick-twitch reflexes. Native Americans considered them ghosts for their ability to slip out of sight. They have a running back's ability to take three quick steps, then vanish. Blink and they're gone.

Bears are playful, I find. At Halloween, they will steal the pumpkins off your porch, roll them around a while, then eat them.

They have a chain of command; they are independent thinkers, not herd animals. I have seen them playing on swing sets, or sledding down their bellies in the snow, like children.

In Valley Vista, a subdivision of mega-cabins and other million-dollar homes, just off Meridian Boulevard, the porches all have life-sized hand-carved bears. It's everywhere, this artwork, the way Rio has statues of Jesus.

Nearly every Valley Vista home has a bear story. At one, a caramel-corn mansion made of logs, an older couple spend their last year in a downstairs room, with nurses and hospital beds—a high-end home hospice. They are in their final days, waiting out the inevitable. Every morning, a mother and her cubs keep them company just outside the window, peering in, as if to say, *We're here.* The bears sleep and suckle on the deck. The bears are only about six feet from the old man's bed.

When I ask whether the couple would like me to remove the bears, they reply, "No, we love them." Inadvertently, the bears had become part of their caregiving team.

Bears burrow under giant decks to carve out their dens, gnaw away bottom stairs, kick in crawl space doors. There, in total darkness, they will hibernate—no food, no water, no urination, no defecation—for over five months.

It is amid these dream homes that I have a moment of self-discovery. At this point, I still don't really know what I am doing, and doubters are everywhere in town. Well, at one Valley Vista house, the cubs have created their own snow-play park on the twenty-foot snowplow piles, skidding down on their bellies and butts to create a toboggan run as the sow watches. I never see the mama bear join in. Like many mothers, she prefers to watch over them.

The residents are delighted by this snow show. My chronic pleas to residents not to panic every time they spot a bear have started to kick in. The residents don't dial 9-1-1. They don't merely tolerate the bears; they appreciate them. Moms and dads will stop by at their lunch hours, or when they get home, to watch the bears play.

Some of the most demanding, outspoken people you could ever find have come to accept the bears. It is exhibit A for me, in learning that I don't just have to work with the bears; I have to work with the residents and visitors too.

By now, I am battling every preconceived notion—my own, and those of other people. As I grow more aware, I realize the king of the forest will bluff-charge you to create space—"Hey, leave me alone!"—then will walk away from most confrontations and even fights, gentle almost beyond reason.

I'm finding the so-called experts hand out more misinformation about bears than accurate information. For example, wildlife brochures urge homeowners to store garbage in their freezers till it is ready for trash day. Can you imagine asking your spouse to do that? Or, this chestnut: "Don't run, a bear will chase you." That's completely wrong. A black bear never chased anything in their life.

Note that their enormous strength makes no sense, given how docile, even sheepish, they are. You take a head of lettuce from a rhino, it'll stomp you to death. Swipe a head of lettuce from a bear, and it'll just shrug and go off looking for some more lettuce.

"Thanks for taking my lettuce. Nice to see ya. Bye."

Oddly—and perhaps a lesson for us—a bear's power isn't in its massive shoulders or the steel in its well-muscled back.

A bear's true power is in its patience and tolerance.

Knowing this makes me more interested in their relationships and emotions, and I decide that understanding their triggers and their temperaments will help me in my work.

I also spend a fair amount of time on the basic biology of bears. A sow's pregnancy lasts seven months. Before hibernating, they eat twenty-three hours a day and consume sixty thousand calories to last them through the long winter. I learn how, as winter approaches, they use a special diet to shut down their metabolism for the five or six months they spend in their dens. I watch them scoop dirt into their mouths and eat their own fur to plug up their systems. Then, at first frost, I see them disappear into their dens, the bigger bears claiming the nicer spots, part of the natural hierarchy.

Crawling into their dens with cameras and microphones, I see how they will essentially build big condor nests, and that they sleep upside down, as if holding a somersault tuck. This helps neutralize their digestive systems as well, using gravity to put their digestive processes on hold.

After hibernation, I watch them step out of their dens, not particularly hungry or horny or desperate, as you might expect. At this point, they methodically eat only foods that will scrub their systems—the colon, the rectum—for 1.5 months, before turning to eat their regular diets of fruit, nuts, wasps, dandelions, mule's ear, tree roots, honeycomb, insects, and carrion. Currants as well. Even ants.

I learn how a sow, after a seven-month pregnancy, spends two years with her cubs, from the time she births them, usually in summer when food is plentiful, to the time she pushes them off to be on their own.

After she sets them free, she becomes fertile again, or "in season."

Breeding is when their gentle nature disappears. It's rough. They do it doggy style. The male will bite her back and neck. I don't mean to sound prurient, or gratuitous, but in one round, he'll knock out seven to eight orgasms. This doesn't reflect the bears' raw lust or sense of domination. It merely speaks to nature's determination to perpetuate the species.

Exhausted, the male will lie down, and sometimes another male will take his place. When she's had enough of all this, the female will sit down, and the lusty male will bite her on the neck to gain access again.

When she's young and skinny, the semen is mostly just a nutrient. Mother Nature will not pull the pregnancy trigger till she feels the female is robust enough to support another life.

If she's Big Bertha, Mother Nature might give her two cubs. If she's robust, yet not a giant, she'll have one or none. If she's not ready physically to bear a cub, the eggs will lie dormant and not implant into the uterine wall.

The babies are tiny. Small as rats. The birthing process isn't agonizing. It takes minutes. Compared to humans, the birth is a non-event.

This next fact freaks people out, because it seems counter to the survival of any species: a male bear will actually kill a cub to make a mother available to breed again. He doesn't know if the cub is his cub; there is no marker for that. So to ensure his seed promulgates to its fullest extent, he kills the cub. The mother will then breed with her cub's killer. Ugly and unsettling, but a sign of nature's determination to survive.

In their heyday, when bears are more abundant, a dozen cubs are born in town. Every year, the number becomes more manageable. Near the end of my career, we had one year when the town registered zero cubs. We shut off the flow of free human food, and Mother Nature responded by dialing back the birth rate. My feeling is that nature somehow gauged the size of the females and realized the habitat wasn't enough to sustain a new crop of bears. Does that seem omniscient? Of course it does. People love cubs, and they love to hear my annual report on the number born that year. But that's exactly what we want: sustainable growth, at a rate that doesn't exceed the natural food supply.

The bear population in California is roughly one per square mile in suitable habitat. In Mammoth, it often comes out to many more than that. Why? Look at that man-made habitat: the koi ponds, the hiding places under the decks, the lush golf courses. There is more food, hence more bears. Obviously, nutrition, water, and habitat are critical to all living things. In our case, something known as social carrying capacity also plays into it—essentially, the willingness of a town to host and care for its wildlife.

In a scruffy-dry pine forest, we're the honey pot.

Add in one semi-confused wildlife officer trying these new nonlethal ways of making them behave and learn.

Early on, residents and town officials describe my tactics as hazing. I resent that implication. By definition, hazing is unnecessary. It doesn't teach anyone anything. At one point, a Mammoth cop comes up to me, so proud. He tells me he's just zapped a bear in the butt with a rubber bullet to try to get him away from some trash. "He never even saw it coming. I fucking shot him right in the ass!"

I have to stroke his ego. He means well, and he is using the tools I introduced. I tell him, "Good job, buddy. Now, let's think about this a minute. Did you help anything? This bear sleeps under sixty feet of snow, he gets jabbed with sticks and bitten by animals on a regular basis. What did one rubber bullet really accomplish?"

Shooting that bear is what I would call hazing. It is shortsighted and a little cruel.

To me, this incident could be a teachable moment. In this situation, I would yell to the culprit, "Hey! What are you doing? Hurry up, get out of there." I might chase him with my truck, blow an airhorn, swat him with my shotgun barrel. I want to get the whole population of bears to worry about me more than they crave an easy meal. That would be an achievement, to get them to set aside the thing that's most important in their life: food. After all, they only have six months to eat a year's worth of calories.

Because I'm a wingnut, I grow more and more obsessed. Almost like an undercover cop, I drive around in different cars, so that the bears aren't afraid of this one guy—me—so that they'll be afraid of and respectful to humans in general. I change up what I wear and what I drive, so the bears won't recognize me. I need the bears to wonder whether I am the trusting tourist who just arrived in town or the ornery bear master with the pocket full of firecrackers. I want the bears to respect all people.

At a certain point, I notice that when citizens spot my standard-issue shotgun, they react fearfully and unpredictably. It amps up every situation. When I switch to an orange shotgun, they relax, assuming the colorful shotgun fires Twinkies and lavender farts. On my part, it is pure human psychology. They have no idea this type of gun, carried in every cop car in America, can blow a hole in a car door if necessary. I certainly can't go into a situation where human life is at stake with a fart-thrower.

So, although I am experimenting with nonlethal ammo, I still carry lethal shells as well. I need the lethal ammo as a fallback. I would use it only as a last resort, with great care and only in the ugliest of circumstances.

Bottom line: a human life will always be worth more than a bear's life. If necessary, I am always prepared to shoot to kill. My mind is preset for that situation. I can't waver; this is heavy stuff. I have to act in the moment. I am no Supreme Court justice pondering the nuances of a case.

As the saying goes, the roads are littered with flattened squirrels that couldn't make up their minds.

Yet, the orange shotgun is a sign that, little by little, I am learning the ropes and how to best use all the tools at my disposal—to manage the bears as well as the humans.

Along the way, I also develop what I call SCAT (special control and aversive tactics) kits. Of course, it's also a synonym for bear poop. I know an unusual acronym like this will draw interest from officers.

I should've made a fortune on the kits. Through the years, dozens of manufacturers have contacted me about everything from nonlethal tricks to bear spray, hoping for my endorsement, my input, and they're willing to pay. The nonlethal ammo kits alone could make me a fortune. I always say

no. My instinct, my heart, my soul all tell me to give this away. It is a gift
for me to work with wildlife, and I want everyone to benefit from it. To
monetize something like that seems inherently wrong.

But the kits are always a hit. I start using them when I work with the
cops, hold clinics, show them my nonlethal tricks. My clinics include brochures and stickers, but what really gets the cops' juices flowing are all the
whiz-bang pyrotechnics that are part of the kits, most fired from shotguns.
They range from fairly harmless noisemakers to flash-bang devices, to
rubber buckshot, to rubber slugs, all the way to nine-pellet buckshot and
the thumb-sized rifle slugs that could drop a bear.

Each day brings a new lesson. One morning, we are called to a construction site on the edge of town, where real estate maven Stacey Bardfield is
building a large home for herself. Stacey is a pioneer in Mammoth real
estate. From what I can tell, she works so hard that she barely sleeps. She's
earned a showplace like this for herself, after finding condos and homes
for thousands of clients over the years.

On this day, the dispatcher gets a call that there is a sow and some cubs
on the property, no doubt attracted by the food and wrappers that the
construction workers always leave lying around—the half-eaten donuts
frozen in the snow, a mustardy disk of tomato someone tossed onto a pile
of lumber scraps. To a mama bear feeding in the early spring, famished
from a long winter in the den and looking to feed her cubs, those little
handouts would prove irresistible.

When I arrive, the site is clear of workers. I immediately call for
backup from the Mammoth Police, given the unpredictability of calls
involving cubs. The officer and I pull out our sidearms as we come
blindly around the half-finished house, following the snowy tracks of
the mama and the two cubs. The tracks give us an edge in knowing
where they were.

All is good, no cause for alarm, when suddenly the tracks of three bears
become the tracks of just one. Whoa. I'm still learning the ropes, and fear

is my default. We reel around, knowing that the other two bears have to be somewhere behind us, maybe a few feet away. They will have the jump on us if they are frightened and desperate to reach their mother. My mind is spinning: Why did they peel off from her? Is the mom wounded or hurt or sick? Is she trying to be a decoy and draw us away from the cubs? The routine call gets sticky in a hurry. The key concern now: Where the hell are they?

Our heads on swivels, we continue to follow the remaining tracks, certain from the size of them that we are following the mother. When we get to the edge of the property, we see Mama looking back at us, with her two cubs riding gleefully on her back.

Again, our presumptions are tossed upside down. The creativity and playfulness of this sow has gotten the best of us. I snarl at her, shoo her away from the construction site, and make a note to scold the foreman for inadvertently baiting the bears. Unless he wants to crawl under this house one day and bump noses with a 450-pound mother bear, he'd best have his workers clean up after themselves.

Bears in cars turn out to be a special challenge for me as well. Lured by the smell of french fries or a wedge of Gruyere, they gnaw off a tail light to gain entry to a trunk. They fiddle with a door to get inside, then freak out when the door swings closed behind them, trapping them. At that point they go nuts, ripping out the seats, the airbags, steaming the windows as they literally lose their shit, a sign of how scared they are. The experience is so foreign to them that they are at wit's end.

In these early years, I really struggle to harness my fears during these kinds of calls. The bears are highly agitated as they tear the car to shreds. We always have both lethal and nonlethal guns standing by. I am always looking for an edge or a tactic to keep everyone safe. I learn to use a C-clamp and a parachute cord to pull open the car doors from a distance, in hopes of avoiding a bear that is desperate and probably furious at being caged up like that. Sometimes, I stand on the car's roof, as far away as I can get.

I mean, imagine the situation. This wild bear has been locked in the car, sometimes for many hours; the windows are fogged up, the seats and cushion material are everywhere, giant wads of foam and fabric. You can't even see where the animal is.

In one case, it takes me fifteen minutes to get the car door safely open. The big bear races out, then starts to circle back toward me, a huffy and aggressive maneuver I haven't experienced before.

"Holy shit, you get out of here!" I yell. "Bad bear! Bad bear! I will fucking light you up!"

And I do. I ping her with some nonlethal bullets, finally chase her off. I am pissed off and mystified over the fact that she has challenged me so directly like this. Very strange behavior for a mother bear, even under stressful conditions.

When I inspect the car, it all starts to make sense. Hiding under the brake pedal, I find her cub, about sixteen inches long, round as a coffee can, cowering down and terrified from watching Mom tear up the car for so long.

I scoop the cub up, walk it to the end of the parking lot, and off it scampers into the woods with its mother.

Among the lessons I am picking up, one of the most important I learn: bears don't want revenge the way we might. When they're locked in a car, they just want to be free. There is no pent-up rage or need to lash out.

After all my early efforts to stay out of harm's way, I finally learn that I can walk up and calmly open the door, and the bear will race out, not giving me a second look. Now I get it.

By this time, I am developing this public persona around town. To get out my message of coexistence, I speak to a lot of groups, and residents know me from articles and TV. They enjoy my stories and my jokes. They are taken by the props I bring, including the animal skins. "Hey, kids, is this a bobcat, here? A cougar? A skunk?"

Standing in front of them, dressed in denim, leather, and heavy boots, they think I'm Davy Crockett.

In reality, I'm a very reserved and private person. A lonely person—that's just my natural state, my preference. But everywhere I go, people are starting to pat me on the back.

More and more, my comfort zone is the bears. They like being in the shadows, being by themselves, left alone. So do I. I think that's why I am increasingly drawn to them and working so hard to become their advocate and protector.

CHAPTER NINE

I HATE FEAR

P oets and songwriters claim that love is our most irrational emotion. I nominate fear.

I hate fear. I hate what it does to me, what it does to any of us, certainly what it did to me back in those early days.

The brake-pedal cub shows what happens when you make any sort of assumptions. It also sums up what I am now learning about the very nature of fear itself. Our twitchy fight-or-flight mechanisms seem better suited to earlier times—of tribal warfare, of wolves circling a campfire. These days, our fight-or-flight responses are still so ingrained that they preempt rational thought. In turn, irrational emotions make us jumpy and quick to demonize anything we don't understand. To me, that kind of circuity is obsolete. It seems humans have a deep, nonsensical need to be afraid of something. We may change what we're afraid of, but it seems to be in our nature to need something to fight against. We seem to seek out things to fear.

As I learn that a bear trapped inside a car harbors no ill will, no pent-up rage, I am starting to wonder: what else are we afraid of that we shouldn't be?

Obviously I am a bit of a roughneck philosopher. Maybe it's the beautiful vistas, the heavenly views that make me reflective? In any case, I can't help seeing little lessons or life tips, gleaned from creatures who sometimes have more things figured out than we do.

Unlike us, bears do not have the capacity for revenge. For all my own personal struggles, I am learning that a sense of revenge gets us nowhere. I can't say enough about how useless it is—a byproduct of fear, hatred, and all our other senseless and irresponsible emotions.

People of different cultures, different lifestyles, people who clip safety pins in their noses? People who scrawl tattoos on their necks? People of different pigments, people who wear funny hats, or talk weird, or have different ideas about what constitutes God?

As with the bears, what if we took time to know these people a little, rather than just lash out based out on all our preconceptions? What would happen then? Could we conquer hate and fear?

At this point, I still have holes in my psyche that I don't know how to fill. But I sure am learning about the uselessness of fear. I am learning to loathe fear.

CHAPTER TEN

BIG RUNS FOR HIS LIFE

Big—the bear that taught me about pecking order and respect—must be a majestic sight on this summer day, up here on the outskirts of town, on the edge of the forest, a forest he rules with great ease and quiet dignity. He might be building a daybed for his afternoon nap, pulling the grasses, decades of decomposing pine cones, all into a natural quilt on which to snooze away the summer heat. That's when he probably first hears the barking.

Big is more than massive. He is also a very intelligent bear, so he understands that there are often loose dogs in the residential areas of Mammoth Lakes. He can triangulate their position and determine when they're roaming free, not on leashes. In this case, the barking is moving too fast, closing the distance from when he first hears them to where they are a minute later. Suddenly, the 650-pound bear does something he has never had to do: Big begins to run for his life, through heavy pine forest, juking and zigzagging around rocks and trees.

As he runs, he hears the dogs getting closer. He is confused and disoriented by the barking; an unfamiliar weakness starts to burn in his legs. As he tires, he stumbles, losing his footing in the loose rock. Perhaps for the first time in his life, the king of the forest starts to feel fear. His mind and body go into overdrive. Why are they chasing me? What evil deed have I done?

On this day, in the mountains overlooking the Knolls, his quest for an afternoon nap turns into a nightmare. The dogs are getting closer and closer, his enormous legs heavier and heavier. The fear he first felt a few minutes ago starts to build. His lungs hurt. Fast as he is, the dogs are faster, younger, better suited to long distances. They are high-tech hunting dogs, with GPS collars featuring mini cameras. And now, they can see him through the trees, this beautiful bear running for his life, kicking up pine cones, needles, and dust, heading for the town of Mammoth, his home, the place where he was born . . . his paradise, his Shangri-La.

As they close in on him, Big hops atop a boulder. A half dozen hunting dogs in orange collars surround him. There are no hunters yet, but he hears the sound of approaching humans. Then their voices. The dogs are frantic. Big spins completely around, trying to keep them in sight. He spins some more, they bark and snap. Bloodlust. Gnashing teeth. Fear Big can feel in his throat.

Big has chosen the biggest outcropping on the hill, Christmas Tree Rock, the same boulder we stand on when we put up the town tree each December, a prominent twenty-five-foot-high boulder overlooking the valley and the town. It's probably a quarter of a mile up, on a steep slope surrounded by manzanita, scrub brush, and pine.

The hunters, in full camouflage, finally catch up to the dogs. Most residents would be shocked by this sight, that something like this is still legal in California. To my knowledge, California has the longest bear season in the nation, running from early October to late December.

These hunters are what are known as "houndsmen." The tech and the $5,000 rifles they use are considered by hunting foes as violations of "fair chase" protocols, meaning their gear and firepower give them an unethical advantage over the animals. The houndsmen use laptops to track their dogs, and they ride around in specialized trucks, rolling kennels, really, filled with barking dogs. As the houndsmen search for bears, the lead dog will stand atop the truck, sniffing the fire roads. When he picks up the scent, the hunters will turn him and the other dogs loose to tree the bear—or in this case, chase him atop a boulder. He's essentially been cornered, at a high point, technically "at bay." Winded. Exhausted. Done. Done. Done.

Till this moment, the bear that would inspire me has led a long and wonderful life—the equivalent of an extended summer camp. Big's thighs are as fat around as your waist. Humans hold him in awe, as do other bears. While most bears are trying to establish themselves in the ursine hierarchy, Big is the obvious homecoming king. Females love him; they are biologically programmed to pursue the biggest males. So, daily life has always come easily to him. Big eats well; he loves well; he doesn't waste his time brawling with other bears. He has nothing to prove. The other bears know to steer clear.

I've known Big a long time. After my initial encounter with him, that epiphany in the town dump, I spot him about once a week, while making my rounds. From a distance, his sheer size makes it easy to identify him. Plus, he has a fighter pilot's swagger, though he isn't a bully. You or I, given Hercules's strength, might flip over a Volkswagen just because. The adulation might lead to hubris and perhaps make us less-decent characters. Not Big. He does not provoke encounters. He carries himself with confidence and class, almost a role model. Imagine that, a bear with presence, a humble hero, a well-meaning brute.

He lives up in the Knolls, amid the nice homes on the hillside at the edge of town, where the lots are good sized and folks can't overhear their next-door neighbors clanging pots in the kitchen or singing in the shower. A handsome area, full of koi ponds and pines; there are no ugly bins or dirty dumpsters sitting sideways out front of the homes. Bear-proof trash cans are tucked away in garages, as you often find in the better neighborhoods.

This is where Big has settled and made his life.

Now, these hunters have caught up to Big and their dogs, using all their high-tech wizardry. Technically, they are out of bounds; you can't hunt this close to town, an ordinance adopted after a stray bullet once hit a teacher standing at her chalkboard. As students watched, a deer hunter's bullet zipped under a door of a classroom and ricocheted into her wrist. That bizarre incident led to the no-hunting zone that extends for a mile beyond the town limits. On this particular day, while chasing Big, the hunters started in legal territory, lost track of their whereabouts, and entered the no-hunt halo.

Nearby, residents are out washing their cars, stacking firewood, going about their mountain lives when they hear the barking. Because of the acoustics of the canyon and the prevailing winds, they can hear the hunters, but the hunters cannot hear them. The houndsmen don't realize that the residents are gathering at the foot of the mountain, furious over what is going on in a no-hunt zone right by all these homes. Protective of their bears, protective of their own safety, the residents have a clear line of sight at all that is happening. They are screaming at them from far below as the hunters admire their giant prey. A dozen residents are yelling: *"Don't shoot! Don't shoot!"* The hunters can't hear any of this.

As the residents and I watch in horror, the hunters high-five each other, then one of the houndsmen pulls out a .44 Magnum, walks to the boulder, and calmly pops the bear. The pain is excruciating but quick. Down goes Big in a heap on the boulder. The hunters congratulate each other, pet their highly trained and high-strung dogs. They are in no hurry and still don't know the fury that awaits them. Their trucks are miles away. They decide that the best way to get the bear off the mountain is to roll him down the hill, so they push him off the giant boulder. Big's body tumbles a bit before snagging on a branch. A hunter kicks him off the branch, and Big somersaults down the jagged hill toward the horrified residents below, pretty much a worst-case scenario for out-of-bounds hunters.

Soon, everyone is standing around what looks like another boulder on the rocky hill. He is all wadded up and filthy from somersaulting down the hill. It's a bad scene. Every time you blast a bear, it always draws a crowd. The residents are a vigilante posse at this point, spitting mad. All they are missing is pitchforks.

As a professional, I can go home and cry in the shower, but not in the field. I have to hold my mud, figure out the situation, try to assess who is right, who is wrong. I also have to work within the laws of the state, which allow bear hunting. If I can't do that, I have to find a different line of work. My feelings about right and wrong are very strong. The only way I can maintain my job is to know what is allowed by the law and force myself to abide by that. Some people make the laws; others enforce them. As contentious as I could be over the safety of bears, I realize the reality of the situation: at the time, hunting with hounds is legal. Killing bears like this is legal.

Despite their bloody hobby, the hunters don't come off as dark-hearted or arrogant. They know their stuff and are claiming it was an honest mistake, that they followed all the laws to a tee, but wandered out of bounds while in hot pursuit. By this point, with residents pointing fingers, spitting at them and demanding justice, the Fish and Game folks just want to get the hunters out of there fast. Six of us use ropes to pull Big into the back of a Fish and Game truck, so they can take him to the station, where we will continue the interviews and investigation.

At the station, we watch the video from the dogs' collar cameras. From the footage, you can see they started after Big in legal territory, which looked much like the habitat where they eventually bouldered the bear. The hunters insist that they didn't realize that the town was watching them, or how far off the mark they were, despite all their tech. The officers interrogate them some more, hassle them a bit.

Now, I have to tell you that a dead bear isn't much use to anyone. To butcher one for food, you have to cut through all the layers of fat to finally reach the deep-red meat. Though extremely high in protein and nutrients such as riboflavin, iron, and thiamin, bear meat will never be confused with a juicy rib eye. Some hunters make sausage of it; even then it's pretty vile. Some cultures believe dried bear gallbladder is some sort of miracle health aid, an aphrodisiac, but I think the interest in that is really overstated. Certainly, in some places they do poach bears and make a small incision to pull out the gallbladder, which then goes to the black market. People call me about it, make claims, but I have never been able to confirm it happening up here.

In the 1600s, a bear was a valuable commodity—for food, clothing, tools. Today, hunting a bear is all about the kill.

Surprisingly, the authorities end up giving Big back to the houndsmen. The massive bear, the king of kings, is carted away as a trophy, probably a contender for a coveted Boone and Crockett Club game record.

It's still in my head today, the way the world looks when the town mascot is gunned down—where the sun is in the sky, which way the wind is blowing, how everything smells.

To me, it is a death in the family. Losing a dog is agonizing. This is even worse. Once home, I cry till the shower runs cold.

CHRIS CUTS IN AGAIN . . .

As a critic once asked of E. E. Cummings: "What is wrong with a man who writes like this?"

Beats me. Everything?

Two years before this project came along, my wife and older son died six months apart—my son in a traffic accident, my wife after a long struggle with abdominal cancer. This book is to be a way of dealing with the emotional wallop of all that, to take my mind off my own struggles. A book is like landing a plane, requiring all your concentration, all your reflexes. Some might see that as denial or avoidance. Well, exactly. The only way I can cope is to not let the totality of the twin tragedies reach me all at once, to accept the situation in increments, to get on with my work, to dote on my three surviving kids, who need me more than ever with their mother gone.

So, as noted earlier, I am damaged goods. We all are. Even Steve, tall and smirky, with that wicked sense of humor, a gun on his hip. We all are.

These days, if you're not crying once in a while, are you even alive? Are there dead zones in your heart? Even the manliest of mountain men like Steve will cry.

At least once a week, sometimes more, Steve chokes up while telling me another new story. He apologizes. "Shut up," I say.

Despite my early misgivings, this project has a certain gravitational pull. I spent years writing breezy personal essays for the Los Angeles Times. *They were odes to the suburbs. If you think life in an American suburb is occasionally stultifying, imagine writing about it every week over three decades. After the deaths of my wife and son, I felt a need to raise the sails a bit, to sample a different prevailing wind.*

That's what this book represents to me. It became a sailing trip through Steve's supple mind.

Seldom in the suburbs do you meet a character like Steve Searles. Is that a good thing? You decide. To me, he is America—stubborn, free thinking, independent as hell. He's not a cookie-cutter, state-school kid who looks just like everybody else, buys the same soap, gushes over the Monday night game. He's more comfortable outdoors than in. He's lived a little, which usually makes men and women far more interesting. Through his ups and downs, he's stayed resilient and playful.

Like a doctor, I try to build some trust and rapport.

Here's our writing process: Steve's in Mammoth Lakes; I'm five hours away in Los Angeles. Over the phone, Steve tells a story. I jot down some notes. I turn the jottings into a new chapter. Steve reads the new chapter. He yells at me over the phone. I yell back. We fix the mistakes. I tell a dirty limerick: "There once was a man from Madras . . ." He begins to go off on why the American working class is screwed.

We're a Harlequin bromance. We're a Second City skit.

It's a septic process. Steve is fond of what his brother once dubbed "skip-talking," meaning he'll jump from topic to topic. As a columnist, I am famous for my abstract stream-of-consciousness ramblings. This makes any sort of narrative nearly impossible to achieve. At one point, we must have three hundred pages of entertaining asides.

"I'm skip-talking again," he'll say, catching himself darting from story to story.

"Doesn't matter," I say.

"Why not?"

"I quit," I say.

We argue over naming his tormentors. We argue over how we handle his personal demons. We argue over punctuation, particularly commas.

Me: "No more tequila!" is way different from "No, more tequila!"

Steve: I like tequila.

Me: That's not the point!

We are the oddest of odd couples. My laptop is probably worth more than his entire wardrobe. His guns are worth more than my house.

When I visit his cabin home, we set up a corkboard with index cards marked for each chapter. While sipping way too much Folgers, we splice together his long, difficult life. "This bear belongs here." "That New Jersey scene—move it up there." We pour more coffee. When things get tough, we add a splash of Baileys.

And little by little, stitch by stitch, we create Steve's quilt.

Little by little, nail by nail, we build his house.

One tree at a time, we pull together the incredible magic forest in which he thrives.

Indeed, on the coldest nights, Mammoth looks like moonlight through a martini, a milky paradise. Beneath that? Black ice and hard truths.

Little by little, we are finding those hard truths.

Damn, this is an agonizing task we've taken on. I have calluses on my frontal cortex. Steve is sniffling again. He apologizes.

"Shut up," I say.

CHAPTER ELEVEN

WILDERNESS JESUS

Here I am, this ponytailed loudmouth up in Mammoth Lakes, California, a nobody in a no place town—a foul-mouthed former hunter—preaching coexistence with bears, making small inroads, sometimes spinning my wheels, ordering bumper stickers, chasing bears out of hotels and out of luxury SUVs, wondering if I am doing the right thing with my life, their lives, this area, which on weekends is a slapstick comedy of tourists stumbling over their ski poles . . .

One morning, I respond to a bear call at a local hotel to find a Russian tourist standing out front, with a gorgeous girlfriend and the kind of Corvette convertible that's always made me drool. I suppose there isn't anything about his life I don't envy: his looks, his money, his lady friend, his ride. Only, the car has just been totaled, torn to shreds by a hungry bear lured by the cooler full of fine meats and cheeses he left out. The tourist comes down in the morning to find that a bear shredded the convertible top, then did a number on the seats and interior.

I genuinely feel bad for the guy and his situation. The car is trashed, undriveable. I apologize on behalf of the bear, tell him how sorry I am to see their vacation ruined, offer him and his girlfriend a ride to the airport.

He just shrugs. "It's a rental," he says. "I'll just have them bring me another one."

Two worlds, theirs and mine. The visitors are like dogs off leash, frisky and happy for their freedom. We locals are lucky for their never-ending interest and their loyalty to this mountain paradise.

At this stage, my life is full of encounters with them, me the bearded civil serf trying to protect both the locals and these weekend warriors, working quietly, grinding out a blue-collar life.

One of my biggest breaks: the *Los Angeles Times* calls.

Now, I have already done some stories for small local newspapers, though none of them really get much notice or move the needle for me.

But now, reflecting my growing presence, comes a piece by *Los Angeles Times* environmental writer Frank Clifford, in the Sunday edition, "above the fold" as they say in newspapers, meaning it is featured prominently high on the front page.

This article butters my bread. It changes my life.

Clifford writes:

> *[Bears are] everywhere: beneath the former Jehovah's Witnesses meeting house, in the foundation of the Travelodge, in the breezeway of the local halfway house, underneath scores of homes and abandoned buildings.*

The article isn't just a profile of me and my odd job. It reaches more broadly and discusses how bears are becoming a problem in residential areas across the nation.

> *As the outer limits of modern society bump up against once remote forests and mountain ranges, wild animals discover that civilization is often a more reliable food source than nature.*

The article goes on to describe how nuisance bears like these were once shot without much provocation, but that today's live-and-let-live policies have resulted in population explosions in residential areas, at density rates far higher than those found in the wilderness.

Then it explains how Mammoth Lakes has addressed the problem by hiring me.

A lifelong trapper and hunter, he has taken to his job like a stern uncle saddled with a brood of overgrown delinquents.

Since readers on the East Coast see the piece first, before sunrise in the West, I stand in my robe in the kitchen, answering call after early call from TV producers, anchors, and other media outlets. The second I hang up, the phone rings again.

I don't want to spend too much time with any of them, for fear of missing out on others. Luckily, I have a stack of five-by-seven cards on the kitchen counter, and I decide to jot down names and numbers, then promise to get back to them later.

As Debs walks into the kitchen, I am hanging up a bit abruptly on one caller. She watches me scribble down the caller's name, in choppy block letters: BRIAN TAGUMBL . . . She looks it over, puzzles over it for a few seconds, then shouts: "Wait . . . Bryant Gumbel? You just hung up on Bryant Gumbel?" I don't even know who the big-shot NBC anchor is, but she sure does. Immediately, the phone rings again.

In fact, the phone rings for hours. When the East Coast producers and assignment editors are done, the Midwest starts calling, then the West Coast. Obviously, I have severely underestimated the LA paper's national reach, at its peak back then, with millions of readers and tens of millions reading its syndicated content. The bounce I get from it—and the vast amount of media interest—catches me unprepared. I have no publicist. I don't even know whether the news outlets will pay me or not . . . I don't know the rules of the news business (as I learn, the more reputable the outlet, the less likely they are to pay you). The whole experience leaves me a little shaky. It blows me away.

At the time, I don't realize that the five-by-seven cards will contain more than a year's worth of interviews and media segments. Their short, mostly fluffy pieces, all total, will add up to a home run.

The well-regarded *Today* show visits as well. The producers and camera people are confident pros, but I can sense that they think I am this *Duck Dynasty* bumpkin who sleeps out in the canyons with the bears, which is true, or that I am an undereducated hayseed who can't put two words together, which isn't. Even at this point, I've started to understand the power of a good quip, aka sound bite. Yet, as with bears, folks have their preconceptions. Based on instant judgments, they think they know me.

When the *Today* camera crew and producers come to me, they talk slowly so that I will understand, as if I were a five-year-old. Would I take them to see some bears? they ask. "Steve, is that something you think we could make happen?"

I shrug and hem and haw a bit, kick at the ground, then tell them— "Aw shucks, sure, we'll get in my Land Cruiser, I'll see if we can find y'all some bears."

That night, with them packed into my Land Cruiser, I drive them to a nearby restaurant where the bins have yet to be secured. As they watch with widening eyes, I rev the engine and plow my five-seat Toyota right into the side of a dumpster. Bam! As I sit calmly watching, a bear flies out of the dumpster, as I knew he would, and trampolines off the hood of the vehicle and off to the side.

The NBC crew is gasping for breath, their eyes as big as saucers: *Whoa!* They look like the audience in a sci-fi flick, pushing back in their seats as the monster comes at them—an involuntary reflex. I mind-melded them like Spock.

Softly, I say, "You guys get that OK?"

They race to get their gear out. They aren't filming because they never saw it coming.

I calmly explain to the TV crew that, for all the drama, for all the schtick, ramming a bin like that provides a teachable moment for the bears. It teaches them to listen for cars and the sound of revving engines, so that later when they are out along the roads, they might stay clear of cars and trucks. It isn't "hazing," as I mentioned earlier. I tell the network crew that every tactic has a point.

So in an instant, I've changed their opinions of me and the world in which I work. Sure, they can underestimate the rube all they want. But I might actually surprise them. And there is a sliver of a chance I might be smarter about the outdoors than they are.

Millions and millions of people react to the segment, but not my wife. She works at a bookstore that has an electronics section with a wall of TVs. On the morning I am featured, every single TV is tuned to the *Today* show. Debs doesn't even pause to watch. She just waits on a customer, ringing up a book. That's just Debs, unfazed by anything, taking her mountain life in stride.

I drag another camera crew, from *Real TV*, up to the Ski and Racquet Club condos, built into the side of the mountain, a ski-in, ski-out resort. It's a canyon of condos latched to the side of the hill, three stories high, with a long row of the kind of garages that always attract wild bears.

Inside each garage door is a trash can. As I patrol, I find each door open to the height of a bear that recently entered. I keep going till I reach one that is still closed. I know that will be the bear's next target.

A huge crawl space also runs the length of the building—you could play handball down there. The bears use it as a hideout, easily entering through a four-by-four-foot door. I position the camera crew atop a nearby retaining wall, out of harm's way. When they're ready, I take a flashlight and my baseball bat down to the other end of the crawl space and start bellowing. As the camera rolls, a female bear lumbers out of the other end, followed by me with my bat and my flashlight, having flushed the bear.

"Hey, you get the shot?" I ask.

No doubt, the media outlets ate up this yup-yup-yo mountain guy with the orange shotgun (says "Less Lethal" on the side). I am so different, so unlike most of their interviews. I can't type, I have a limited vocabulary. To them, that just adds to the wilderness aura and sense of authenticity. The media is always drawn to something fresh and different. Aren't we all?

Plus, I know some stuff about bears. And the visuals? There is no close-up quite as powerful as a bear cub on a branch, yawning a little, her eyes shimmering like sequins after her afternoon nap.

Outlets from all over the country show up at my doorstep, and I spend a day with them—at least the bigger ones. *Nightly News* with Tom Brokaw (the word of God) does a segment, as does *Inside Edition*. The *Times* piece is circulated all over the world, and the frenzy just snowballs. The *Boston Globe* does a piece, as does the *Denver Post*. Fresh and different becomes my brand.

"It's hard to know if the bears are his spirit animal, or it's the other way around," environmental studies professor Peter Alagona tells the *Los Angeles Times* in one of several pieces they run on me over the years.

In no time, I've become a media hustler, not much better than a Kardashian. They always come in here with their ideas of what I do, and I flip that on its nose, and get my message across. And the more they love me, the bolder I get. To know that my approach is worthy of a national audience boosts my confidence. I start to feel better about my mission, as they portray me as some sort of savior, a kind of "Wilderness Jesus," a portrayal I find unnerving and feel undeserving of.

In moments of reflection, I justify my media outreach for the attention it calls to the fondness Mammoth Lakes has for its bears. I think the town deserves some recognition for that, and I can only hope it will help change the way communities outside of Mammoth interact with their bears or other wildlife.

In further moments of reflection, I also have to wonder about how seldom reporters and producers question my tactics and approach. Sure, we've had some genuine, quantifiable success at this point. The bear population is headed in the right direction, toward a population that can be sustained by natural food supplies. But the media just swallows up everything I say. I'm sure the fact that an esteemed paper such as the *Los Angeles Times* has done a long and thorough article bolsters their confidence in what I am doing. Yet, why wouldn't some reporter with some balls confront me a little: "Hey, you're really just Steve, a former surfer with a knack and a passion for bears. No formal training?"

In my darker moments, I really fear that too. I am still just Steve.

Yet, I consider every offer, screening the requests myself, chauffeuring the reporters and photogs around town. The national chapter of the Humane Society sees the coverage and brings me in to discuss a lecture circuit on my nonlethal tactics for dealing with wild animals in populated areas.

I sit at the head of a table in a meeting room in Maryland, surrounded by nice, earnest folks in suits. They say, "Steve, we want to employ you." They're very businesslike, with their day planners out and open. I don't care. I'm just being me, dropping f-bombs left and right, as I'm prone to do.

They offer to pay me $50,000, plus expenses, for a series of lectures around the country.

They even offer to send me a handler. I mean, I'm fine with being a foot away from a wild bear. But to be honest, new cities scare me, so I accept.

The Humane Society sends me all over the country. They handle all the pre-appearance promotional stuff: "Appearing this Friday, from Mammoth Lakes, California, Steve Searles."

Unlike most presenters, I don't have a laptop, a PowerPoint presentation, or a laser pointer. My visuals are a few poster boards listing bear facts in colored ink. I duct tape them up on a wall, then rant profanely when one of them falls to the floor, to the amusement of the audience. Like the producers and reporters, audiences have never seen anything quite like it. I am Wild Bill Hickok crossed with George Carlin. If I get nervous, I get louder. I jump up on a table to demo how I confront a misbehaving animal. I rack my orange shotgun, as if preparing to fire. Just the *cha-chaaaaang* of that always gets their attention. Most of them have never heard a shotgun's chilling metallic snap in person. It also reinforces that, although I keep my presentations fun, this is serious business.

I appear before a lot of animal activists, a lot of gun-happy wildlife officers. I appear before pissed-off rednecks who don't really want to hear from some hippie-looking conservationist from California.

They're a tough crowd, reluctant to buy in, till I tell them, "Hey, let's go out into the parking lot, I've got some cool ammo I want to show you."

Outside, I dig out my flash-bang pyrotechnics, my rubber-bullet shells, show them how I scare bears out of culverts. I show them all the pyrotechnics I have at my disposal. Also the lethal. I teach them how to kill when absolutely necessary. That makes me even more credible among the doubters. "If these nonlethal steps don't work out . . ." Then I show them how to destroy the animals. I'm not exactly Thoreau. I carry guns. I mean business when I work with bears. The animals have to know I am the alpha.

Bottom line, the media attention gives me incentive to keep moving forward, to keep working on my big bag of unconventional bear tricks back in Mammoth Lakes. I have the run of the area, the growing support of residents. There are gates to ranches and property to restrict public access. I have a key to every gate, duplicating keys that aren't supposed to be duplicated.

I do public service announcements for the local radio station—I know the FCC regulations require them to give me the time. So they sit me down in the sound booth, another chance to get the message across. One time, I recite the word for bear in ten different languages, then say, "Whatever language you speak, wherever you're from, please don't feed our bears."

The public education is nonstop. So many problems are education problems. Every single music festival, every event, I talk to families and hand out stickers. I look over and see there is a line of people waiting to speak to me. I feel like Willie Mays.

An elementary school in Ohio is so taken with my work, they hold a bake sale and send the proceeds to me. It's not a lot, $60. I send it back. Again, I don't want to profit from something that belongs to everyone.

My daily life has changed, people making a fuss, by mail, in person, going through a lot of trouble to pat me on the back.

Despite being flattered by the attention, I'm very reserved and pretty private. My comfort zone is still the bears.

CHAPTER TWELVE

SPREADING THE WORD

The audience is mostly cops, lots of good old boys chewing tobacco and spitting into paper cups. I take a deep breath and start my spiel for this out-of-town department of fish and wildlife in Maryland. Their body language is pretty clear: "Screw you, Searles. Screw you and the horse you rode in on."

You know how people are. They distrust newcomers. Especially know-it-all newcomers from sunny and chirpy California. If I were them, I would too.

I take my time, don't try too hard to impress them. I start with a story about a VW van and a hippie, high as a kite. A bear is chomping on the hippie's junk in the van, and the hippie is going nuts. His stuff is total crud—belts and vests and bellbottoms with rainbows and peace signs. Lots of macramé and scruffy thread. But, you know, it's his stuff, maybe all he has in the world. The guy looks like a *Laugh-In* hippie, a satire on hippies. "Do something," he pleads with me, half-crying. "Easy," I say. "We got this."

The cops are still kind of dead-eyed—tough—but I've got them chuckling a little, I've managed to get them listening. Yeah, a hippie. They can get into that. The hippie and the bear. I know cops. I've worked with them, hung around with them. I happen to like cops, so I know what they're probably thinking: *This bear expert looks like a hippie too. What's he really know about guns and bears?*

I explain to them all the sad ways something like the hippie incident usually goes down: the officer whips out his Remington shotgun—every squad car in America has one. I mean, it's all you got, really. The hippie's screaming about the bear, the bear seems out of control, a possible menace. Law enforcement is there to preserve the order, to make the streets safe, right? So the cop raises the shotgun and he smokes the bear in front of a bunch of frightened onlookers.

"What happens next in a case like this?" I ask the audience.

Then I tell them a typical outcome: the hippie is freaking out even worse, and now you have all these reports and forms to do. Plus, you got the cold, dead bear on the asphalt. Where do you put him, how do you even lift it into a truck? What truck? Bystanders are milling around, calling you a motherfuckin' maniac, a cold-blooded killer.

You get home, tell your wife, and she tells you you're a piece of shit. Your kid asks, "What's wrong, Mommy? Why are you crying?" And your wife explains how Daddy just smoked Paddington Bear. The dog, your former best friend, takes a crap on the carpet—he's mad at you too.

Now, I ask, "Imagine if the cop had nonlethal alternatives in his squad car?"

I explain how they'd load the shotgun with a beanbag cartridge. You'd ping the bear on the ass. If it doesn't get the message, you pull out the pepper spray. Done. No blood. No screaming. The bear scampers off, crying a little, but he's learned his lesson: don't mess with hippie vans.

Now you're a hero. You've turned a lose-lose-lose into a win-win-win. The hippie loves you, offers you a little weed (thanks, no thanks). The local paper does a hero story. You go home, your kid thinks you're Superman. That night, you might even get laid.

Bottom line: instead of feeling crappy about yourself, you feel pretty good. And you look forward to the next bear call, instead of dreading it.

"Because now you have the tools," I tell them.

This begins to define my career—finding the right tools for the ethical treatment of wild animals. In turn, it benefits the officers as well.

I am learning how to change minds without lecturing and scolding. Instead of talking about a bunch of touchy-feely topics that the cops would snarl about, I've recreated a situation they can relate to. It just plugs into a better outcome.

I never dig my heels in, insist this will have to be the way. I give them examples and let them reach their own conclusions.

"Dead bears suck, dead bears don't learn anything," I tell them for emphasis. "I'm not saying you don't have to kill one once in a while. I'm just saying try these other ways first."

"Try it," I tell them. "If I'm full of shit, go ahead and kill the bear. Then send me a text telling me I'm full of shit and why. Here's my number: 760-937-BEAR."

I never get a single one of those texts.

How many bears do I save with presentations like this? More importantly, how many officers, constantly berated and demonized these days, find a better way to go about their work, go home happier at the end of the long shift, roughhouse with the kids, are kinder to their husband or wife? I am hoping it works on a lot of levels.

As my reputation grows in California, as I handle Mammoth's bear issues in enlightened and novel ways, I start getting invites from municipalities dealing with bears from Canada to the East Coast. I sign the contracts with the Humane Society, with an animal rights association in New Jersey. Even if my message doesn't exactly match theirs, they are still asking me to come in. By now, they are paying me, after years of me giving away my time and expertise.

I often tell them: go make friends with the hunter or the guy running a trapline. Ask them questions. Ride in their trucks. Share a thermos of coffee. Ask about their kids. Don't just squirt ketchup on their clothes.

Maybe tone all that murderer shit down. Get their side of the story, just as you'd like them to hear yours. If you want to save animals, go talk to the guy who's killing them.

I am in their headquarters getting paid to talk to them this way.

I always bring the SCAT kits I mentioned earlier. I do a classroom session, then we go out onto a range, sometimes just a parking lot, and I demo the various nonlethal and lethal tactics. I scratch my balls and rack the shotgun. Good old boys like when you do that. It's something they can relate to. Trust me, if you're giving a presentation, and you're feeling like you're losing your audience a little, there's nothing more effective than racking a shotgun to make everyone sit upright. Most cops never shoot in the line of duty. To hear from someone who does immediately gets their attention.

Hey, it isn't always a success. One of the shells I had was all gunpowder, with no projectile. It was just a giant noisemaker, with plenty of pow and smoke. In one session, I fired it and every car alarm went off. Hey, I come from a little town in the California mountains. We don't even need car alarms.

Another session, I hand a shell to another cop, who fires it; the blast knocks the sight right off the Remington 870, normally a pretty rugged gun. Oops.

At one presentation on the East Coast, I use an explosive with a six-second delay. It is loud, like a cherry bomb. You'd fire it, count to six, and the thing would flush any bear or coyote within earshot. Only, this time, it doesn't just go boom, it starts a fire at the gun range. I just keep talking, while stomping the fire out with my white tennis shoes.

At a Yosemite ski area, the Department of the Interior brings me in to explain my nonlethal tactics. They set up this range with a bunch of bear cutouts, for dramatic effect, I guess. I ask a federal parks officer to demo a lethal round, and his shot skips off some ice, goes across the ski run, and hits a ski lift tower. *Boooooooooooooonnnnnng.* The steel tower vibrates for about ten seconds. "Class dismissed!" I say. To this day, there's a big, mysterious dent in that tower.

Invariably, though, these nonlethal info sessions are well received, the good old boys put their spit cups down to shake my hand. They applaud. They take me for lunch and a cold beer. At the end, I receive a big check.

What a trippy thing. My ego and confidence grow. The attention I am getting continues to annoy various agencies. I have a track record, my methods work. But this is typical of the pushback I always get from the so-called experts who have a spotty record with bears themselves. Of course, that's just my opinion. Still, I am never worried about what wildlife officials think, only the people in my town. The local papers eat it up.

At some point, the US Forest Service tells town officials that I can do my thing in the city limits, but not in the federal land that surrounds it—the busy campgrounds, food basket for the bears. This handcuffs me, since that's where the real need is, where half or more of my calls come from. That's where bears learn bad habits before they go into homes in town. It set me up for failure.

They even persuade the Mammoth City Council to hold a meeting on what I am doing. At the hearing, everyone has their say about these non-lethal tactics. The implication is that I've just pulled it all out of my ass, that I haven't fully tested these methods. Their concern is understandable. It also plays into my thoughts about fears and how you demonize anything you don't quite understand.

At the hearing I let everyone voice their concerns about the children's toys I am using, the paintballs, the flashy noisemakers. They finish by telling me that these nonlethal methods could be more dangerous than real bullets, which is just ludicrous.

When I finally get my chance to talk, I prattle on a little about coexistence. Then I pull out some of the nonlethal weapons, these fuzzy-feathery projectiles I use to ping the bears. To prove how harmless they are, I start tossing them at the audience. The audience laughs and starts tossing them back at me. Then I start tossing them at the council members, who can see firsthand that this is nothing to worry about.

What a shit show, what a grandstanding spectacle. But that is just my way: Use humor and demonstrations to make my point. Seeing is believing.

And it always comes back around to what I told the cops: dead bears suck.

A little addendum: Though the Feds don't want me on federal land, I go right back. If I get a call for a buck with a broken leg, I go. It's the only humane thing.

CHAPTER THIRTEEN

NEW JERSEY NEEDS HELP

I n 2000, animal advocates in New Jersey fly me in to testify against a proposal to allow black bears to be hunted again.

Now, outsiders might not think of New Jersey as bear country, which tends to be chiseled with mountains and pretty rugged. Yet, the forests and meadows of much of the state once supported three thousand bears, till they hunted them nearly to extinction. In 1971, the state banned hunting.

When I visit in 2000, three hundred bears are back, trickling in from surrounding states, establishing a foothold in the forest, and occasionally showing up in suburban areas. The state's Department of Fish and Game wants to hunt them, in a bogus attempt at population control. In essence, folks like to shoot stuff. It's fun, and there are few trophies to rival a full-grown bear.

Animal rights activists and lobbyists, led by Lynda Logan, hire me to come in as an expert witness on behalf of the bears. They see me as this mountain-man savior from California who can educate the flatlanders on the ways of bears and the nonlethal options for controlling them.

So here I am, all in denim, with the hippie hair and the beard. They realize right away they aren't dealing with a Republican or a Democrat, a lobbyist or a resident activist. They probably aren't positive I can read. But they know they have a bear expert in their midst with growing renown, a straight shooter from California who doesn't actually give a rat's ass about New Jersey. I think they kind of like that. With my growly voice, I sound like a garbage disposal chewing up a spoon. In looks and actions, I'm like no one they have ever seen. They look at me as if they might spook me, as if I'm a reindeer or an elk.

I charge them $1,000 a day, plus expenses, which I consider to be a lot. They don't even blink over the price. My hosts set up media sessions and meet-and-greets. They even build a tiny shooting range with life-size cutouts of black bears, where I can demo my nonlethal tactics for the police and the press. The cutouts look more like large black pigs than bears. I sight them with my gun, stand firm, squeeze the trigger, and ping the targets with beanbags, just to show how I would get bears out of harm's way, to teach them where they couldn't go. I also demo flash-bang devices, rubber buckshot, rubber slugs. I demonstrate fifteen different rounds. After an extra-loud pop, I ask, "Would that drive you away?" It is disturbing, like warfare.

Strange audience combo, animal activists and seasoned street cops. The demo seems to impress them both, though. From the cops, I earn respect. They can see I can shoot. For the activists, this swift nonlethal kick in the butt is far superior to laying the bears out.

The kits I give law enforcement, and demonstrate here, rank order all the options, from most peaceful—a whistle—to the most dramatic, a lethal shotgun shell. It serves as my PowerPoint presentation.

But the main event is a fact-finding appearance in Trenton, at the state capitol building. On the day of the event, with politicians and wildlife officials, my hosts drive me into these large underground caverns, park the car, and walk me through a maze of halls and eventually outside to the New Jersey statehouse steps. As I step out, blinking into the sunlight, I see the street is filled with protesters of the bear hunt. They've brought in buses of them, many carrying signs. The crowd sees us and starts chanting. This is the animal-rights crowd, no one wearing camo. The organizers say a few words, then introduce me. I'm standing off behind a big pillar, trying to disappear. I approach the microphones. "Stay strong and fight the good fight," I tell them. Big fist pump. They roar. Whoa, what is this? I feel like Abbie Hoffman.

From there, things get . . . interesting and weird. We enter the capitol, wind our way down some hallways, and head straight into a security checkpoint. I'm already anxious from the huge crowd outside and a little amped up about the upcoming session. There is lots of media, lots of entourage. And suddenly everything grinds to a halt when security—these state cops with those *Smokey and the Bandit* hats—say, "Sorry, this gent can't go in. He's got to have a suit and tie. Those are the rules."

I'm wearing my best clothes: a freshly ironed shirt, clean Levi's, and a bear buckle on my belt. I don't look like some scruffy camper. It's not that I forgot to bring a coat and tie; I don't even *own* a coat and tie. If they had told me about the dress code ahead of time, I would've just said, "Hell no, I'm not coming. That's not me." Ironically, the women who are accompanying me are all wearing pantsuits, no ties, outfits made of rayon and other fabrics that fall funny. But OK, rules are rules. I'll just turn around and go home now. If I can ever find my way out of this maze of hallways.

Big hubbub, big drama, and I haven't said a single word to the lawmakers, haven't even dropped an f-bomb.

Security and my handlers go off by themselves in some back room to figure things out, to see if they come up with some compromise on the suit-and-tie infraction. The handlers who are waiting outside with me are spinning this way and that, frantic that I'm being banned over a dress code violation.

Finally, they let me in. Carrying my SCAT kit full of demo items, I follow officers in. I have a security escort, like I'm some big deal. The marble, the elegant architecture—I see quickly that I'm out of my element.

They take me into an ornate chamber full of pillars. Forest of microphones. A raised platform for the big shots, the standard pitcher of water in front of them. I'm down in front of them, like a Senate witness. They are very gracious. The show starts. They welcome me. The chairperson notes I have traveled a long way, offers to let me talk as long as I need, no time limits.

Well, OK then . . .

I put my demo kit down, my beaten-up briefcase, and scan the room. Dozens of uniformed Fish and Game folks line the walls, accompanied by state police. I sure have their attention.

At times like this, I kind of just wing it. I say, "Look at all these fine guys," pointing at the Fish and Game. "Look at all the work they did to get three hundred bears back after the three thousand you killed off.

"They have worked so hard. They deserve to shoot a few, don't you think?"

I tell them that nobody hunts a bear for food anymore. Nobody hunts for a bitchin' jacket. The only reason to hunt is because it's fun.

The animal activists are looking at me, then each other, aghast. They are starting to hyperventilate.

"That's why they brought me in here," I say. "I want to support them."

I am just teeing them up, playing both sides. As everyone stands there stunned, I let loose the wrecking ball. I mention that under the proposed new law, children ten and older would be allowed to hunt down bears.

I say, "Senators and distinguished guests, I don't want to tell you your business. But I can tell you this: shooting a bear never goes right. It's never one round, and when the bear starts screaming, it can really affect your psyche and affect your next shot.

"Again, I don't want to tell you your business, but whoever thought kids as young as ten should be killing bears is sadly mistaken."

After some awkward murmuring, they go, "Mr. Searles, thank you." A few have questions. The chairman gets last-ups, and he says, "I've got to know what's in that box you brought."

My SCAT kit of demo stuff is propped up on the table. It has a "Mean People Suck" sticker on it, positioned so all the lawmakers can see it. I hadn't referred to it during my talk, never reached for it, never opened it. But I made sure they could all see the kit and wonder what was in there.

I open it up, take out a protective layer of foam insulation. In the kit are the brass ends of fifty shotgun shells, lethal and nonlethal. I hold up a flash-bang device, the way I always do when I teach newcomers, and explain how it works. I also explain the lethal shells, saying that when situations call for it, I want officers to have the rounds to take a bear down quickly and humanely. Human safety always comes first, I say. I tell them that I adore the bears, but I would shoot ten bears before I would let a bear hurt a single person. People are more important than bears.

Before I go, Fish and Game does its standard spiel about bears becoming more leery and standoffish when we hunt them. The logic is that wild bears learn to keep their distance when they are hunted.

"What do you think about that, Mr. Searles?"

Obviously, I say, there is no next of kin when you kill a bear, no obit in the paper. There's just a hide next to your fireplace. The hundreds of other bears aren't aware of the killing. The death makes no difference in their behavior; they have no way of knowing about it.

I tell them that people should not put their own dark thoughts upon the poor bears. I assure them that bears don't go on killing sprees. They don't abduct children or keep victims in boxes in basements. Only humans do that. I urge them not to let their bogus fears dictate public policy. Once you remove the misunderstandings and the false threats, doesn't that take the justification out of hunting?

Shoot them for the fun of hunting if you must, I say. Just be real about it. That's a legitimate stance; hunting is an amazing hobby. People love it. But don't tell me it's for the public safety, because it isn't.

"Hunting will not make New Jersey safer," I say.

Finally, I tell them that if the bears were a real-time threat, you'd never be able to get all these devoted Fish and Game officers here. They wouldn't be standing here against the back wall; they'd be out there on the front lines fighting off the invasion of the bears. "But there is no front line. There is no invasion . . . no immediate threat. Their stance is preposterous."

"Thank you," I say. "Any questions?"

They cancel the hunt.

In the press room, shortly after, they take me before a small army of East Coast reporters and photographers—strobes and flashes everywhere. The country mouse is in the city, and the city is digging it.

I use humor and common sense, mixed with all my experience, to win over both sides. As I always say, so many problems are education problems. I believe that when people have access to the right information, they will come together to make the right decision. Or, at least they have a fighting chance. Things go haywire when each side brings in its own set of "facts." And that feeds the unfounded fears.

Everyone seems pleased. I go out for drinks and dinner with the animal rights people. The next day, I leave the hotel for coffee and a pack of smokes. At the newsstand, nearly every paper in the New York metropolitan area has a photo of me on its cover: me, the ponytailed wack job from California, preaching tolerance for New Jersey's bears.

One by one, I go down the line, grabbing a copy of each paper. I bring home one of each. I am overwhelmed.

CHAPTER FOURTEEN

THE SUPER BOWL OF BEARS

B y now, I'm starting to feel like a Forrest Gump of the wildlife kingdom, a man with uncanny good luck. Unlike Forrest, I have no saintly strength of character that would explain why the universe seems to smile down on me, or my string of lucky accomplishments. I'm more of a broken Forrest Gump. But what a winning streak I'm on—the guy with the ninth grade education has become some sort of scientific authority. No question I am using my work to fill some missing ingredient in my life. Till I realize what that ingredient might be, I am using professional success, pretty much the only success I know.

Coming off my New Jersey trip, I'm invited to speak to the International Association for Bear Research, made up of more than five hundred biologists and wildlife officers from some sixty nations, at their symposium in Jackson Hole, Wyoming. Known by its scrambled acronym, the IBA, the organization is holding the equivalent of a Super Bowl of bear experts.

The Humane Society flies me in, pays my expenses, and sponsors my appearance, considering it part of their public education initiative.

Let me just say that the enormity of this invitation is apparent. It's not lost on me that a shoplifting, pot-smoking high school dropout is now about to speak to folks with twenty years or more of formal education apiece. Academics have usually viewed me with a wary eye. Hell, I don't even own a bow tie or a tweedy vest.

Honestly, I will gladly crawl into bear dens or under houses to roust bears. But the times I am most scared is when I travel. At that point, I'm a fish out of water. Just to give you an idea of how uneasy I am with making my way through airports and strange hotels, I take a dozen ironed shirts, and halfway through the day I change into a fresh, less sweaty one.

In the days leading up to the bear summit, I try to remind myself that Jack London had only an eighth grade education before he wrote so famously about wolves. Or that Jane Goodall didn't have a college degree when she went off to do groundbreaking work with chimps.

I remind myself that noted conservationist Marjory Stoneman Douglas worked in department stores before writing her prize-winning pieces on the Everglades, including her *River of Grass*. To my mind, formal training in a particular topic is less important than a passion that will literally push you into the field to learn firsthand. Charles Darwin, the father of modern biology, was actually a geologist with very little standing in the field of animals. I even take solace that Quentin Tarantino never went to film school. He worked in a video store, surrounding himself with friends who had a similar love for movies, while immersing himself in the subject.

Far as I am concerned, I've paid my dues, done my ten thousand hours—Malcolm Gladwell's baseline for mastering almost any given field.

Nothing against advanced academic studies—it is the basis of our shared body of knowledge. But they tend to produce people who think the same way. As jazz legend Billie Holiday once said, "If I'm going to sing like someone else, then I don't need to sing at all."

That's how I rationalize—even take pride in—my lack of formal training as I head to the Super Bowl of bears. As usual, I'm a bundle of nerves, but very honored and flattered that the world's most esteemed experts on bears want to hear my side of this subject. In the end, I'm certain that our mutual passion will unite us in important ways. In the end, it's all about the bears.

I walk into the hotel banquet hall, cookies and coffee on the table, a big podium in the front. I'm sweating I'm so scared. I'm scouting the early presentations. For days, I marvel at their sophisticated PowerPoint lectures. Every participant goes about their presentation in the same format: hypothesis, findings, theory, conclusion—a standard academic approach. Each night on the phone, I complain to Debs how basic my presentation is going to seem and how worried I am. In my hotel room, I reshuffle my cardboard presentation to try to match the way they did it.

Finally, it's showtime.

Audience members walk in to find poster boards duct-taped to the wall.

Now, in stiff and formal situations, where protocol and self-importance are the general rule, it probably doesn't help that I speak like I am—casually, off the cuff, and from the heart. As in New Jersey, I'm more effective when I wing it. Starting speeches always freaks me out a little. But I'm fine once I get going. Occasionally, an f-bomb will fly, even across a room of stiff academics. I'm dressed like a college kid. I look like I sleep in the woods. If nothing else, I'm authentic.

My presentation is a sellout, not an empty seat . . . lots of interest in the Searles show. Holy cow.

In my opening statement, I talk about how happy people in my community feel in the presence of bears, that we feel blessed when we see one in the yard while we stir our morning coffee. I explain that because I didn't go to college, I learned from the bears, and the people in my community—the only teachers I ever had. I tell how I tried to emulate Mother Nature rather than try to change things, to see the world through the bears' eyes.

I tell the world's biggest bear experts how Mammoth Lakes considers its bears to be residents, not interlopers, that they are part of our everyday life. We don't want to ever have to put them in barrel traps, I say. I explain how I teach the bears to learn to live with us, while reinstilling the bears' natural fear of humans. Appropriate measures, I say, are critical—the right level of pyrotechnics, appropriate amounts of response. I talk about love and hate, fear and respect to a bunch of scientists who insist on numbering bears instead of naming them. The number of teeth they have doesn't really matter to me, but their emotions do.

I try to paint a picture of our town, how food, water, habitat, and the buy-in of residents are in abundance. That if you live with them, instead of shooting them, it stops the influx of new bears and avoids the sinkhole effect—new bears coming in to replace old ones that are shot. Most residents would rather see a cop shot than a bear—an overstatement, sure, but reflective of my town's love for bears.

Ninety minutes into my lecture, a couple of audience members begin to showboat. One turns to another audience member and questions my findings out loud, calls my research anecdotal, a word I'm not familiar with. I think it's a compliment.

"Thank you, sir," I say.

An argument begins that doesn't include me. Most of the crowd is thoughtful and respectful, but a couple of guys are going at it.

One says that my experience has no merit compared to the research he's done in his own state.

I respond calmly, "Sir, I do not question what you know or what you've seen in other places. I'm just telling you what I found in Mammoth Lakes, California."

The presentation ends abruptly. As it turns out, tweedy professors make damn good hecklers. I return to my room, put on a fresh shirt, and go down to a dark downstairs bar to get liquored up with a biologist I met from Louisiana.

Man, oh man, am I bummed. It is as if I've struck out with the bases loaded, in the biggest game of my life. Once again, I feel like that loser kid in the outfield with the gopher in his glove, everyone yelling.

Back in my room, I call Debs. "Get me out of here fast." In addition to her other duties, Debs is a travel agent at the time, and I beg her to get me on the next flight out of Wyoming, of which there are fewer than you can imagine.

Next morning, before leaving for the airport, I duck downstairs to grab something to eat. Dr. Stephen Herrero, a renowned honcho with the bear group, invites me to join him and his wife. Dr. Herrero is gracious about the previous day. He knew I was feeling out of place. But he salutes my novel ways of dealing with bears and my use of nonlethal methods. "What you talked about and what you presented is here to stay," he says.

"Hey, Steve, got a second?" someone else asks. Standing at our table, another expert is handing me his card.

"When you have a moment sometime, I'd like to hear more," the stranger says.

It is the oddest turn of events. One by one, in that breakfast room, the world's most renowned bear experts begin to draw me aside and hand me their contact info.

By the time they are done, I have twenty-three business cards from experts who want to know more about my novel, boots-on-the-ground experiences with bears. Of those twenty-three cards, I end up not talking to most of the experts—just didn't have the time for that. But they all affect me in a positive way. It makes me wonder how many little gestures in the course of a day or a week can impact people, and we don't even realize it? We can make a difference just by saying, "Hey, what you're doing is interesting. Let's chat."

You know, the initial response from the biologists (or at least some of them) was my worst nightmare come true, the fruition of all my self-doubts. But that appearance turns into something wonderful. No, I haven't received an ovation, haven't come close to the rock-star status I enjoyed in New Jersey. But before a very skeptical crowd, in a very different venue, I feel like I've been heard.

I end up staying the week.

CHRIS WEIGHS IN AGAIN . . .

These interruptions must sound like the liner notes on backs of album covers in the seventies. Remember those? The writer would explain where the tracks were recorded, how many groupies attended the session, which Peggy Lipton lookalike inspired—then ruined— the lead guitarist.

Liner notes were breezy, rat-a-tat-tat musings on music and life. They are how I learned to write, lying back on the bed, while Pink Floyd or Dexter Gordon washed over me, often enjoying the liner notes more than the music. Now largely gone, liner notes were once so significant they began to reward them with a special Grammy.

In the hands of Pete Hamill or Dan Morgenstern, liner notes often contained a wisp of cowboy poetry—and an appreciation for fresh ideas—that is largely absent from anywhere I look these days.

Sigh.

American culture. Is it even culture?

Steve and I would often open our writing sessions with some tiny gripe about it. So predictable, right? Two past-their-prime boomers kibbitzing over how our leaders and the media have forsaken the common person. It is a warm-up, a great way for us to get comfortable sharing.

It is liner notes.

"Aren't we lucky," I say more than once, "to have lived when we lived, the movies, the books, the music."

"Especially the music," Steve would say.

"Especially," I'd say.

Troubling times now, to be sure. Monsters come in every shape, every size, as they say. No one can agree on anything.

That's probably why chapter 9, "I Hate Fear," resonates deeply with me. It speaks to Steve's uncommon grace and his Yoda-like philosophies, gleaned from decades of seeing bears and humans at their best and worst.

"People of different cultures, different lifestyles, people who would clip safety pins in their noses . . .

"As with the bears, wonder if we took time to know these people a little, rather than just lash out based on all our preconceptions? What would happen then? Could we conquer hate and fear?"

For Steve and me, this becomes a theme. Maybe all we can ask of our tormentors is to slow down. To not be so angry, rash, impulsive, and thoughtless. To maybe listen to what we have to offer.

And shouldn't we do the same for them? I think that's Steve *philosophy in a nutshell. Do unto others . . .*

Meanwhile, in pulling this book together, different feelings about the wilderness are beginning to drop. I'd always thought of the wilderness with great reverence, as you would a cathedral—perhaps the greatest cathedral of them all.

Now, I'm discovering that we can expect too much from it. As Steve proves, wilderness is no escape from the mundane issues of modern life—bad bosses, family tensions, money woes. Wilderness can't repair a broken egg. It has no greater purpose than to try to take care of itself. We're the only ones who can repair the egg, especially since we were the ones that broke it. The wilderness can be a balm, a demulcent. The great outdoors is also, occasionally, stronger than we can ever be. Thoreau and Muir had it almost right, solitude and sunlight are a road to salvation. But maybe it's not quite that simple. The heart and mind play major roles as well.

That's all for now.

But for the record, Steve hates the "Wilderness Jesus" tag I gave him. Insists I take it out.

I leave it in because I think it gets at what he brings home to us from the wilderness—a wider view of life, an artful sense of forgiveness, a deeper understanding of our place in the universe. Of course, Steve is more of a mystic than a messiah. But he has some of the same tendencies. For one, he speaks plainly and to great effect. For another, the more he lives, the better he gets.

Hey, isn't that what we all should aspire to: the more we live, the better we get?

CHAPTER FIFTEEN

DON'T FEED OUR BEARS

B ack home in the California mountains, where I belong, I am the bears' dietician, their shrink, their primary care physician, and—sadly at times—their undertaker and the person who gives their eulogy.

More than anything, I am obsessed with their eating habits, just as they are obsessed with eating. If your dog wandered the neighborhood every day accepting handouts, how long would he last? First of all, he'd eat way more than he needed. Second, he'd eat a bunch of junk, grow fat, die early, just as we all would if we ate nothing but Oreo cookies all day. After all, we are what we eat. And bears are just stomachs with feet. When tourists and locals see a bear, they are always eating.

So, many of my initial efforts go into controlling what these bears eat. More than anything, their well-being—their futures here in town—are closely tied to my ability to shut down the pipeline of free snacks and dinners they are constantly offered. I study their natural foods, and their calorie intakes, in hopes of pointing them toward a more sustainable and healthy diet. When I see flowers and plants come into bloom, I watch carefully to see which ones the bears prefer.

A key development: the bumper stickers I create that say "Don't Feed Our Bears." That word *our* and how much difference it makes cannot be overstated. It emphasizes the entire town's stewardship. In the early days of my career, residents would call and say, "Come get the bear out of my trash." Actually, it was their bear. And their trash. That subliminal turn, without having to force it down their throats, makes a huge difference in what a million people needed to shoulder. *Our* bears. Not *the* bears. Quit blaming the bears. Own the issue. In a lot of instances, on a lot of calls, they want to see me come do my magic. It is their magic. I try to mess with their minds too.

The Department of Fish and Game (now known as Fish and Wildlife) didn't like us using *our*. They believed it wasn't good for the community to think of the bears as theirs. I argued that using *our bears* would create that sense of stewardship and responsibility.

Indeed, the stickers change the conversation. Generally, the residents are receptive, and the "Don't Feed Our Bears" bumper stickers start showing up all over Mammoth Lakes and cities far away. It seems complex, but it is really very simple. It is just a matter of getting people to help me paint the fence.

Now, if you've ever fed a bear, you know it's wonderful, it's bitchin'. You're having a good time; the bear is having a good time. Feeding a bear is like staring into a campfire—it puts you into a trance. As we've noted, there's something transcendent about being in the presence of a bear . . , something spiritual. In a way, you're having coffee with Mother Nature.

Now I have to teach folks not to do something that's uniquely satisfying. And the Forest Service is no help. For some reason, they ban the stickers from the places they are most needed, visitor centers and bear-proof lockers. I have my work cut out for me.

Everywhere I go, I hand out these simple ten-cent stickers. I'm making my rounds, talking at schools, libraries, civic luncheons, explaining what I'm about, asking for help, answering all kinds of stupid questions. From my experience as a glass salesman, I learned a few tricks. To make them laugh, for one. And how when you finish a meet-up, you should always leave something behind—a sample, a keychain, a business card. In this case, it was a bear sticker.

I chat up churches, hospitals, cops. I always wear a double-pocket shirt. When I step out of my truck, my pockets are filled with stickers. I am finding my groove. Remember, most problems are education problems, right? The stickers are on every car, every cash register. Like a poker dealer, I deal them out to every table at a restaurant. Is someone in town for ten minutes, or a full-time resident? I don't care. I park in the center of a mall and walk around with a stack of stickers, hit up every single customer, every single clerk. I work both floors of the mall, door to door. "How are you today? Here, have this cool sticker." I am a freak about it. "Stick a sticker, help a bear," I urge store owners. "You're part of the cure now," I add. To track my progress, I take a real estate map of the town and color-code it to the places I hit.

One year, we have a big town party at the park, packed with locals and alcohol. I slip a bear sticker under every windshield wiper in the lot.

As usual, once I start doing something, I do it to excess.

I go to the schools—elementary through high school—and spend an hour slipping stickers under every single car wiper in the lot. Since these are the people teaching our kids, it is extra important for me to have this message on their minds. I walk to the teacher lounge and poker deal the stickers into every mail cubby. Don't feed our bears. Pretty conniving. I don't have permission. You shouldn't litter cars like that. Still, no one ever gives me any grief about it.

The stickers come in bundles of two hundred. Every time I remove a rubber band to open another stack, I put it on my wrist. At the end of the day, I look like a hippie girl. That way, I can track how many I've handed out—my version of an abacus. Some quirky accounting, sure, but it works.

In the staff lockers at the ski school, I slip them through the vents in the locker. The stickers start showing up on snowboards, lift towers, shovels. They need to be part of the landscape.

In my frequent public sessions, I find that a sixty-five-year-old Lions Club member asks the same silly question as a fourth grader. I kick it around with residents at the Breakfast Club diner, where I eat almost every morning. In audiences of adults, I see their eyebrows rise as I rattle off my bear stories, in my typically profane and earthy way. I like to think they enjoy hearing from a real person rather than the slick, blow-dried town bureaucrats who often stop by.

Slowly, folks buy in. Word gets around. The bears and the town benefit in huge ways from the "Don't Feed Our Bears" campaign. At first, there is just the generic "Don't Feed Our Bears" on the stickers. Then I add the word *Mammoth* to it, in the old serif font the ski mountain has been using for years. At that point, they really take off. I go on social media and prompt people to post photos of their stickers from locations around the world. They send photos from Japan, Australia, the Philippines. They are becoming as common as the Sex Wax stickers I used to see on so many surfboards as a kid.

Over time, I give out eighty-five thousand of those bumper stickers, one at a time, about a dime apiece, initially out of my own pocket. Since then, I've seen photos of the stickers on cars on every continent. Countries that don't have bears have them on taxis, buses, and trains. I think it speaks yet again about our unique kinship with bears.

But keeping the bears out of the garbage bins? I may as well have been teaching them the trombone.

Now, I'll admit that it's nuts to lock up your trash as if it contained gold coins. It's counterintuitive. Why would you secure trash? Honestly, if someone stole your trash each week, wouldn't you be stoked, kind of flattered, happy to avoid the trouble of putting it out? But locking down trash is something we have to do to address the bear surge, minus any sort of financial incentive for those who have to go through the trouble.

We have to do it because it is the right thing. Since when does that ever work?

Lots of luck, right? "The right thing" can be a hard sell. Eat your dandelion greens. Exercise daily. In my experience, most solutions involve a significant financial incentive before anyone gets interested. Or it somehow develops some sexy, trendy, everybody's-doing-it appeal. With locking up the trash, we don't have either of those.

The food pipeline is still staying open 24/7, in dumpsters behind restaurants and hotels, where the bears constantly binge. I see the bears balancing like ballerinas on the one-inch ledge of the big metal bins, intoxicated on french fry oil. They don't just feast, they frolic. They look like a chorus line of dancing bears from an old Disney cartoon.

And one by one, residents stop and—not realizing the bears are mucking around in the bins—dump their trash right over their heads. Other times, I make my rounds in the morning and find that someone propped a dumpster lid open with a piece of firewood, in order to get a good photo of a binge-eating bear. Often, "Don't Feed Our Bears" stickers are plastered all over the dumpster. If irony were gold, I'd be King Midas.

Occasionally, a bear is feeding in a bin when the trash truck arrives and proceeds to inadvertently scoop the bear into the truck. Inevitably, the stunned bear wiggles loose from the debris. Sometimes they stand atop the heap, as in a sci-fi thriller, as the truck rolls through town. I get the call, show up, open the back of the enormous truck, and push that giant loaf of garbage back so the bear can climb out. Then the trash company has to find a front loader and refill the truck. I must've responded to sixty of these kinds of calls over the years.

I think to myself, *These open dumpsters are a ticking bomb of a situation. I've got to fix it, or I'm going to have to wind up shooting some bears.* I do not want lethal action to be part of my methodology. So far, nothing has gone lousy, I've never had to shoot a healthy bear. I need to keep my winning streak intact.

One night, I respond to a 9-1-1 call at a condo with some underground parking, where they keep the dumpsters. It's a screwy trap for a bear—you don't want one in underground parking. This is a perfect example of why.

"I got one!" a dude screams as I get out of my truck.

"What?"

"I got one, I got one," he says proudly, like he's fishing for trout. "I caught a big one!"

He keeps going on and on. His adult son has a camcorder with the kind of annoying light that gives you a headache. It is the oddest thing. The dad has latched the bear-proof dumpster with the bear in it. Before I get there, they have watched and waited, and when the bear climbs in, they lock it inside.

Idiots. I call for backup. The cops pull up, lights going, blocking the driveway. It's a busy weekend, people everywhere in this giant condo complex.

Out of earshot of father and son, the two cops and I talk. One cop says, "Hey, it's on wheels, let's just push it down the street."

That's one way to get the bear out of a crowded situation. I veto that. You'd have to push it a mile before you reach a place where you could safely release him. To his credit, he's thinking on his feet. Then the cop suggests getting a little stinger truck, the kind that ferries dumpsters around so the bigger trucks can get at them. So, yeah, we're still looking for solutions at this point.

The commanding officer goes over and kicks the kid with the camera out. He asks the dad, "Did you lock a bear in the dumpster?"

The guy says yes. The lieutenant gets in his face and says, "You locked him in there, you let him out."

The dumpster is walled off, to get it out of sight, and for safety. I've opened a lot of dumpsters at this point in my career, so I know the trapped bear will fly out. Not angrily. But if he happens to land on you . . .

The guy looks at the lieutenant like he's nuts. The guy is confused: Why would you let a bear out? Why would you make me do it? Aren't you going to take him to the zoo?

When he refuses, the commanding officer tells him to get the hell out of there.

Nearby, there are people in a condo Jacuzzi, drinking, having a weekend. We clear the area—it is that sensitive. No one knows where the bear will go once released. The partiers climb out with their towels and their glasses of wine.

Drumroll, please. I approach the dumpster. I am worried. I throw open the lid with a baseball bat. I peek in. The bear is lying on his stomach eating, completely oblivious to what has been going on, no threat to anyone. He isn't going anywhere. He is chowing down on some mutton, or something. In his entire life, he's probably never been happier, thank you very much.

I start beating on the side of the dumpster with the bat, rousting him. I don't want him all comfortable in there; that will just lead to more encounters like this. I don't want him to think the inside of a dumpster is a safe haven, or some kind of Michelin-star restaurant. Over the side he goes and off into the forest.

Obviously, we need to keep them out of the big bins in the first place.

Bears are unexpectedly adept at futzing with pins and clips. Though they lack opposable thumbs, their fingers are strong and they are persistent—and they are far more patient than most humans would be in puzzling out any sort of wires or chains that secure the lids.

"There is considerable overlap between the intelligence of the smartest bears and the dumbest tourists," a Yosemite ranger once explained.

If so, that would seem to make the job easier. In fact, the range of capabilities of humans and bears is one of the biggest challenges.

I've sat in the darkness, without the bears knowing I'm there, and seen them play with a pin or lock for hours. With car handles, they'd swipe left, swipe right, then pull up. Bingo. I learn that they will figure out any lever-type of lock that doesn't require a thumb. For example, some homeowners like big front doors with heavy levers. If you have a lever like that, a bear will be in your house before you blink. In Mammoth, soon as you buy your home, you have to change it out to knobs.

Any avid camper knows that you need a thumb to open a bear-proof canister, the heavy plastic buckets that campers use to store and protect their food. That is key to our understanding of making bear-proof dumpsters.

The problem wasn't just the bear. If we fix lids so a bear can't get in, then humans might have a problem opening them. How about a padlock? Well, residents, restaurants and hotels need quick and easy access to the giant dumpsters, so that type of lock is out.

There are so many of the damn trash bins, 450 at this point, all across town.

We try everything. We fight cultural hurdles; we fight sheer stupidity. In Yosemite, they used carabiners, the springy clamps favored by rock climbers, to secure the lids; visitors stole them as souvenirs. Stupid, right? You could buy them anywhere for fifty-seven cents. If we used those, we'd need to weld them in ways to thwart the petty thieves.

So that's two wild species we have to balance: the bears and the tourists. I deal with both the dumbest and smartest creatures on Earth—the two-legged and the four-legged kinds. Dumb bears are all dead. They do things like wander in front of cars, or make themselves a nuisance and get shot. It's Darwinism, pure and simple.

An enormous part of the problem is that up to thirty-five thousand visitors come into town on busy winter weekends. We spend millions in marketing money to lure them from London and Sydney, any place we can. You see them come in on Highway 203, driving on the wrong side of the road, because that's how they do it back home. Most of them are good, God-fearing people eager for a taste of the mountains. They're temps, and even if they happen to care about local customs, which many do, they're here so briefly that we don't get a chance to teach them about being around bears. Generally, the summer visitors are a little more savvy about being out in nature; in winter, we get the skiers, who appreciate their surroundings, yet don't have the necessary experience with the weather or the wildlife.

They'll leave a bag of trash next to the dumpster. So what? They don't even know they have done anything wrong. I get furious to the point where I just need to step back and realize that the nicest people can do the dumbest things. Breathe, brother, breathe.

One of the challenges we face is making the clip easy enough that a human holding a bag of trash in one hand can unfasten it with the other using cold, drunk, numb fingers in the middle of winter, on a too-dark street of a mountain town. As it is, lots of folks leave the garbage on the ground in front of the dumpster, where the bags invariably get torn into by raccoons, ravens, and bears.

The dumpsters have light metal split lids. Sometimes, the bear will sit on the edge of one, wiggle his paws in the gap between the two lids, get a whiff of the treasures inside, and pull up on the other side. Instead of the other lid lifting, the one she's sitting on buckles into a V and she will slide right in. Not only does the bear have access to the food, now she's crumpled the metal lid into the dumpster, damaging the lid to the point where it can't be easily repaired. A one-piece heavy-gauge steel top is vital, though you can't make it so heavy that humans can't lift it.

After years of trial and error, we come up with a spring-loaded carabiner clip through an I-bolt to pin shut the now-heavier lids. Welded to a three-link piece of chain, so they can't be stolen, the carabiners can be unsnapped and resnapped with one hand in seconds.

Success! At great cost and requiring an enormous amount of time, we convert all the troublesome T-bars—the metal bars that previously secured the lids—to the new carabiner latches. Takes years. We start refitting the restaurants, move on to the hotels that serve food. You can still go to a condo and watch the bears have an all-night feeding frenzy. They will eat like college kids—at one A.M. Eventually, we get to the condos too, though. Not the sexiest work, to be sure. But vital to saving the bears.

Who pays for all this? Fortunately, the trash company plays along, and the significant cost is quietly passed along to the consumers. Takes years, but we finally fix our chronic dumpster issue. The bears are now forced to eat grass, currants, and seeds, which winds up reducing the bear breeding to numbers that won't overwhelm the town. Their population will now be governed by the laws of nature, rather than random pizza crusts and bags of curly fries. Less food, and a natural diet, cuts the birth rate dramatically.

Archimedes has found his lever.

As with the bumper stickers, I have to rely on many others for help. In this whole process, I kind of con them into trying different solutions to the lids, into springing for the conversions, into hauling away the damaged bins. I can't do it alone for our bears.

CHAPTER SIXTEEN

LOCALS VS. TOURISTS

The more I learn about the bears, the more I learn about human nature and this quirky mountain retreat. We're not a wholesome, Little League town. The snow is dry and glistens like sequins. But that doesn't translate into anything pure.

You come to these silver hills to get your party on, to get laid, to get your rage, and to get out. Visitors come for fun, then they return to Brentwood or Newport Beach, after blowing off steam, and blowing off the outstanding warrants. Out of sight, out of mind.

"Come for vacation, leave on probation," a local saying goes.

At the police headquarters, I once saw someone call up all the outstanding warrants; there were six thousand, an astounding number for a four-square-mile town with seven thousand official residents, though I've always suspected that four thousand is probably a more accurate number, if you're counting permanent residents.

Many of the locals work for the government—local, county, state, and federal; others work at the hospital, at the ski mountain, or in local businesses. Cooks, servers, lift operators, and ski teachers make up a significant chunk of the population. Mix in the well-off folks who drop in for a weekend here and there, and you get a diverse and dynamic populace.

Every little town has a dark side, mountain towns maybe more than most. All told, this is a marvelous place to make a life. For all its quirks, Mammoth Lakes is a life-changing paradise for a guy like me, who feels privileged and proud to have a role in daily life here.

Working with the bears in a public position changes my stature, for the good and for the bad. Going in, I know all the officials, the residents, the cops. And, it comes as no surprise that, in the early years of working with the bears, residents stand out on their porches and mock me.

"Bad bear! Bad bear!" they echo, as I scold a bear and her cubs down the street. That is my mantra, my one hit song: "Bad bear! Bad bear!"

Think of the vocabulary of a good dog: "Get in the car." "Off the couch!" It's got to be forty words. Bears' instincts and capabilities are higher than your dog's. No surprise to me that the bears can pick up on the words I use. Hand signals are a big part of my arsenal too. As with pets, a voice command accompanied by a gesture is far more effective than a voice command alone.

One bear I work with, Rasta, has gone completely deaf. She's an odd-looking bear, as big around as she is tall, with an abundance of guard hairs, the thistle-like protective hairs. We call her Rasta because when she turns to show her profile, these wild hairs show up, hanging down her sides, making her look like she has Jamaican dreadlocks.

She's a good bear, a bear everybody likes. Tourists can't rattle her, no matter how silly their behavior. A patient and slow-moving bear, Rasta has a routine like clockwork. Grew up here, knows her way around. Rasta doesn't care much for exercise, kind of a slug, actually. Her favorite food court is the shorelines of our lakes, where anglers leave stringers of fish at the water's edge. She enjoys countless meals that way, for not much effort. No one complains. The stocked lakes feature beautiful fish, but the trout are farm raised, fed on cat kibble, hardly the most organic diet. Sure, Rasta baby, have yourself a few cat-kibble trout. *Chef's kiss.*

Well, in the six or seven years she's around, we realize that we are having to raise our voices to Rasta, as you do with Grandma and Grandpa as they age, find their good ear, repeat yourself, almost yell to be heard. It's very rare for bears to lose their senses like that, the way we do. For bears, there is very little physical decline—nature won't tolerate it. Once an aging bear can't fend for herself, off she goes into the forest to die or be killed. Older bears just wander off and don't come back.

Not only is it unusual to come across a deaf bear, but Rasta's hearing loss is incremental; takes us a while to realize she responds only to hand signals, not voice commands. I learn to point this way and that, to guide her away from trouble. If I see her heading to a camp or a group of fishermen, I traffic cop her around.

One day when I'm not around, Officer Doug Hornbeck finds Rasta locked in a staircase at an apartment complex and uses the same hand signals he picked up from me to guide the bear to freedom.

"Hey, Steve, you won't believe what just happened . . ." Hornbeck says the next time he sees me.

Like watching your kid grow, in the moment we don't always appreciate all this wildlife work. But when you look back at the magic little moments and the milestones, with the clarity that time can offer, you think: *Wow, that actually happened?* In this case, we actually learned to communicate with a deaf wild animal.

So, early on, the obvious revelation: Why wouldn't we use language to coexist with the bears, one of the smartest animals in the world? Instead, we take the low road as we often do when faced with new situations we don't understand: we panic, we throw stones, we yell, we call 9-1-1.

All the years I worked with bears, when I'd say "Good boy, good boy," people would laugh and wonder why I would do that; they'd think I was a fluffy weirdo—like those folks who pet whales. You're with a bear for twenty years, you learn to communicate . . . the good, the bad.

When I roll through a neighborhood in my truck, making my rounds, they spot me and yell "Bad bear!" like some sort of battle cry. Over time, "Bad bear!" goes from derisive to an affectionate appreciation of my work.

They are aware and grateful for the progress we've made together so quickly. Their love and fascination with bears wins out. They buy in, even if their normal default emotions are ridicule and a general distrust of authority figures of any kind. (You have to kind of admire that.) This love and fascination doesn't just apply to bears; it starts to apply to other wild animals. It even streams down to the chipmunks, porcupines, all the creatures we took for granted. They call me the Bear Whisperer? We all are bear whisperers. Earlier in human history, humans knew the right ways to deal with wild animals. Your great-grandparents likely knew not to pet a buffalo or hand-feed bears or leave food lying around for the raccoons. They were better with animals. They lived among them in rural areas. That's what we're after here.

The whole paradigm change happens in a short period. It is a chapter out of a storybook.

Doesn't hurt that I am so much like the residents here—a wiseguy with a bit of an attitude, always quick with a flip remark. My stewardship of these bears amuses them. To their minds, I am like a pied piper of an odd and hairy cult.

"Bad bear!" they'd shout, then point directly toward me. I'd smile.

Tricky audience, for sure—a crusty, hardworking demographic with a gift for a snide remark. At first glance, Mammoth Lakes looks like an overly gentrified Swiss village, a slick snow globe. In truth, it's a little more like the morose and secretive town in that eccentric TV show *Twin Peaks*.

In 2011, a popular daycare provider is sentenced to sixty years in prison after pleading guilty to four counts of child molestation.

Shortly afterward, another major case roils the community when a prominent local surgeon is charged with having a sexual relationship with a fourteen-year-old girl. The forty-six-year-old doctor leaves his hospital job and resigns his school board seat after the charges. While awaiting trial, he injects himself with a lethal amount of drugs in a popular wilderness area near the Mammoth Airport.

Residents are divided over whether there should be a memorial for the sex predator / super doc. To many, he is still a hero who skillfully saved lives. Indeed, one thousand mourners show up to a big tent service near chair 15, a controversial event to this day.

My point is that you think you can escape to the mountains and leave creepy human behavior three hundred miles away. You can't. Where there are humans, there will be creepy human behavior.

The town consists of two major groups, the locals and the tourists. They're codependent and mostly tolerant of the other side. It's a class clash. Also, a values clash. Also, I think each side envies the other a little bit: the tourists envy the townies' outdoorsy lifestyle; the locals envy the tourists' heaping gobs of vacation cash. To be fair, many of our visitors are just as hardworking as I am, or more so. They've brought the family up and are trying to stretch a buck, just as I would. As the saying goes, skiing is like standing in a cold shower and tearing up $100 bills. I am grateful for their presence. Folks like that built this place.

The party boys are another story. I don't have too much in common with the ones who drink too much tequila and suddenly decide to jump naked (and steaming) from the Jacuzzi into a nearby pile of snow, amid the cackles of their pals and sweethearts. You see stuff like that all the time up here—this Jacuzzi-to-the-snow stunt. Hey, what do I care? If it restarts the guy's engine, fine.

It's certainly better than some of the things they could be doing. There are plenty of drugs up here, as there are in any raging party town.

The locals? A little crabby, truth be told. It's a hard life. Forty miles south, in Bishop, the elevation is low enough that the big snows don't pound them. By comparison, we're the North Pole.

In a typical year, there is so much snow that you have to shovel your roof to keep the rafters and trusses from collapsing. You open a door after a big blizzard to find the doorway filled with a wall of snow, a flat and perfect rectangle except for the hole the doorknob left. You're literally snowed in, yet the dog needs out and the kids have to get to school. Start digging, Mom and Dad. Oh wait, the shovel's outside on the porch? Of course, the shovel is outside. Who brings a shovel inside a cabin? Well, in Mammoth, the veterans do. So you're ready to dig yourself out of the next blizzard.

As noted, we even wax our shovels, as you would a surfboard, warming the metal blade over the stove and rubbing the butt end of a candle across it. With the wax, the snow slides right off, making the grueling task a bit easier, as we move tons of the stuff by hand each year.

I once shoveled off my home's steep sheet metal roof, walked along the ridge line clearing a row at the very top. As I learned in my snow removal days, once you clip that very top row of snow, gravity carries both sheets of snow gliding to the ground. So I'm walking like a duck with both of my size 15 boots through the three feet of rooftop snow. Along the ridge line, I'm shoveling a line all the way down the ridge when a sheet of the snow begins to go, carrying me with it. Rather than fight it, I sit with my feet facing down, as you do if you go overboard while white-water rafting, and let go of the shovel. The mini-avalanche sweeps me past a protruding vent pipe I can't see, which fillets my hand open like a fish. Meanwhile, the shovel lands blade first in the drift at the side of the house, so that when I fall on it seconds later, the handle whams me in the ribs, like a bad pole vault. Dazed and bleeding, I stumble a few steps, then fall eight feet from the drift to the pavement.

Ooooof. "Debs! Help!" A bad day, to be sure, including two hours in the emergency room getting stitched. Almost a cartoon moment, this sequence of lousy luck. Still, typical of the types of mountain hardships we constantly face. No wonder the bears opt to sleep through winter. Sometimes this place isn't fit for a snowman.

You slip on black ice and bruise your butt, feeling lucky you didn't crack an elbow or a wrist.

Car doors freeze shut, and once inside, the engine won't crank. Twenty-five-foot plow piles block drivers' vision at intersections. Most years, it snows so much crews have to load it into trucks and dump it on the out-skirts of town, because there's nowhere else in the village for the big plows to push it out of the way.

Each weekend, armies of L.A. people descend, filling the restaurants, emptying store shelves, and turning the town's only supermarket into a version of Mardi Gras. Hooray, that's why we're here. Their bread is our butter.

Now, if you visit Las Vegas or a resort town in Mexico, you'll find remarkable customer service. The moment you finish your beer, someone is there to sweep up the empty: "Would you like another, sir?"

In Mammoth, the level of service is a little less. Many folks are working three jobs, which causes a certain amount of tension between the townfolk and the visitors.

Mammoth's customer service once got so snarky that the town funded employee charm school, essentially people-skill classes on how to be more polite to visitors. Normally, that comes naturally to people. Here, it's some-times a conscious effort.

The snow and the cold, the short days, the early evenings that start around two, all of that wears on everyone who lives here. Housing is expensive, especially for those doing blue-collar work. The lifties and the checkout clerks—the guys chugging coffee while driving plows through the night—they all might be working three jobs, in addition to dealing with the horrific winter weather. Then they still struggle to make ends meet, sharpening their edgy outlook.

The long winters end, and a new crowd descends, leaving no time for a breather. There is almost no off-season anymore, no leisurely tempo. Winter dovetails into spring, when the mountain bikers arrive. In the last couple of decades, the mountain bikers have given the hill fresh life, a warm-weather, adrenaline-charged alternative to skiing. The tradeoff: no one gets an intermission after the backbreaking work of winter; it's just on to the next season.

We can't hire enough people. The ski resort spends a lot of money recruiting workers from as far away as Australia; foreigners come in, work hard, party harder, and leave in a year or less.

You move into town, buy a little A-frame on a shady street, and you wonder "Why are the locals so standoffish?"

It's partly because of how transient the population is. Newcomers seldom last. We know in six months, or a year, you'll be gone. The number of people who last up here for twenty or thirty years is very small.

Still, they come. Still, the snow flows. Still, for all the cantankerous folks who run and work a ski village, my work with bears strikes a stunningly harmonious chord.

Well, mostly.

CHAPTER SEVENTEEN

THIS BEAR CHANGES EVERYTHING

A crisp October dawn in 2001, only a month after September 11. It's still early in my stint as Mammoth's wildlife officer when a creepy and anonymous call comes in at the crack of dawn: "Steve, they've shot six bears."

Click.

I race outside. In the semi-darkness, in a lot near my house, I spot a bear badly hurt, walking on three legs. From fifteen feet away, I can see he is wounded in the right rear hip. I recognize the bear by the distinctive Nike swish on the side of his snout. He's an average bear, a standoffish bear, kind of a cranky coot. I've never used him in the video segments I've begun to do because he is such a raggedy-looking bear. In his defense though, I've never had a 9-1-1 call of him causing any trouble. He's such a routine, anonymous bear that I hadn't even given him a name.

At this point, I haven't darted a bear. Drugged bears don't learn a thing. I want bears sober and paying attention and learning every day. Though common in wildlife management, the only way I would resort to drugs would be so we could repair the bear, or diagnose a wound. Perhaps find the head of a hunter's arrow that we can pull out, that sort of thing.

My buddy Kevin Peterson loads up on ketamine from the vet, and Kevin and police sergeant Paul Dostie race to the local hospital so they can transfer it into barbed syringes for the police department's pneumatic tranquilizer gun. I stay behind with the wounded bear so that he can't wander off to where we might not be able to find him.

When Peterson and Dostie return, we load the syringes in the gun, pump it up, and dart the injured bear in the rump. He instantly starts hopping on three legs through the backyards of town straight to my house, a half mile away. Dogs barking, people gawking. What if a stray dog starts biting him? Even Debs and Ty come out on the porch when we arrive. I yell for them to get back inside. The poor bear lies down in my yard, and we whack him again with the ketamine, a serious pain-killer they used on wounded soldiers in Vietnam. On three legs, he limps off to a nearby golf course and ducks into a gaping drainage culvert.

At this point, he must feel caught up in some war himself, everyone shooting him. As he limp-hops off on three good legs, you can see the fluorescent-orange syringes flapping in his rump. It is a scene, and I'm running the show. I am very intense and very focused.

Deep into his underground hideout he goes. The bears use the culverts as lairs. They are dark, they are ominous. In these caves, the bears know they will usually be left alone, and they often go to the center point, as far from civilization as they can.

Remember how I'd drop down a manhole with a flashlight to study the bears, find their safe places, learn their habits? That is paying off now as I track this bear to his refuge, where he probably plans to die quietly, without that loudmouth Steve to hassle him.

Well, I hassle him. I protect him too. In the end, I advocate that we shoot him to put him out of his misery, an act of compassion for a suffering bear that I believe to this day needed to be done. This point of view is not universally shared, as you'll soon see.

A lot goes on before that showdown. The attack on this bear will be, to me, the saga of all sagas, and nearly my final saga. This event captures all the angst, the challenges, the frustrations of my job. It nearly does me in. As always, it ends up not being a bear problem. Essentially, it will be a people problem, and one that encapsulates the ignorance, all the well-intended missteps that human beings make in their relationship with nature. It showcases my own people-skill shortcomings, especially when dealing with hidebound state officials. It is, from the very outset, a colossal mess and—by the time it is over—an international story that brings nature lovers to tears.

Fortunately, we never find any other wounded bears, just this one. The initial bloodbath I feared doesn't materialize. But it is still on my mind as I deal with this injured bear in the culvert—the possibility that there are more out there. Till then, I sure have my hands full with this one.

I grab a long climbing rope and give the other end to Kevin. My plan: find the wounded bear underground, tie the rope to his leg, and drag him out so that we can see how badly he is hurt. If he is beyond repair, we'll euthanize him. Otherwise, we'll get him all the help we can.

In the pitch-black tunnel, I come face to face with the bear. He's lying down, eyes open, immobilized. He's staring me in the eye. Ketamine has made him motionless—it freezes up a bear's muscles. But he's conscious. I think that, at any moment, he'll muster a surge of strength and rip my face off. Kevin is outside the culvert watching me—for him, it's like looking down a milkshake straw. "You OK?" he keeps asking. "You OK in there?"

I'm not OK. I tell him I'm afraid. I'm five feet away from the bear, and Kevin is eighty to a hundred feet away in the mouth of the culvert.

Kevin is one of my best buddies, a reliable outdoorsman, the kind of guy you want next to you in a foxhole. And you know what Kevin says to me? He says, "If it goes really bad, you lie down on your stomach and I'll shoot right over you."

This is a super-dark tunnel, and our plan B is for him to shoot the bear off of me? Fuck that. I don't want anyone pulling me out of there with a rope.

I start crawling backward out of the pipe real quick.

At this point, our struggles to save the bear have taken up most of the day—to acquire the ketamine, to trail him to the tunnel, to find him deep in the dark. It's almost night by now, and Kevin and I agree to come back in the morning.

At first light, I call the police chief, who sends out another cop as backup. And I check in with Fish and Game: "This is what we got, this is what we're doing."

Well, Fish and Game official Eric Wong goes ballistic. Ketamine is illegal in the fall, during bear hunting season. The theory, valid or not: if someone darts a bear with ketamine, then a hunter shoots him, turns him into sausage or steaks, and throws him on the barbecue, the hunter and his buddies could end up consuming the ketamine.

I find that extremely far-fetched—certainly nobody is going to butcher this wounded bear and turn him into steaks. But it's a serious infraction nonetheless. Fish and Game takes it so seriously that they record me confessing to the ketamine, which I didn't like using in the first place.

To me, this is how frivolous this all is. Chemically, ketamine degrades by 50 percent with every hour that passes. In addition, it is illegal to shoot in the city limits of Mammoth Lakes, or within a mile of its perimeter, making it preposterous to think that someone could hunt down this three-legged bear, skin him, and consume him in a way that would be lethal.

Still, I am the one who is cooked. The state's wildlife law enforcement arm starts to investigate how Kevin, Dostie, and I tranquilized the bear, a task that only state-sanctioned experts are supposed to perform. Keep in mind that I'm not some rogue vigilante, running around darting bears. I'm the town wildlife specialist, and I am with Dostie, a police sergeant. The state prepares to charge me, the vet who gave us the ketamine, and Dostie.

In my mind, Fish and Game already has it out for me because of all the publicity I've gotten for working with bears, the TV stuff, the newspaper articles, all that. I skipped any sort of formal training, so they are extra leery of my unconventional tactics. In their mind, I haven't paid the same dues they have, read the same books, crammed all night for exams. Nor do I have a crew cut.

Before I know it, we're a week into this, and the bear isn't getting any better. Despite the state hullabaloo, we keep tending to the poor bear, who by now is almost an afterthought. Al Zamudio, a close friend and former game warden, helps me deliver care packages with antibiotics, honey, and high-grade dog food to keep his strength up. To help fight off the infection, we roll apples full of antibiotics to him in the culvert. What option do we have? He isn't able to fend for himself, to find food, and is getting weaker every day.

I sit sideways in the culvert, slice open the bags of honeyed kibble, and feed the injured bear. Then I turn and talk to Zamudio, who by this time is working as a cameraman for a local TV station and filming daily interviews. Also in my favor, USC is in the midst of doing its documentary *Affairs with Bears*, and they start filming this chain of events. Because they're barbed, the fluorescent darts are still stuck in the bear's butt. The cameras catch all that. It is good television, shown on local channels, with some of the feeds shared with L.A. and other major outlets. Awareness escalates very fast. Each day, I give the media a progress report. With the bear looking over my shoulder and my gangly legs propped on the opposite wall of the forty-inch culvert, I turn to the camera:

"We're on day 11. It's time for justice for this bear, to put him out of his misery or get him the help he needs . . ."

As is my way, I get very emotional. I am both sad and tense during my self-righteous rants. To see this bear rotting in this culvert, bleeding, infected from the wound. Bear fur is dirty to begin with, and when a bear is shot, the bacteria on the fur and skin gets carried inside and flows into the bloodstream.

State officials and I are at a standoff: I believe we need to put him out of his misery or get him out and treat him. The state wants to let nature take its course, to leave him where he is to die a slow death. I tell Fish and Game officials, rather emphatically, that nature didn't put those shotgun pellets in him; that was mankind, and now humans need to make it right. State officials insist there is no evidence he was shot.

"Except for the bleeding gunshot wound," I say sarcastically.

We know that the public has started responding to the media reports. Friends and colleagues, more clear-headed than me in the moment, know this story is going to get even bigger. They also know more about fighting state agencies than I do. One night on the phone, Dostie urges me: "Name the bear, name the bear, do it now, tonight." Up to that point the bear has no name. As I noted, he is just a typical bear. Generally, only the trouble-makers earn nicknames.

Dostie says that naming the bear will make him more sympathetic, more real. Ann Bryant, the Tahoe bear advocate, suggests Arthur for his name. A very smart woman, she thinks it is especially appropriate: Arthur, hero-warrior, symbol of chivalry and moral righteousness.

Arthur it is.

In many ways this is a turning point. I am convinced we never could have rallied support had we not named the bear. It is genius-level public relations and the right thing to do.

Meanwhile, the situation is becoming as ugly as ugly gets, as the growing media attention puts everyone on edge. I am spitting mad, dealing with a bunch of armed and angry men, each side insisting they are taking the moral high ground. The difference of opinion is philosophical, ethical, and territorial. I believe I have jurisdiction and a better feel for the needs of Mammoth's bears. The state feels it has more wildlife knowledge, more responsibility for public safety, and an obligation to take the lead in the case, based on its resources and legal authority.

And his plight is getting worse by the hour, with unexpected twists. One evening, when the golfers are off the course, I crawl into the tunnel with Arthur's usual care package: kibble laced with honey and meds. Expecting Arthur, I come face-to-face with another bear. He and Arthur have been brawling, and he's shredded across his chest. Arthur is nowhere to be seen.

"What-the-fuck, what-the-fuck, what-the . . ."

Believe me, I am becoming an expert at backpedaling out of tunnels in a hurry.

Just as things can't get worse, they have. The predator bear, who I'd named Half-Nose during previous encounters, has always been a brawler, and his nickname probably gives you a sense of his long-damaged schnoz. The two bears tore into each other overnight, and Half-Nose is now bloody in the face and chest. On one side, his face appears fine. If he turns his head to the left, you can see right into his damaged nasal passages. In the dark, with the inherent spookiness of flashlights and a head lamp, he looks like Halloween.

Once we find Arthur, we see that he is scratched up too, though not as badly.

By now, I am coming face-to-face with some humans as well, namely the state officials who have way different ideas on how to handle Arthur.

In week 3, the California National Guard flies in a huge cargo plane to whisk Arthur away. Bryant, of the Lake Tahoe Bear League, comes in, a woman with a huge amount of influence; she has a thousand millionaires who support her. Bryant brings along a noted vet with a big background in bears.

As the situation reaches critical mass, state officials demand a meeting at the police department. On a whiteboard, I explain what needs to be done. I draw the drainage tunnel, mark where the bear is. I tell them how I'm going to go in there and lead him out, like Dr. Doolittle. And then we'll have the vet look at him, and we'll either euthanize him or transport him out, at the doctor's discretion.

"This is how we're going to deal with our bear," I keep saying.

This sense of ownership does not go over well. After about the fifth time I say "our bear," the Fish and Game staffers storm out, slamming doors. Police chief Randy Schienle comes to me and says that I can't keep referring to Arthur as "our bear." I insist that they are *our bears*, they belong to us, they are town residents. We've invested in, protected, cared for these bears, possibly like no American city ever has before.

The chief says, "No, man. You're really freaking them out . . . let's try to make peace with them."

Cut to a big convoy of state wildlife cars, police cruisers, all following me back over to the culvert. I am wearing a Ruger Security-6 .357 Magnum, which I normally never wear. It's a hand cannon I bought from a cop. If we have to put Arthur down in tight quarters, it's better suited to the task. We find that Arthur has moved closer to the opening of the culvert. At this point, he is having good days and bad. This is a bad one.

As we kneel on the ground, near the bear, I ask the vet whether he has any problem with euthanasia by my .357 Magnum, rather than by drugs. He says not at all. Meanwhile, another state expert, a biologist, is standing three pickup truck lengths away, so scared that he's following all this with binoculars.

I go into the culvert—I'm crying behind my glasses, I'm that upset. The idea is to flush Arthur out of the culvert, watch him walk on his three good legs, and then make a decision. I drop behind him in the long culvert, get down with him, and I say, "Hey buddy, just hang on. It's only going to be a couple of minutes and we'll take care of you."

I slowly prod him out of the tunnel, to the daylight, where there's a dozen people waiting.

Arthur takes one look at this wide-eyed welcome party and does a buttonhook into an adjacent tunnel. When I emerge, Arthur is gone. "Damn, where'd he go?" I ask.

Suddenly, the presiding officer from Fish and Game calls a halt to every-thing. We have to let nature take its course, he says, and orders everyone to leave. Again, I tell them that Mother Nature didn't shoot this bear's back end; a human had done that. The officer insists we haven't confirmed the cause. I'm adamant: "He wasn't hit by lightning! This was caused by humans. It's up to us to fix him, or put him out of his misery. We can't leave him here in a public place, an injured bear who's been shot, on a golf course," I say.

Nope, the official says: We're all leaving right now. Anyone who hangs around is subject to arrest.

The police agree to leave, the National Guard leaves, Bryant is ready to leave. I am so incensed. Every molecule in my body is pinging. I tell the state biologist, the guy driving their decisions: "I'm going to take my gun off right now, strip down to my underwear, and I'm going to kick your ass."

Whoa, whoa, whoa. The cops do a U-turn and step in, escort me to my truck, tell me to go down to the police department to cool off. Fish and Game officials get together with the police chief, and Schienle decides to put me under house arrest through the following day. Tells me not to go any farther than my own porch. My head is spinning. My wife is freaking out.

"Our typical reaction is to first see if an injured wild animal can make it on its own," Patrick Foy, a Fish and Game Department spokesman, would explain later. "This isn't an unusual situation. We're typically at odds with the animal rights community as to when wildlife needs help and when it should be left to its own devices."

Just after the showdown, Zamudio interviews an Air National Guard pilot on camera. Even he is with me. The pilot turns his uniform jacket inside out so he can speak freely and candidly about how offended he is about the state's stance on this.

Viewers and readers are eating up the coverage. Phones are ringing off the hook, callers insisting they can't leave a wounded bear to suffer and die.

Seems almost everybody, rich or poor, Republican or Democrat, sharp or stupid, agrees that we can't leave a wounded bear to suffer and die.

On November 14, almost a month after the saga starts, state wildlife officers go to find Arthur; it takes a long time to locate him. Once they have him, a state wildlife veterinarian shoots Arthur with a tranquilizer dart, then loads him into a steel barrel with the help of trappers, in preparation for sending him to the Fish and Game's Wildlife Lab near Sacramento, four hours away.

The last time I see Arthur before he leaves town is in that trap, in the center of town, surrounded by trappers, state police, and wildlife officials. They have a huge presence, hoping to deter a confrontation with residents, who are riled up by now, not wanting to see the bear placed in captivity. The whole scene scorches my heart. I can see that he's muzzled and shackled, like Hannibal Lecter. What's wrong with letting him wiggle around? The cages are solid, sturdy, hard as bombs.

The trappers haul Arthur to the state lab, where the plan is to do some medical tests, to see how they can treat him. X-rays show copper shotgun pellets in his back end.

At this point, a "Free Arthur" campaign is reaching a fever pitch. Thanks to all the media coverage, those who have followed Arthur's saga are wearing "Free Arthur" T-shirts and hats. Media outlets near and far are following the backlash. To many folks, Arthur's trip to the state lab feels like a kidnapping.

PETA has also shown up, militant in these matters, to say the least. They send a mass phone message to various California area codes calling on animal lovers to reach out on Arthur's behalf. It is highly disruptive to local phone service. The district attorney, who to that point has been pretty patient with me, forcefully tells me to make it stop—*now!*—even though I have nothing to do with the phones.

The uproar grows, drawing national animal rights groups ranging from the Humane Society of the United States to PETA. The extremist and often-violent Animal Liberation Front contacts me, drawing the notice of the FBI. Far as I know, the animal liberation folks never show up, but the FBI reportedly does, that's how wary they are of ALF. Amid all this, state lawmakers are besieged with calls and emails.

Days after Arthur is taken away, my wife, Debs, comes into my home office: "Steve, you'd better come out here right now."

"Why?"

"Because there's a bunch of Indians in the front yard."

Out front, I find a large group of Native Americans. Unknown to me at that point, many of them are members of the Paiute Bear Clan, who continue to honor nature and bears through ancient ceremony and dance.

In my emotional fog and exhaustion, all I see are a bunch of braids and turquoise and silver.

Now, you need to understand that the Native Americans have appreciated the bear spirit for thousands of years. Largely unknown and unseen, there are still Bear Clans operating across the West, from the flatlands to the mountains, performing dances and rituals for an animal they have always honored.

Why? What is behind this special bond? What do Native Americans see in the bears that connects so closely? Well, bears, monkeys, and elephants have always been the rock stars of nature movements. That's a given. In addition, I suspect this: When we see a bunch of folks dancing around a fire, it unsettles us, even scares us. When we see a bear in the yard, it scares us too. To me, that's part of their bond. Because they're not understood, the bears and the Native Americans have both been demonized.

"I'm Shorty Stone," their leader tells me on my porch. "And we're here to help you."

Shorty is the son of Raymond Stone, a legendary orator and spiritual leader in the Paiute tribe. Shorty tells me that they want me to meet with them in two days. In the meantime, he leaves behind a woman, Sherriee, to stay at our place to look after me. Well, OK, I guess. Debs is cool with it.

In talking to Sherriee day after day, I realize she knows it all: the language, my story with Arthur, what they were going to ask of me.

Two days later, we head over to the Vons supermarket to see Shorty. In the parking lot is a protest scene right out of a Billy Jack movie. Various tribes from across the West—Shoshone, Miwoks, Paiutes—have brought their families to a parking lot, circled their trucks like a wagon train near the supermarket. In the nearby Carl's Jr., each booth is full of tribesmen and women. Everyone has silver or turquoise, lots of braids. Men, women, and children. At midday, they tell me, there will be a ceremony.

Typically, the Bear Clan is active across the West until the bears go into den in late fall, then the clan members stay idle, as do the bears, for six months. At this point in the fall, the Bear Clan has put the bears away for the season, through an elaborate ritual. But Shorty has called them out again. Shorty asks for their help, and they go through all the steps for the Bear Clan members to come back into action like this.

Ideally, they'd want a fire—the customary way to carry their prayers to the creator. But they don't have a permit. So they're using a huge six-man powwow drum as their centerpiece and are lighting smudge sticks, wrapped sage, one at a time. The bear dancers are there, a half dozen of them dressed out in bearskins. They've carefully finger-painted white mud—*coso*—on their faces, per tradition.

It looks like a museum display come to life: the Native Americans dance barefoot in the lot, wearing bear hides and leather, dried *coso* mud on their legs and cheeks, the big drum pounding, leaving the twenty-first century behind.

This Free Arthur rally is cross-cultural, involving the Natives and the whites. It stems from interest in Arthur's case, staged by activists upset with what the government is doing. Everyone knows it's going to be a big day. The Native Americans end up being the profound centerpiece of it and—for me—the start of a wonderful personal journey.

I'm tripping. I'm still a mess from the ordeal with Arthur—spent, tired, drained, and armed—and the situation is very heavy and fraught. Now this. I've never seen anything so surreal. In a four-part ceremony, they "dress out" in their ceremonial regalia, light their sage, creating a smoky autumnal haze.

Helpers known as wingmen are taking sage, in groups of thirty to forty sticks, lighting them quickly. The wingmen move actively among the dancers, waving eagle wings to get the smoky sage, and the prayers, into our lungs—as I explained earlier, burning sage is an ancient spiritual whisk broom.

The leader announces a "hook-up."

To the sound of the drums, the Native Americans start to dance in a circle, spiraling out. They "hook" together, a hand on the shoulder of the person in front, everybody linked. I've been watching, leaning against the wheel of a truck. Sherriee takes me by the hand, walks me out to the dance, puts my hand on the right shoulder of a bear dancer by the name of Pete, big as a house. I feel a hand on my shoulder. Soon, this dance line is fifteen rows deep, everyone looking down, mimicking the dance steps of the person in front of them as we all dance together.

When I turn back, I see that my buddies Al and Kevin are right behind me. Hundreds are rotating with us, round and round in the concentric dance circles, young and old. Hippies, trust-funders, folks who just happen by. Everyone is hunched over, doing the two-step. I'm crying, it's so moving. You can feel it. All the sacred subsets are here: sun dancers, medicine men, the drummers—traditional roles you might think vanished 150 years ago. Shoppers are coming out of the Vons supermarket to find this ancient dance party. They peek through rows of cars, amazed at what they're witnessing just blocks from their condos.

The power of it, the history of it—all happening in real life. Fear, energy, and prayers are colliding in a paved parking lot. At the center of the ceremony: six people with two-foot-long drumsticks surround the powwow drum, sitting on folding chairs. Song after song. Ringing the drummers are the "song carriers," performing in the native Paiute tongue. They are singing the bear songs to bring healing and health in a desperate situation that they know will go bad. They instinctively know the antidote to the insanity that is happening, without teaching me . . . they just bring me in and show me.

The Tahoe bear advocates in town—led by Ann Bryant—begin a protest march down Old Mammoth Road, one of the main streets in the middle of town. The cops are cool, carefully escorting the peaceful protesters, handing out water on the too-warm November day.

I don't talk much that day. I just thank everybody for their support. Strangers are joining the cause from all over, not knowing me. I'm not a religious man. But when you have that many people praying together, you can feel it.

You can imagine how this hazy ancient dance in a supermarket parking lot, surrounded by the amazing mountains and big trees, would make headlines across the nation. At this point, the "Free Arthur" campaign is making international news.

Hours later, as I'm leaving, one remaining Native American stands waiting for me. He's a big man, six and a half feet tall. I walk up and say, "Chief, party's over. We're done here." His name is Marshall Jack, he tells me, and he's waited for hours to talk to me. "Steve, you're in harm's way," he says. He reaches into a bag and pulls out a carved stone of a female bear. He tells me to place it next to my bed that night. "It will keep you safe."

But will it?

Amid all this, Arthur advocates are still writing from all over the world, essentially of the same mind: kill him or set him free. In coming weeks, the office of Governor Gray Davis holds a hearing in Sacramento to try to figure out what has stirred so many people up and why the backlash is lingering.

In the end, despite criminal investigations and hearings, nothing changes. Arthur is first held at the state lab, fifteen miles outside Sacramento. Arthur's keepers discover his diet has included lots of garbage.

Among the items they find in his scat are food packaging and even a dis-carded sock. They insist that, if released, he'll revert to his old ways and become a garbage bear, a neighborhood nuisance. Remember, though, I never once had a problem with him before the shooting.

Fish and Game officials also said they found bone growth in the right rear leg, in the same area as the shotgun pellets. They blamed the bone injury for his lameness.

John Hadidian, director of the Humane Society's urban wildlife pro-gram, disagrees.

"The bulk of the evidence does suggest the gunshot had a big, big role to play in this," he says.

Later, they take Arthur to Galt, California, to PAWS, a refuge for exotic animals that had been abandoned as pets or abused in attractions and various facilities. When I visit him, I spot an elephant chained to a stump. A blind lion has worn a dirt path in the grass from pacing in his long rectangular cage; I can see the cataracts over both eyes.

Before I leave Mammoth, I spend days cutting bouquets of all the plants Arthur would've had access to in Mammoth. I figure this will meet his natural nutritional needs, assist his healing. I am hoping to see what he is drawn to, then bring him a truckload more of it. When I get to Galt, they won't let me into Arthur's cage.

With the chain link between us, I sit with Arthur. He hobbles over, a three-legged bear, his injured leg atrophied and tucked up, unusable. Arthur knows it's me. He huffs and blows his breath on me, typical of bears. As much as he's blowing out, he's breathing in. As noted, their noses are their control panels. They process everything through scent and smell.

After all the drama, Arthur would live—if you call what he had a life. In bad circumstances, I don't think dying is scary; living is scary, for mortally sick people and for injured animals. This was one of those cases. I feel so guilty over this . . . heartsick. I decide right then: never again would I allow a bear to go to jail on my watch.

In Galt, they slip his food through the kind of slot you find in a prison, along the floor. As I watch that day, they slide in a cafeteria tray of Fig Newtons and sliced fruit. Ironically enough, they are giving him junk food.

As you would expect, Arthur grows fat and lethargic: a neglected prisoner, sentenced to life in a welded-shut cage for doing nothing more than getting shot.

It never leaves my heart, or my mind, that this insane stuff they do to Arthur—tossing this bear into solitary confinement—appears to be motivated by a personal vendetta against me, which adds to my anguish.

Arthur dies an old bear. In captivity.

Though they're called black bears, in California they are rarely black. They come in variations of reds, browns, or cinnamon, much like these three. *Image by Tim Bartley.*

ABOVE: A beautiful bear known as Blondie went on a rampage after losing her second cub. Her troubled life ended in an early and dramatic death. *Image by Brooke Hartnett.* BELOW: A dead bear in the back of my truck, with a bundle of sage. By waving burning sage, I send a victim into the afterlife with care and respect. *Image by Steve Searles.*

The odd-looking bear I dubbed Rasta. When she had grown completely deaf, we substituted hand signals to keep her out of harm's way. *Image by Heather Kemper.*

When mountain towns grow, they add attractive habitat for young bears, which den under decks and in crawl spaces. *Image by Ellen Fox.*

Bears look for fish off a dock in Lake Mary. You could wash your baby in these pristine lakes. You could use them to make soup. *Image by Skip George.*

RIGHT: Besides bears, what else are we needlessly afraid of? BELOW: These stickers changed the game. Residents pasted them on ski towers, on cash registers.

MAMMOTH DON'T FEED OUR BEARS

ABOVE: Their sense of smell is extraordinary, leading them to back porches and barbecue grills. *Image by Kathy Watson.* BELOW: Bears patrol the shorelines, often snatching anglers' fish from the well-stocked lakes. *Image by Skip George.*

To a bear, an open dumpster is an all-you-can eat buffet. The drawback: a fat bear is an attractive bear, and that leads to overbreeding. *Image by Henry Gembitz.*

ABOVE: The region's raw beauty is captured in Lake Ediza, between Mammoth Lakes and Yosemite. Sierra summers are warm, the winters long and sometimes brutal. *Image by Skip George.* LEFT: Bears in vehicles are a constant problem. They will tear the airbags out of cars; they will trash truck lockers. *Image by Henry Gembitz.*

Black bears are playful. They have a chain of command; they are independent thinkers, not herd animals. *Image by Carroll-Sue Jones.*

Grizzlies eat everything. But black bears like these are primarily herbivores that graze on vegetation and the occasional Big Mac. *Image by Carroll-Sue Jones.*

A nursing sow and her cub. A mother spends about two years with her cubs, from the time she births them to the time she pushes them off to be on their own. *Image by Carroll-Sue Jones.*

Eliminating human food from their diets kept the bear population manageable. They feed full time, especially in autumn, before shutting down in winter. *Image by Carroll-Sue Jones.*

Black bears climb trees to escape danger; grizzlies do not. Campers and hikers are often unaware of the bears hovering high above them. *Top image by Skip George, bottom image by Carroll-Sue Jones.*

Though well-intended, bird feeders often lure wild bears. Done with that, they'll head over the railing and into the house. *Image by Jim Thomsen.*

I learned that the king of the forest will bluff-charge you to create space—"Hey, leave me alone!"—yet walk away from most confrontations. *Image by Heather Kemper.*

ABOVE: Heavy snows start around Halloween. In midwinter, you can open your cabin door to a wall of snow in the morning, then be forced to dig your way out to go to work or school. *Image by Cynthia Hayes.* RIGHT: Mammoth Lakes' bears are known to slip through the automatic doors of a supermarket and snatch what they want. *Image by Mike Dacosta.*

CHAPTER EIGHTEEN

DANCES WITH BEARS

I suddenly feel seven hundred years old.

I'd already been reeling from the death of my first son, who we'd lost over his severe heart defect in the third trimester, an agonizing experience for Debs and me that led to much grief and emotional trauma. They handed me his birth certificate and death certificate at the same time. You crash your car, you get a new one. But something like that does not go away. It changes me forever.

The loss of my first son, followed shortly after by the Arthur epoch, prompted me to ask all the questions we ask ourselves in middle age: Have I made a difference? Am I doing good work? Am I a good man and father? Why aren't I more at ease, happier, more content?

Still grieving over my son, Arthur's saga has pushed me to the edge. My confidence is severely shaken. I'm not eating, not sleeping. If your nervous system is aflame, you will be too.

Marshall Jack, the Paiute who handed me the carved bear in the parking lot, also asked me to meet him on the outskirts of town. I am leery. He seems to sense something in me. "Steve, you're in harm's way," I remember him saying at the end of the rally. I wasn't sure in what sense. From outside forces? From myself? But the next day I meet him, as directed, at a place called Lost Lake, ironically enough.

There, Jack draws me a map to a spot in Big Pine, a little town—kind of pretty, kind of barren—an hour to the south.

With 1,700 residents, Big Pine is one of a stretch of small towns between L.A. and Mammoth. Some Californians see these little outposts as a slice of Americana, while others see them as drab and forgotten places lost to time. In truth, they're a little bit of both. There is certainly a rustic charm and a reluctance to change. Chain restaurants are few. Instead, steer skulls and split-rail fences line the roads, toasted and bleached from the fabled California sun.

It's cowboy country, rich and fascinating, far more than first meets the eye. A half hour away are the oldest living trees on Earth, the ancient bristlecone pines. Some five thousand years old, these trees survive despite poor soil and dry, harsh conditions. Mostly known for nearby fishing and camping, Big Pine is also a hub of the Paiute tribes, and the hangout of Shorty Stone, my spiritual adviser during the Arthur experience.

Every single town has a sign for a reservation, the site usually marked by a casino, a tribal gas station, and abject poverty. I pull onto the reservation in Big Pine, into an area near some government land, the Owens River close by. Trailers and RVs serve as homes. Sprinklers are hissing in an effort to fight off the dust and high desert dryness. Hummingbird feeders, dogs off leash and roaming freely on the mostly bare dirt lots. Basic as basic could be. The kind of place you keep an eye out for rattlesnakes.

Like someone coming out of a dream, I rub my eyes. I've arrived on this late-fall day to a health spa directly out of the 1600s, a rustic complex of longhouse dining halls and ceremonial gathering places, all surrounding the centerpiece of the place: a sweat lodge, a ferocious sauna fueled by volcanic rock. Smoke from the ceremonial fires adds to the gauzy, sepia-toned scene.

In short, a sweat lodge is a place where tribal members and select outside guests like me can gather regularly to sweat out the physical and spiritual crud that brings us down. Part spa, part altar, you come out different from when you went in.

In with the good, out with the bad, a place to remember what is deep within us. As I get out of the truck, I smudge my trademark white tennis shoes with a burning wrap of white sage.

Look at me, the ultimate cynic, about to go dancing with the wolves. I stand there, dust covering my Reeboks, thinking how ancient this scene is—the light filtering through the smoke, the crackle of the fire super-heating the rocks to the point where you can see right through them.

The roundhouse I'm seeing for the first time today may harken to dwellings first erected in this region ten thousand years ago. The past is prologue, as they say. Right in front of me now, a bonfire heats the rocks that will power "the sweat."

Now, I may not believe in God the same way you might. By temperament, I am a skeptic. I am skeptical of every institution, every mass belief, every conventional wisdom, every hymn. And as you can tell, I am hugely suspect of authority figures in general. So many have let me down.

Yet, to me all the good we see in the world represents God. I believe that heaven exists in our hearts, in the kindnesses we offer, in Rembrandt's paintings, in a mother's kiss, in a hospice caregiver's reassuring touch.

Do I pray? Well, I pray that all my friends collectively think good thoughts. When you are in a church full of praying people, or singing a hymn in the town square at Christmas, you can feel it then: God—and good—at work.

With that as my touchstone, the Native Americans' rituals and passion speak to me from the very start. I already realize they have a reverence for the bears that appeals to me—the Bear Clan is among the most active tribal subsets. They also have a humble appreciation for their place in the universe. They don't feel superior or subservient to the physical world—merely a part of it.

One of the most distinctive traits is this: many of the world's organized religions discourage members from praying for themselves. Instead, your prayers and healing thoughts are directed at others. Not here. The theory is simple: if you don't take care of yourself, you're no good to anyone else. Self-preservation is encouraged. Shorty says this over and over. Broken people are in no place to help other broken people. You need to stay strong so that you can help a neighbor or loved one.

As I explore the site, a drum begins to pound—the heartbeat of Mother Earth.

The centerpiece of the complex is the sweat lodge, though it is surrounded by eating and meeting facilities as well. The lodge is round. Take a woven basket, flip it upside down, add a door, and that's your lodge.

Made by hand, only about four feet high and twenty feet across, the sweat lodge is crafted of two-inch willow poles, stripped of their bark and rainbowed into anchor holes in the ground, where they'd put a pinch of tobacco as a token of thanks. They have space for up to forty folks, sitting on reeds brought from the nearby river.

The roofs are made with handmade blankets and military tarps. Like a sauna, they are designed to be roasting dens that purify and cleanse.

Someone yells "Sweat!" and the participants begin to pour from trailers and homes. There is no guide, no one to show me around. I merely follow the leader . . . I find a line, I blend in. I bow my head, I don't ask questions. There are pairs of sandals that participants have kicked off before entering. How out of place the plastic sandals are. How out of place am I?

The women and girls wear the most unflattering down-to-the-ankle sweat dresses, or sometimes long-sleeve shirts and skirts. It's striking and lovely, not high fashion, very plain but carried in such grace. The men wear trunks, like board shorts, go in bare chested—no shoes, no sandals, no jewelry.

Once the ceremony begins, the sweat leader enters first.

With eight-foot tools, the "rock men" begin to pull the stones off a fiery outside pile, knock off any ash or debris that would cause them to smoke, and bring the ancient rocks inside, where they carefully ladle water on the rocks to draw the steam—generating heat and steam in incredible amounts. We pat our chests and hearts. "Rock men, leave out ten, bring in the rest," the sweat leader says, as they bring in twenty more blazing rocks. They close the door. The ceremony begins. We offer prayers for the ancestors that came before us, and the loved ones yet to come.

When they are done, the tarp closes. Inside, it is completely dark . . . the blackest black, ten times darker than any campsite or movie theater you've ever been in. The darkness completely steals your visual senses, and the other senses compensate: your hearing, sense of smell, your mind.

The sweat itself is very short. How it affects you is very long.

At times, the drum is pounding so furiously that it gets your heart going. Like when you put your ear to your lover's chest—*that* powerful, maybe even more so. During songs, the quiet moments, the drum stops completely. During bear songs, more physical and aggressive, the drum kicks up again. So primal. Just that deep, methodical thump.

Five minutes into the ceremony, my eyeballs begin to sweat. To keep the heat up, they continue to pour water on the lava rocks. I'm not sure how much more I can take. Just when it becomes unbearable, it becomes slightly bearable again.

The ceremony continues. Following the lead of others, I ask permission to speak: "My name is Steve. I am a weak man. I need prayers for the wild bears I watch over."

The fire tenders continue to bring in new rocks. With the door open, I can see them use three-point deer antlers to position them in the pit, part of the optics that make this of another time. They close the door again, and ladle water over the rocks. No smoke. Just steam and prayers billowing in the darkness. They add cedar dust to the hot rocks, brought in from

Yosemite—an incense, a myrrh. When they sprinkle it on the rocks, the cedar dust flickers up, swirling like fireflies.

All my senses begin to ping. I can feel the water running down my back. I go from bone dry, in this dusty-dry land, to sitting in the mud of my own sweat.

I feel I have jumped from the hot Jacuzzi into the fresh snow.

Someone passes around the *coso* mud, the white goo the Native Americans have worn for ceremonies. Another person passes around a jar of bear grease, used as a balm. Put it where it hurts, someone says. I dab it on my temples, my head. In the heat, it starts to warm, like Bengay.

I learn how everything the Native Americans do is in sets of four, in honor of the four directions, in honor of the seasons.

Hence, there are four rounds to each sweat session. In the first round, we will sing four songs. The first one begins (my phonetic interpretation): "Doya, doya, quinn . . ."

New as it is to me, I can already see that they are radiating exactly what I need.

The second round is the doctoring round, a time for prayers for those facing mental and physical hardships. It's quickly clear to me this is the firecracker round—the hottest round. They add more of the ceremonial lava rocks—each rock is hand selected and carried like a newborn in a very respectful way.

In the third round, there are four more songs and prayers. By the fourth round, people are maxing out in the heat, some lying on their backs on the ground, nearest the comfort and healing of Mother Earth. At a certain point in time, this was like taking a Zoloft. In time, I learn to find an emotional balance point during this, much like discovering a centerline of riding a bike, almost a Native American version of a Zen state.

It's profound and healthful but also challenging. I often feel that it is too much, that I might pass out. Everything is interconnected; time passes quickly. The four rounds take maybe ninety minutes.

This was the happiest and most supportive ceremony I'd ever experienced. I was so thirsty and starving for this. A little at a time, the sweat lodge begins to soothe some deep spiritual gulf that goes back to the beginning of my life.

In the coming months and years, I will learn some of the duties I see for the first time today. They will put me to work, splitting and stacking firewood, fetching rocks. I am a doorman for a while, ushering people in and out. I learn the ceremonial way to set up a fire, in a starburst pattern, alternating rocks and firewood, in a twenty-foot circle. The prep and setup is an important part of the ceremony itself, giving me time to get my head straight. Eventually, I help cut poles and build the lodges.

After a sweat, we share a meal; it's considered part of the ritual. I bring food from home. Bags of pasta, beans. Apple juice. Most of these people have little, and they are allowing me into their culture—into a world you don't see on any religious channel, a world cloaked and protected and poignant. I want to reciprocate.

Clearly, the Natives' struggle is the bears' struggle . . . is my struggle. We are a league of our own—with a history of being mistreated and misunderstood. Yet, with a quiet confidence, without grandstanding, the Native Americans stay the course and show their strength, which helps guide me toward gratitude, humility, appreciation for the winged ones—those that hop, those that crawl. Their kindness toward the crickets and the bees extends to people of every creed, ethnicity, and color.

They have much of what the modern world needs. We just never respected them enough to ask.

The touchstones that are missing in my life, the Paiutes have in triplicate. The guy who could never get enough family and structure starts to find it here. As the Grateful Dead song goes, "The bus came by and I got on."

In time, as they grow more comfortable with me and understand my commitment, I fill a soccer van full of family and friends to share these rich and generous rituals. How could I not? I hadn't found the secret to eternal youth, but I'd found a secret to making the most of the life we have before us. I bring the Paiutes more apple juice and pasta. In return, they give me guidance without guiding, helping me find my way. I've never been lectured by anyone in the tribe.

Obviously, the Natives end up doing way more for me than I ever do for them. They respect my kinship with the bears. My knowledge of bears, my advocacy, is the equivalent of my town key, the gateway into their world. But not all tribal members are accepting of outsiders. Who could blame them? They've been cheated and tricked throughout their history. On a moonlit night in 1863, soldiers chased thirty-five Paiute into nearby Owens Lake. Those who weren't shot drowned as they tried to escape the massacre. Since then they were bought off with beads and trinkets, given the most arid cropland. Almost 140 years later, younger tribal members are repulsed by the notion of the white man now relying on their culture to find solace.

I hear the arguments and side with the folks who don't think I belong. I'm not sure I belong either. What gives me the right? It represents cultural appropriation at the highest level.

Well, Shorty Stone thinks I belong. Like his esteemed late father, Raymond Stone, he is a very special leader. They are proud of their culture and inclusive with others, a quality missing in many religions and cultures. The Stone family is quick to share the magic. Black, white, yellow, green—they don't care about your skin tone. When I voice my concerns to Shorty that I probably won't be welcome once he is gone, he pulls out a folding knife he always carries.

"How about this," he says, holding the knife against his hand. "I'm going to cut me, and then I'm going to cut you. Will we both bleed red?"

"Of course," I say.

"Then I don't want to ever hear of this again," he says, putting his knife away.

Not just a special leader, a special man. Shorty Stone feels that all people are equal, all welcome. There is constant conflict among the Paiute over his tactics and insistence on inclusion, some of it violent. But Shorty will not budge. His principles are his principles. As far as he is concerned, his beliefs demand that of him.

In an addendum to my sweat lodge experience, a ten-passenger van full of the Stone clan shows up one day in Mammoth. They are escorting a young song carrier (a singer) by the name of Ambrosia Stone, a young teen who is part of the famed Stone clan in Big Pine. All her aunties and her grandma come along to escort and support her. She's a lovely young lady, and she has all these Paiute songs memorized, hundreds.

There are many job descriptions in Paiute lore. There are sun dancers and pipe carriers. Well, a song carrier is someone who is gifted in music. Ambie is a savant, a natural song carrier. Since she was tiny, she could remember the words to all the songs in Paiute and sing them with a clear, show-stopping voice.

My favorite cameraman and close buddy Al Zamudio is there to record and preserve the performance, in which Ambie is planning to serenade some Mammoth bears. I locate two subadult males playing at the golf course a short walk from the house. As part of the ceremony, Ambie has an eagle feather in each hand. For the sake of the shot, I turn her so the bears are behind her. She hasn't had much experience around bears, so she keeps looking over her shoulder, at these creatures. She is there to sing to them these tender songs, to honor these bears and all bears—the bear spirit. That doesn't mean she quite trusts them; she's a little skittish, glancing warily at them.

So there she is, little Ambie in her buckskin dress with beads and moccasins. After she is done singing, she wants to honor the nearby waters. I lead her out over some rocks to the boulder where she can do that. It is an ideal spot to film, with water all around, cascading over rocks . . . very pretty. She begins to sing again, at top volume, in her youthful alto. Ambie stands on the rock and begins to sing to these trickling headwaters, urging them to keep flowing so they can help those in need downstream. She thanks, honors, and blesses the water coming from what is the Continental Divide of California, with these pure and ancient songs that are never about lost love or cool cars, or even booty calls. They aren't about Christmas or another person. They are about water, hummingbirds, the earth.

Ambie's songs are meant for the bears, but aren't they meant for all of us? Ambie sings her heart out on this flawless day. And one note at a time, I heal a little more.

CHAPTER NINETEEN

NO QUICK FIXES

For a man to conquer himself is the noblest of victories.

—Plato

B ack home, I tell Debs about my journey to the spiritual hothouse, and she accepts it, as she does all my obsessions, even feels connected to the rituals in some ways, given her New Zealand background and knowledge of the Māori. She is in a process of her own—dealing with me, and with the fretfulness of having a new baby (Tyler) after having lost the first one so traumatically. Think of all she's been through. Now her husband is joining some sort of Native American health club, bouncing town to Big Pine a few times a week to soothe his crazy.

In the movies, the Native American hothouses would be an instant cure, a hallelujah moment. In real life, progress happens much more slowly. At the sweat lodges, I get a taste of honey. I am like a blind man seeing color for the first time. There is way more work to do. My ass is still kicked. Regularly, I am still blubbering in the shower.

Unfortunately, I carry grudges. I am still pissed off and angry over Arthur, a dangerous place to be for a guy who carries a knife and two guns to work instead of a briefcase. I turn back to Marshall Jack, the big Native American who drew the map to the sweat lodge in the first place, whose basic decency and wisdom will always be a balm. He tells me, "Steve, that anger is good. Real good. Save that for your son, for your wife . . . use it to protect them. We as men keep that put away, then pull it out when we need it. You can't waste it being furious at a state agency. That's futile and not helping you heal."

According to Native Americans, if you are searching for the path, you are already on the path. I wasn't up to speed, yet was learning the tools I needed. If I was indeed on the so-called Red Road, I had a lot of steps to go.

Sometimes I self-sabotage. My sense of empathy is off the charts. I think I have a disease where I can feel others' pain too much. You probably shouldn't be a wildlife officer if you have very deep feelings about pain and suffering. Like many people, the wounds of my childhood linger far into adulthood. I begin to wonder if anything can fill the void.

In the moment, I can still get my work done; I can rise to the occasion, save a bear, or put one down if it is hurt. I can wade into volatile situations involving man and beast, keep my wits about me, make it all work. Privately, I am still struggling to appear OK, to hold it all together.

Through all this, the forest remains my safe haven. The bears are my comfort zone.

People often ask me what they should do when they see a bear.

"Maybe say a prayer of thanks?" I say. "Or, how about you look around and remember the moment, because you'll remember it the rest of your life?"

That's how I still feel when I encounter a bear. Blessed, in the midst of something I don't quite understand, yet fully appreciate. Take the moment. Sometimes it's all we need.

My line of work helps me deal with things, and also it doesn't. I find myself sitting with the bears a lot—that gives me solace. I study every aspect, their love lives, their nutrition, the places they sneak off to nap, how they play with stolen pumpkins every Halloween.

When we have to put an injured animal down, I sometimes keep the skull, boil it as you would soup, remove the tissue and the hair so that I can study the jaws, the way their teeth mesh . . . what is worn, what isn't. This is more like a lab study an anthropologist might do. I always take my time, it is respectful, prayerful even—none of these bears died of natural causes. It is not lost on me that there are sometimes bullet holes in the skull where I ended their suffering.

I need to see everything firsthand to really understand it. When I boil the skulls, all the tissue, all the gums melt away and the teeth fall out. I have a bleached skull and a big pile of teeth. One by one, I rebuild the mouth as if doing a jigsaw puzzle, trying to get the right teeth in the right sockets. I find they can only fit in the proper socket, nowhere else. I do all this with the purpose of doing better, of being better. In the middle of cementing an incisor in place, I get another call of a bear misbehaving, or a lion, hawk, raccoon, deer, or any of the other animals that might've been trapped in a house or clipped by a car.

At this point, bears aren't the only world I am studying. I am also learning how to be a father. Because of my upbringing, I feel ill-equipped. I come from a world where if you spill your milk, you are spanked till it leaves a mark. I worry that some of that is still in me, that I am also capable of harsh, uncontrolled anger. At this stage, Debs and I are both tense parents.

I escape to work while Debs does everything for me. As a man, I am doing what we were taught to do in that era of parenting: bringing home the bacon. We realize now that's not enough. It's a farce—and a relic from an earlier age—that we used to think that a paycheck alone made you a good father.

When I begin to work with wildlife in the mid-nineties, my wife is as committed to the cause as I am. If a bear is killed in traffic, all too common in our area, I bring it home, and Debs participates in the traditional Native American rite of smudging, waving burning sage over the carcass. Tenderly, she runs her fingers through its deep, shaggy coat. Nature doesn't produce bears as easily as it does bugs or sparrows or squirrels. As such, a bear death takes on added significance. These premature deaths sadden her as much as they do me. It is part of our bond.

At this point, I am very busy with Country Glass, a multimillion-dollar window company I co-own. We win some military contracts, and I scramble to fill the orders. In the midst of that, I learn my business partner is keeping two sets of books, one to throw me off of what the business is really pulling in. I quit that day. To me, wrong is wrong and right is right. My hardheadedness can serve me well in some respects, but it can also be a detriment. "Steve, pump the brakes," friends urge. "I ain't pumping no fucking brakes," I snap back. The glass company embezzlement gives me even more to be mad about. As they say, a fish would never get in trouble if it just learned to keep its mouth shut. I could never keep my mouth shut. I am no fish.

So here I am, still learning to manage my emotions, and now jobless because I quit the glass company, with a wife and small child counting on me. My bear work is contract work and doesn't pay enough for us to live on. I am no longer bringing home enough bacon.

Total shock. We never see the big stuff coming. If we did, we'd tighten our belts, be prepared. When life blindsides us, it can take us a week, a month, a year to catch up to the fight we didn't see coming. It jolts us out of our workaday stupor. Hot Jacuzzi into the powdered snow.

Like many of us, I can easily take a bad situation and make it worse. At the time, I had yet to learn that when bad stuff happens, you need to focus on your response, not the unfairness of it, or the injustice.

Just the response, minus any sort of self-pity. More than anything, I needed to add that to my spiritual tool kit.

CHAPTER TWENTY

A WOBBLY LITTLE CUB

To be blunt (again): My comfort zone isn't in front of a camera crew. I come to all this pretty raw, with no training. In general, the TV and newspaper folks are more enamored with my big, gruff persona than they are with what I have to say. In the end, I use them, they use me. In Media Studies 101, they should teach that quid pro quo the very first day; media is much like the oldest profession.

I much prefer to be out chasing bears out of saloons. I'm finding that they are my comfort zone, if something like that exists in this line of work. Each call is something almost entirely different. Keeps me on my toes. Also keeps me grounded.

Bear cubs become a bit of a specialty for me, and the Mammoth police are quick to call for help in those situations. In most cases, the police find bear calls to be a nuisance. Cubs add a layer of unpredictability to the situations. Only half of bear cubs make it past age two. Their curiosity, their innocence, and their occasionally inattentive mothers are all to blame. Plus, sometimes their own daddies kill them. Rough world for bears in general; even rougher when you are too young to understand the threats posed by cars, raging streams, fences, or packs of dogs.

One of their bad habits: sticking their heads into barrels and buckets in search of food. "Hey look, a tater tot!"

One of my most memorable calls is for a young cub with his head jammed into a Costco party mix container. He looks like a short and hairy astronaut.

The jar fits him like a bad tux, too tight around the neck. For days, I get calls and photos from all over town about this wobbly bear cub, staggering around in a daze with his brother and mother. By the time I race over, they are always gone. It makes me remember the Native Americans' observation about how bears sometimes seem to vanish into thin air.

For four warm summer days, the young cub wanders the village of Mammoth Lakes with the plastic snack jar stuck on his head, banging it on rocks, clawing at it with his inch-and-a-half nails, unable to see out of his fogged-up helmet.

You can't really miss a sow and two cubs. But somehow I have. After four days, I am jumpy and frustrated at not being able to find the distressed young bear, which I know will be growing hungrier, more frantic and dehydrated by the minute. At that age, they need to eat every chance they get. If they're not playing or sleeping, they're eating.

Bears are constant eaters, and this one is still suckling. I worry also about the sow's behavior. Young black bears die all the time, that's part of the cycle. The mothers know it. They are not as ferocious about their offspring as many people think. But they are unpredictable. This was a situation she hadn't seen before. The mother had to feel the cub's growing sense of panic. She had to know that life was draining out of the young cub, hour by hour, minute by minute.

I have seen this happen before—bears getting their heads stuck in big jars. They are naturally curious, and when food is involved, they lose any sense of caution, if they have any to begin with. This is a juvenile bear, after all, maybe seven months old. They are born feeders. They will pry the taillight off a car just to get into the trunk for a wedge of leftover taco.

In this case, word about the Costco cub gets around town, and the calls keep coming. The cub isn't big—I could've tucked it in my coat. You can't miss the jar on his head. Folks are invested. Who doesn't want to help a young bear having a Winnie the Pooh moment?

The cops and I gear up, drive around town for days looking for the cursed little bear. We throw the world at it.

I have all but given up on the poor animal when a call comes in at eleven P.M., on a warm July night, just as the visiting campers, hikers, and other tourists are dousing their fires and sliding into their sleeping bags. I hurry to the garage, round up extra equipment, including capture poles and welder's gloves to keep from being sawed up by the bear's Freddy Krueger claws.

When I reach the scene, the bear is fifty feet up a Jeffrey pine. A couple of Mammoth Lakes' finest are tensely pacing, guns drawn, worried about the mama, who is lurking in the dark behind a plank fence thirty paces away, where two planks are missing, kicked out by schoolkids seeking a shortcut.

At the center of this well-armed scrum is the cub and Mammoth police sergeant Joe Vetter.

Before I arrive, Vetter made an attempt on his own. Body-cam footage later shows the tall and husky officer valiantly grabbing the plastic jar with his left hand and trying to palm the jar off.

But the freaked-out bear's butt and legs flap everywhere. He looks almost human. *"Waaa, waaaa, waaaaaaaa!"* the frightened bear wails. In the video, the sergeant is palming the jar like a basketball, trying to shake the poor cub loose, while using his cruiser door as a fence between himself and the sow. With his right hand, he is pointing his .45 in the direction of the mom hearing her baby in distress.

The little bear twists, snorts, and brays—*waaaaa, waaaaaaaaa*—like an angry, befuddled drunk . . . like a drunk with a Costco jar on his head, being lifted two feet off the ground by a stranger. What a stud Vetter is, straight-arming this bear and trying to shake it loose.

"Cover me!" Vetter yells, worried that the sow might blast through at any time.

"Come on, get outta there," he pleads to the cub.

After a few more tries, Vetter lets the cub down and the poor animal scampers off behind the cruiser and toward a fire station a short distance away.

That's the point when I arrive on scene—the bear in the tree, the mom and the other cubs somewhere in the inky-dark perimeter.

In short, and in the vernacular of cops, I show up to a total shit show. And now it is up to me to fix it. That's my job, after all, but things are already out of hand, kind of at a rolling boil. The cops are jittery; I'm jittery.

Nearing midnight, our little ski village is almost pitch black, no street or porch lights. Mammoth Lakes in summer is more serene, less overrun than in ski season. Still, as luck would have it, several current and former firefighters happen to be camping next to the nearby fire station, and they quickly become the peanut gallery. Police flashlights are beaming everywhere, adding to the *Close Encounters* atmosphere. The whole forest is painted with these flashlight beams, darting everywhere, high and low, and across frightened faces.

The mom has scolded the cub up the tree, out of harm's way, at least in her mind. The bear is tired and thirsty and scared out of his wits. He is still bawling—*Waaaaaaa! Waaaaaaaa!*—an enormous methodical racket that the big plastic bucket can't contain. On a super-quiet night, you can hear that cub screaming from a block away, a sound from a horror movie.

I can't see the poor animal's mug, because the cub has fogged the plastic with his hot breath, and snot, and probably a few tears. We aren't even sure how he can breathe, the jar fits so tightly. It appears to be vacuum sealed.

He's a tough little guy, no doubt. He's been through a lot. From fifty feet away, he stinks with fear.

The firefighters camping nearby, with decades and decades of emergency calls between them, probably think they've seen it all. They know I'm the wildlife control officer; they've been waiting for me to show up—the guy at the peak of his career, hitting on all cylinders. The Mammoth police? They are pals, and they are supportive. But they are still cops, tough and edgy, and they can't resist a snide jab in my direction.

I probably would laugh with them as well, if I had the time for it. I'm life-and-death worried for the cub, and what the mom might do, and the officers with their guns drawn. Mama is still somewhere on the other side of a rickety fence, out of range of the flashlight beams that are still darting this way and that.

One cop is keeping his flashlight trained on the hole in the plank fence, but I know that if a mama bear wants to get over or through a fence, there is no telling where she might come. She'd bash her way through anything. The poor cub's crying only adds to the confusion and the high stakes.

Trying to play things cool, I pull on my heavy welder's gloves, which reach halfway up my arms.

Now, when cubs go up trees like this, it's often because Mom has yelled at them to scamper up. She is using a low, quiet, guttural grunt—you can barely hear it. I know it's the sound a mother makes when danger is near, produced somewhere in the chest.

Uoonc, uoonc, uoonc . . .

To a bear, the word means to flee. Fortunately, it also means to come back—the same word having two meanings, in the same way *aloha* does. The sound doesn't come from the throat or the vocal box, it comes from within them.

With no other tricks in my bag, I begin to *uoonc* the bear down out of the tree, much to the bemusement of the bystanders. I am keenly aware, amid the bemused emergency workers, that no grown man should go around *uooncing* bears. But what do I have to lose?

Uoonc, uoonc, uoonc . . .

Somehow, it works. Flashlights off, to keep from freaking out the bear. Pitch black.

In less than a minute, bark and needles start falling, the little bear is coming down butt first out of the tree. When he shimmies down to shoulder height, I grab him.

"Lights!" I yell, so I can see what I am doing. The flashlights all come on again, blinding us. Damn.

I don't want to hurt him, and the thick leather welder's gloves make it difficult to get a grip. The little bear squirms free and scoots back up to the very top of the Jeffrey pine, accompanied by world-class cussing from me, a very stressed-out wildlife control officer.

Now I'm really pissed and afraid. I figure I've lost my one and only chance, failed in front of a bunch of professional first responders. I am worried that the cub will stay in the tree for days, if his strength holds out.

"Try again," Vetter says.

"Huh?"

"It worked before, why not again?" he says.

I shrug and take a step toward the tree: *"Uoonc, uoonc, uoonc, uoonc . . ."* I *uoonc* for all I'm worth.

The flashlights go out again.

Sure enough, the scraping sound of claws against bark. The little bear is elevatoring back down the tree, giving me a second chance.

"Watch your perimeter!" I yell to my support troops.

The bear is making all sorts of sounds. In bear language, the little cub is crying out to his mom: *"Kill Steve! Kill Steve!"*

As the flashlights come on again, blinding me and the cub, I pounce on the little bear at shoulder height again, so that I can wrap him up from behind, then bring him carefully to the ground, and hold him while kneeling.

"Cover that fence line," Vetter reminds his colleagues, wary the mother might blast through.

"Grab the snips!" I yell, but Vetter is already there. Carefully, Vetter begins to hook the metal snips up under the rim of the Costco jar, made of the thick, difficult plastic that defies opening on Christmas mornings, the maddening stuff that almost requires a saw.

"Easy guys, we got this," I say. "Take your time."

Vetter cuts the plastic, but can't quite get a long seam going. The bear is squirming and screaming for his life.

"*Kill Steve!*" the little bear screams. "*Mom! Kill Steve!*"

My interpretation, of course. Do I overstate it? No. Holy shit, the screaming is constant and frantic—so loud you can feel it. Everyone is on edge, man and beast. "What in the world?" the mama must be thinking. If the little bear would just shut the fuck up, we will all be good. On a scale of 1 to 10, the drama is a 12.

The whole situation is heightened by the fear of what the sow might do at the sound and sight of all this. Vetter is having trouble cutting the heavy threaded lip of the jar, and the urgency of the situation isn't helping. He may as well have been using nail clippers to saw a log.

One of the officers, Jason Heilman, is brand-new to the department; he's moved his wife and daughter to our sleepy mountain town to get away from the extreme stress of gang warfare. Heilman is Robocop, high and tight, chiseled good looks. And suddenly he's holding a gun on a wild bear, no doubt wondering how he's found himself here and is there anywhere in the world you can go anymore to avoid extreme stress? Evidently, no.

"Watch the perimeter," I remind him.

"I know!" he says.

"It's tough . . . take your time," I say, as the baby bear is still braying to his mama: "*Kill Steve! Kill Steve!*" In my mind, I'm thinking, "Take your time. But hurry."

Finally, steam starts to escape from a six-inch gash in the jar, so I know we are making progress. After a couple more snips . . . "Peel it off!" I yell, and the jar slides off, releasing the bear—and also freeing his teeth. At that point, I assume I might be hugging a revving chainsaw. Fortunately, he just wants his mommy. He goes totally silent, doesn't bite or claw me; he just scampers out into the dark to find her.

"Atta boy," says Sergeant Vetter. High-fives all around.

All the times I'd *uoonc'*d bears through the years, all the years I tried to emulate their communications—all that silliness—it never worked this well. It really paid the bills this time.

Thirty minutes later, I'm home, a glass of merlot in hand. Enjoying a moment of reflection, the adrenaline dump. Shortly before, I'd been what cops in stressful situations call "frosty, icy, cold," all the senses pinging. I'm grateful for the way things turned out. I'm also aware of the risks, the luck involved, and how it could've gone south very easily . . . the awe of it is overwhelming.

You know, in everyday life, I see three important qualities running simultaneously: the way you see yourself, the way others see you, the way you really are.

The more closely those three elements line up, the better you are. Rarely do those three tangents line up for me. Rarely do I feel at peace. That night, considering all that could've gone wrong, I feel that those three elements finally line up for me. It is a comforting moment, almost soulful, a sense of contentment and affirmation.

Am I feeling the bear magic? Or something greater? Is something deep inside me starting to mend?

Well, happy endings don't last long, at least in the rugged Eastern Sierra.

In less than a month, the little bear will be a victim again—not of another bear, or a Costco jar, or a poacher. This time, it is the bane of all wildlife: a speeding car.

A tourist driving up to the Lakes Basin plows into the same cub in the middle of the road—on a sunny day, busy with traffic. The bear I saved is killed instantly. When I arrive, before I even put my truck in park, I know it is the same bear. It is as if the poor animal had a giant target on his young back. This is the harsh reality of what I do. If one threat doesn't get the bears, another often will.

I'm not angry, just disappointed. There isn't anything the driver could've done. I load the little cinnamon bear's body into the bed of my truck, and drive the ten minutes back to the house.

In situations like this, I use a smudge stick, the spiritual whisk broom that I learned about from Native Americans. When a bear dies, I wave a smoldering stick of white sage, wrapped in yarn, over it. So when the last thing a young bear like this sees is the bumper of a speeding Camry, I try to take away that bad image, that negative vision, and replace it with something positive. For the Native Americans, and for me, smudging is a way of sending the victim into the afterlife with care and respect.

Sure, it may sound kooky. How many rituals, religious and otherwise, would sound a little kooky to outsiders? Besides, you think a so-called normal person *uoonc*s bears for a living? With the burning sage, I smudge this jinxed little bear, then drive his body deep into the woods to blend the remains back with nature.

I don't tell the town residents the long sad saga of the bear, that this is the same bear that escaped suffocation in the Costco jar, only to be run down a short time later. It seems too fatalistic. I want residents to believe in the serendipity and magic of these bears and have a sense the animals can have happy outcomes.

Instead, I merely take a photo of the dead cub in the back of my truck and create a flyer with the words "Save a bear. Please slow down."

I post it everywhere.

CHAPTER TWENTY-ONE

PIZZA AND THE BABY

H ot call: 9-1-1 first thing on a summer morning from Coldwater Campground, a popular spot near Lake Mary, a beautiful Alpine setting brimming with campgrounds, fifty-plus lakes within a day's walk, and plenty of trout a little hungover from overindulging on the latest hatch of insects.

I get up to Campground 31, busy at this time of year. I find a family with a brand-new camper truck, plus new gear they just pulled from the boxes: sleeping bags, lanterns, cooking utensils, and ice chest. It looks like a Coleman commercial. Super-nice couple. Also super novices. Brought along a month's worth of food. I can say with total assurance that California's black bears really appreciate that kind of charity.

The night before, they built a bonfire, organized the site. Before they climbed into bed, they slid the giant ice chest under the bumper so bears couldn't get into it, thinking they'd been extra cautious. A few minutes later, they watch in horror as the bear nudges it out from under the truck and begins to feast. From their beds in the back of the camper three feet away, they listen to the whole noisy meal.

"We're so stupid," the campers say when I arrive. "We knew all about the bears . . . we built a big bonfire to keep them away. But the bear came and opened the ice chest and ate all our food."

The couple have a small baby, so they are feeling extra vulnerable, extra protective.

By the time I arrive, the bear is gone. I give them some "Don't Feed Our Bears" stickers and info on how to deal with them if they come back. Tip number 1: Bonfires don't keep bears away; they just provide ambient lighting for their free meal. The bears know that campfires indicate that generous humans, with a carload of Twinkies and marshmallows, have arrived to party.

Next morning, another hot call from Campground 31. I race up there, expecting more of the same. Sure enough, this same young couple is even more apologetic. With Mom holding their tiny baby, they tell me that they are blown away by the fact that the bear could get at the food they stacked so carefully in the middle of the picnic table, with the ice chest placed strategically at the center of it all.

"Strangest thing, he climbed right up on the picnic table and he ate all our food," they say, bewildered.

This time, I scold them. "That bear can climb a hundred-foot tree in about thirty seconds. You really think stacking stuff on your picnic table is going to stop him?"

Day 3. Same thing.

By day 4, all this couple has left from their month's worth of food is the mustard, mayonnaise, pickles, relish, maybe some barbecue sauce. They stack it like a Jenga game, big to small, four levels high, all condiments—seriously?—and go to a popular pizza place in town, Giovanni's, for an extra-large takeout pizza pie . . . the works. Before they leave, they stoke the fire.

By the time they return, that pizza must've smelled so good to them, the peppers, the charred bits of ground sausage, the pepperoni curling just so, all melding in the cab of their truck on their way back up to the campsite, the baby in the car seat between them. As they reach Campground 31, the truck headlights wash over the campsite. And there sits their new friend, sitting on top of the table, fiddling with the condiments with his paws and his tongue.

They race out of the truck to confront him—*Bad bear! Bad bear!*—and clap their hands together, just as I advised them to do. Off he goes into the dark. They hug each other, happy to have run him off, proud to have been so brave, to learn the ways of the wilderness. It's pitch black, the stars winking down at them. The only available light is from the truck headlights buttering the campsite. The dome light is also on in the cab because they left the doors all open as they rushed to chase away the bear.

They turn back toward the truck, to get the baby and the pizza. Guess who's sitting in the passenger seat, a pizza on his lap, the happiest diner in town? That's right. The bear has flipped the lid, like you or I would, and he's hammering down the peppers, the cheese, the charred bits of meat as the couple's baby sleeps soundly in the car seat next to him.

As he pulls another slice, the cheese stringing out like it does on the TV commercials, the bear must be thinking: *These people have been sooooo nice to me. Hope they come up here every summer.* Through his eyes, these people really like him. Each night, they're bringing him something new and delicious.

They've been feeding me all week. And now an entire pizza, the cheese soaking into the crust, just the way I like it. I wonder what we're having tomorrow? How are they going to top this?

All doors are open, the dome light is lit, they're looking through the windshield at the baby sitting in the center of the bench seat, with the bear sitting next to it. Of course, the frightened parents yell the bear away. The baby, untouched, sleeps through it all.

On a practical level, the easy solution for this family? The metal bear lockers that are available at every campsite around town. (Bear bags and canisters are primarily used in backpacking.) For some reason, and despite my urging, this couple wouldn't use the lockers.

But imagine being the next set of campers to reserve that same site? The bear will probably be waiting for them on the middle of that picnic table, holding flowers to welcome them to the mountain retreat.

As for the bear, a total mixed message that plays out hundreds of times in the course of a summer season. One moment, the humans are in awe of you, the next they're screaming. Just imagine if other people stopped in their tracks every time they spotted you—they freeze, yelp, and pull out their cameras—the way we do with bears. It would dramatically change how you felt about the simplest social encounters. You'd probably never leave the house.

In any case, how are forest creatures expected to process and make sense of the sort of encounters that we never could? That's why, in these symposiums and clinics, I tell people to think about the emotions of bears—to look at things through their eyes. It elevates our responses, takes them to another level, gives us a chance of understanding the bears rather than having to shoot them.

Also, consider this: if all the myths about the dangers of bears were true, thousands of people would be dead from bear encounters. The innate gentleness of the bear, like the one eating pizza in the passenger seat next to the baby, is the norm, not the exception. As my colleague Dr. Lynn Rogers notes, one of the safest places you can be is in the woods. Your chances of being murdered in North America are sixty thousand times greater than being killed by a black bear. "Chances of being killed by a domestic dog, bees, or lightning are vastly greater."

Honestly, my own troubles stem more from human bosses than from pushy bears. Fish and Game is suspicious of my techniques, which go against convention. Dubious of me and my work, they shadow me, try to catch me screwing up—poaching or mishandling the bears—only to have staffers report back that I am actually saving the agency wildlife calls.

I am a rebel in my tactics and approach. You know how that often goes.

"Steve gets along fine with bears," George Shirk of *Mammoth Monthly* tells the *Los Angeles Times* in 2007. "It's people he sometimes has a problem with."

CHAPTER TWENTY-TWO

"GOOD THOUGHTS ARE TINY PRAYERS"

S horty Stone is dying, yet he finds the time to carve a pipe for me out of stone, symbolic in so many ways, a token of his devotion, of his legacy. That pipe may last forever, as will his impact on me and anyone else who knew him well.

For many of us, Shorty is an inspiration, spiritually and for what it means to be a kind and decent human being.

In all the time I spent with Shorty, the dean of prayers, I didn't know a single one. In his final months, I work up the courage to approach Shorty to see if he'll teach me a Paiute prayer. He responds, "Steve, do you have good thoughts?"

I assure him that I do.

"Those are prayers," he explains. "Good thoughts are tiny prayers."

I thank him, but he can see I'm eager to delve deeper into how his prayers seem to flow into so many souls and how they heal and restore people.

When he finishes whittling the pipe, he finally agrees to teach me a prayer. He is holding the long pipe that he spent hours carving from dense red pipestone, technically catlinite, the sacred clay Native Americans use for ceremonial pipes, chipping away at it a little at a time.

We're in the sweat lodge, with the door open, no smoldering rocks, only the two of us around. This is the very first time the pipe is lit. He is not emotional as he explains this prayer; he is calm and collected. He is Shorty. He lifts the pipe higher than his head, and turns it ninety degrees to his right.

"We pray to the South, for our brown brothers and all they bring to our lives." He then takes a pinch of tobacco and puts it in the pipe's bowl.

He turns the pipe toward the west.

"We pray to the West, to the ocean, where the salt comes from to sustain our life . . ." He reaches in his bag for another pinch of tobacco.

Shorty turns the pipe again with both hands, as he slowly teaches me the prayer. "We pray to the North, where the pure snow comes from," he says. "Each flake is unique, just as we are." He puts in another pinch, and turns it to the east.

"We pray to the East, where the sun rises to start our new day, a new beginning for each of us." He adds another pinch.

Finally, holding the pipe high: "We pray unto the Creator, the father of all fathers." Then he puts in the biggest pinch of all, topping my pipe. He lights it and we share the pipe, the last one he would ever carve. His dad was a carver, Shorty is a carver, each pipe a little different, just as we are.

When Shorty is diagnosed with cancer, he is sick for a while, giving him time to ask a friend to build a casket for him—out of plywood and two-by-twos, very plain but beautiful.

In his final days, he is hooked up to oxygen and one of those medical machines that beep.

In this small, humble home, the bear dancers lead the way into the bedroom. Ambie and Carol, Shorty's wife, are there in this tiny bedroom with a small hospital bed. The bear dancers are in the front row, bent over at the waist hugging him, honoring him. They have their hands on his feet and legs. Others have their hands on his head and chest. They are not just singing; they are bringing all the juice. Those who can't reach Shorty have their hands on the backs of the bear dancers who can. In the next row, same thing. I am in the doorway, and the people behind me also have their hands on my back.

Thus, the hookup.

We're all touching and praying. Ancient bear songs are sung for him as he prepares for the next journey. It just rolls out as natural as can be. I am one of only two white people there. But we all bleed red, remember?

It is so sad, yet so incredibly beautiful . . . the most powerful moment. Those who can't fit in the room are in the doorway, singing with all their love—songs of strength, traveling bear songs. It is such a natural and lovely thing. Their appropriateness is just outstanding. Instead of leaning away from a dying man, they are leaning in. I realize that all my life, I've been afraid of death. Maybe I am wrong about death? Maybe it can be OK.

It is the most advanced masterclass on death and dying that you could ever take—all happening in one hour.

As always, Shorty's admirers pause to pay tribute to the people who have come before us, and the ones who will come after. Late that day, I bid him goodbye and head home. That night he dies.

I arrive the next morning to find the man I'd dubbed "my *togo*"—the Paiute word for maternal grandpa—has died. They have removed all the medical equipment. They have pulled the blankets off and placed Shorty's own bear hide over his chest, his head exposed.

Days later, they place him in the custom plywood casket. Tents go up, cars pour in. The sweats go on for four days and four nights in tribute, the coffin nearby.

Into his coffin, I place a walking staff, a sapling tightly wrapped with yarn taken from bundles of sage. Tiny branch, easily broken, yet once I wrapped it with two years' worth of yarn, it was strong as could be. More lessons: alone we are nothing.

For the burial, we take him down the 395, the main road through the Eastern Sierra. The casket is in the back of his old pickup, with people sitting along the rails of the truck bed. The funeral procession is followed by a long line of friends and admirers from all cultures, all walks of life.

His legacy: no one is ever turned away.

With a humble shovel, I help bury my friend in a Native American cemetery in the barren dessert, no headstone. The setting is spartan: no grass, no sprinklers, no pretty decorations. No sounds except the wind and a single hand drum.

In the cemetery, the drum plays as we bury Shorty, his feet facing east, the direction of new beginnings, new days. His family is surrounding the gravesite, singing his songs as we lower him into the ground with ropes.

With the bears, I restored some innate ursine behavior that humans had undone with our free food and often idiotic behavior toward them. I got them to remember what they were.

Similarly, did Shorty teach me something, or simply get me to remember what had been inside me all along?

CHRIS . . . AGAIN . . .

Mammoth itself has a molten heart. It has a dark and lethal past. During this region's violent birth, magma mixed with groundwater to create a nuclear heat, to fire boulders high into the sky. Sheets of ice gouged the volcanic rock, creating the chutes and bowls that skiers and snowboarders lace through today.

As with Steve, Mammoth's early years weren't all that wonderful.

Sure, there's a lot of grace and beauty to this place, but fall wrong on this mountain and you're suddenly a three-inch obit in your local paper. Some of these ridges are jagged stilettos. What better metaphor do you need? Success in mountains like these requires brute force, a sense of daring, a talent for engineering. Men don't have a lock on those things, never have. But Mammoth sure suits them. In general, men seem more comfortable—at least most alive—in the hollows where danger lurks.

Not me, of course. I'm a city kid. Hate danger. Hate to leave my couch. Yet, now I find myself working daily with this goof who crawled into bear dens for a living, who wrestled Costco jars off snarling cubs' heads, who shoots and spits and cusses as easily as I roll over to take another nap.

You know, I always fancied myself an offshoot of John Updike, who found such farce in the suburbs, all that hypocrisy and frustration, while revealing a deeper understanding of human nature. That's a high bar, to be sure, and I never come close to that. Ironically, I find some deeper human truths up here in these mountains, where with fresh eyes and an open mind, I can think clearly again amid my lingering grief. Sometimes, all it takes is a different place to walk.

Look, ultimately we men can have reptilian hearts. We are more reactive than thoughtful, and we're at our absolute worst when we have nothing much to do.

What we are learning about Steve is that he really needs something to do—some challenge, some goal, some damsel in distress (the hairier and smellier the better).

At this stage in his life, at this point in our book, Steve's challenges have never been greater.

And, as with the rest of us, his greatest challenge might be himself.

CHAPTER TWENTY-THREE

SEARLES, YOU'RE FIRED!

I n the course of my twenty-five-plus year career here, I outlast five police chiefs, seventy-five cops, eleven town managers, and more than a hundred bears. These mountains are my masterpiece, my natural habitat. But this time, I take the bullet.

In March 2007, police chief Randy Schienle fires me. We've had a long and rocky relationship, and I bristle under his command. To his credit, he is the boss who made me a town employee after all my years of contract work. But with that came expectations of me lining up like a good soldier and performing all the usual bureaucratic tasks. He cites job performance and takes away my badge. As if to make a point, he sends all my uniforms to a struggling police department in Mexico.

He explains to his bosses that I won't play by the rules, notify dispatchers of my whereabouts, follow police protocol. To a minute, supervisors want to know where cops are, and for good reason. My job is completely the opposite. I need to adapt to the season, what the animals are up to. It is a completely different form of music. His is rigid and classical; mine is Jimi Hendrix. I share with the bears a sense of secrecy, a need for privacy and to be left alone.

I am convinced my firing has even more to do with my prominence in town and how vocal I am about the town's problems. As a longtime resident who cares deeply, I am always quick to voice my thoughts on the issues of the day. I attend every town council meeting, I stay informed.

I've also stirred things up with some anti-drug bumper stickers I've made. Methamphetamine was growing very popular for locals needing a boost to work long hours and multiple jobs in harsh conditions. Or, maybe they just liked doing drugs. In any case, arrests were skyrocketing. I had some anti-drug stickers made, including "Mammoth, Not Mammeth" and "Mammoth: Locals Against Crime." I'd focus-grouped them at the police station, and with merchants. But the ski execs at Mammoth Mountain, obviously a major power in town, immediately call on me to cease and desist. Like many tourist destinations, they are super-sensitive to negative news. Also, in their defense, I was out of my lane. My job was wildlife control, not drug use. In my zeal to help my town, I'd overstepped.

The disconnect between Schienle and me has been festering for years. I tend to be opinionated, and I don't care much for protocol. I'm a free spirit who works with cops, people who have a set procedure for many situations. Whether you like it or not, police departments have to be capable of paramilitary operations, able to respond to school shootings and terror attacks. Despite the criticism they are always going to receive—and the close scrutiny they are under—the physical confrontations they face require courage and engender an inevitable sense of bravado. I've always gotten along with cops, while appreciating the differences between me and them.

Keep in mind, of forty-five potential officers in a police academy training class, none of them will learn how to get bears out of pantries or a raccoon untangled from someone's backyard hammock. Similarly, I don't have to handle the scum they do—the wife beaters and the drugged-out ex-cons. Oddly, I sometimes get more positive attention for my pied piper moments than they do for putting their lives on the line.

I remember being with a Mammoth officer down at a fireworks show one night when a man he once arrested comes running up holding a blue baby that was choking on something. The officer goes into overdrive, saves the baby, relying on years of EMT experience. No one does an article. Conversely, I walk the bears across Main Street and two days later there's a photo of me on the front page. Not only am I perceived as Wilderness Jesus; I am also thought of as Mammoth's own Mister Rogers—if only for the winsome photo ops that the bears offer.

Because I live in the very center of town, I can respond to calls quicker than the police. I'm not on days, or nights, or the graveyard shift. I am *always* on. When the phone rings, I am in the middle of situations within minutes—sometimes beautiful, sometimes tragic.

I am the populist figure who gets all the breaks and none of the negatives. When I screw up—and I certainly do—no one teases me or rats me out. If you screw up as a cop, they're usually all over you. I think Randy resented that I seemed made of Teflon.

Over the course of my career, I've shot from a moving vehicle, driven on the wrong side of the road, parked on lawns and in red zones—no one ever complains. If you were rich or poor, big or small, an idiot or a saint, if you called, I answered. For all my shortcomings, I have an innate ability to listen to people. I hear residents out and ask them questions that lead them to arrive at the right answer themselves.

I have it down to a science: "Well, did you leave the big bag of dog food in the back of the truck? Bet that bear loves you now." They laugh and realize they've been baiting the bears, accept responsibility, and promise to be more careful.

By contrast, police work often tends to be "demand and compliance."

I tend to be more empathetic. For me, every encounter is ripe for an opportunity to win someone over, create an ally. Ordering people not to feed bears is pretty worthless. Feeding bears is magical. Giving them a donut feels a hundred times better than giving a schnauzer a biscuit or a horse a carrot.

I have enough street sense to get people to want to do the right thing. As time goes on, residents start to snitch on each other about open garage doors, the bane of hungry bears. Over time, I deputize four thousand wild-life officers. A dream or a nightmare? Well, it sure pays off in this David vs. Goliath showdown between me and the town's top cop.

After Schienle fires me in spring 2007, problems like the one at Campground 31 begin to spiral out of control. Instead of me responding, Mammoth police show up, with varying degrees of experience and success. The situation comes to a head five months after my firing, in August, when state wardens have to kill a bear that has broken into several cabins, just the kind of situation I usually was able to defuse. In September, with bear incidents on the rise, a dozen residents call for my return during a tense town council meeting. Maybe the cops didn't get me, or the town's managers and elected officials. But the residents sure did.

"Given the number of bear incidents, it made sense to authorize the police to bring Steve back," town manager Rob Clark told the *Los Angeles Times*.

Bottom line: even though I am rehired, I feel that cloud is still hanging over my head. Yeah, I'd become the biggest, baddest bear in town, as I'd learned to be from Big. You can lose a lot of allies by stepping up and put-ting yourself out there. For all my work, for all the 24/7 shifts I put in, I am still seen by some town officials as a nuisance.

Sure enough, by 2009, when we start filming a life-changing (for me) reality show called *The Bear Whisperer*, my relationship with Randy reaches another breaking point. He fires me yet again.

In the meantime, a county grand jury has begun to investigate possible police misconduct, triggered in part by Mammoth officers' involvement in a bar fight at Rusty's Saloon down in Bishop, an ugly episode that makes big news, in part because there is very little news in this area.

During that inquiry, the anti-meth stickers come up, and seem to play into the general lack of control that critics claim is rampant in the depart-ment, including claims of misconduct by Schienle.

Ultimately, the grand jury finds nothing critical enough to pursue. The town of Mammoth Lakes follows up with a hearing of its own on issues related to the police force. Schienle is under the spotlight again, and my firing is an issue.

At a town hall inquiry, both Schienle and I are fighting for our careers. In a dramatic flourish, Schienle brings in the entire force, some dressed in full unform, presumably to show rank-and-file support for the chief. They stand with their backs to the wall. Reps of the police union step to the microphone to say they don't want me to continue. They wave around a list of officers, sergeants, and secretaries who don't want me to continue.

Finally, I get up to state my case. I've been sweating through my shirts. My hands are wet. My face is flushed. It is such a pivotal moment for me, and I feel so ill at ease. Despite my initial discomfort, I speak from the heart, I don't repeat myself, I straighten my back and hold my chin up. How I kicked into this mode, I'll never know. I feel a hand on my shoulder.

"My tears will dry," I tell them. "What we did as a community for these bears cannot be erased. You people are the ones who made things possible. They can take me out of the equation, but they can't erase what we've all done together."

I begin to go down the line, officer by officer, to explain what I've learned from each one of them. I even mention the secretaries and how they taught me how to sign in on a computer.

I tell the story of the night before my son was born. I got a call that a bear had been hit right on the end of my street. I responded immediately. I could hear the bear screaming. As I charged my gun and went to deal with it, I got physically ill.

The officers that night said "Sit down, sit down . . ." I sat and put my head between my legs, the world was spinning, all the emotions of the moment. About sixty seconds later, I heard a shotgun go off. They'd taken care of it.

"These guys always had my back," I conclude at the town hall.

It is a movie moment, straight out of an old Frank Capra flick. The city council decides to rehire me as a contract employee. Shortly afterward, the town manager, who reports to the council, is pressured to convince Schienle to retire, which he does. Schienle finds out the hard way that the Bear Whisperer has far more influence than the police chief. It shouldn't be that way at all. I'm embarrassed that the situation reaches that point. That's just the way events worked out over time.

I still think Randy is a good guy who got caught up in small-town politics. He said some things to me before he left town that were humble and thoughtful. I listened, shook his hand, and have never seen him since.

Next up: Dan Watson, who comes on as interim police chief, as "a fixer." His mission, direct from the city council, is to bring peace and calm to the department and to share his wisdom and experience.

Watson comes aboard with a heavy-hitter's resume. He worked under some very tough big-city conditions with the LAPD, and as a small-town police chief after leaving the L.A. force. On his first day, I enter his office expecting a high-and-tight, by-the-book LAPD vet. Instead, I find my new boss wearing a Hawaiian shirt.

Watson tells me the terms of the hiring require him to get along with the bear guy.

"So, who the hell are you and what do you want?" Watson asks with a smile.

"I'm easy," I tell him. "I'm on board with whatever you need."

Bit of an exaggeration, sure. But I want to get off on the right foot.

I insist on one thing: I want to be a town employee again. Watson wants me to remain a contract worker, which would give me more freedom to do my job. "You're an artist, not a bureaucrat," he explains.

I knew right then he got me.

I say that's fine, but it doesn't solve my biggest concern: health insurance for my family. For that, I need to be a town employee. He tells me to get several bids from the private sector, and he'll go to the town council to ask them to boost my pay to cover it.

Smart guy. Over the next few months, Dan does such good work as interim chief, the council asks him to stay on permanently as Schienle's replacement. Watson turns out to be like the character Hawkeye Pierce on *M*A*S*H*, restoring confidence in the small-town department and bringing a calming presence.

During his five years as chief, Dan and I chat every day—not just about our jobs. In fact, seldom about work. We learn we have nothing to fear from each other and much to gain.

There's that word again: *fear*. What a lousy and unnecessary emotion.

I work my tail off for Dan Watson.

CHAPTER TWENTY-FOUR

REALITY TV AND ME

I'm walking a golf course with Mike Slee, a contract cameraman for LMNO, the company producing *The Bear Whisperer* reality show, which is about to make me a star on Animal Planet. We're a mile from my truck, just out for a stroll, looking for bears in a place called Crooked Pines, which sounds like one of those weirdo David Lynch TV shows. But it's a sunny day. Bitchin'. Nothing noir about it.

We spot a bear grazing on wildflowers at a condo complex, near the fairway. It's not a good camera position, so we're crouching down in a low spot on the fairway, taking our time, waiting to see what he'll do next. I spot an older woman on the porch of the condo, stealing a quick cigarette.

We're focusing on the bear, watching him eat the flowers, when he turns to the condo, flicks the screen right out of the open window, and climbs right through. Didn't see that coming.

Now, the female smoker can't see us, since we've been out of sight on the golf course. Suddenly, two strangers are running right at her, one with a camera (Mike), the other looking like a cop and carrying a sidearm (me). She has no idea the bear has slipped into her home. Mike pushes her into a corner of the patio, and just shields her with his body as I run in the open door after the bear. No shotgun. I'm nearly empty-handed, having left my shotgun back in my truck a mile away. All I have is my sidearm as I run toward the condo, where a 350-pound male bear has just broken in.

The woman is freaking out. In seconds, this is all happening. We have no chance to explain, only react. To her, it's some sort of horrific home invasion like she hears about on TV.

"Is there anyone else in the condo?" I yell.

"My granddaughter," Grandma says.

For all we know, the bear might bolt out the door any second. As Slee blocks the grandmother in, using his body as a shield, I race into the house, past the kitchen, down the hall, where all the doors are closed. It is like entering a burning building. I open a door on the right and I'm three feet from an adult bear, facing me on all fours, in a confined situation. My mind is racing: *Bad, bad, bad.* I close the door. Shit. I open the door on the left, and there is a tiny baby girl in a onesie standing in her crib, staring at me silently. I've jumped from the hot Jacuzzi to the powdered snow. I carefully grab the baby and go down the hallway, through the kitchen, and out on the porch, where I put the baby in the grandma's arms. Insanity.

Finding nothing to eat, the bear crawls back out the window. Another day, another adventure in the life of the Bear Whisperer.

That's what Animal Planet titled their reality show about my work, and Slee and I are in the midst of our bare-bones first season of it, starting in 2009. If the 1997 article in the *Los Angeles Times* put me on the map, the reality show *The Bear Whisperer* expanded the map and gave me a global presence.

You know, at this point, after all the press I've received, I get frequent requests for TV segments and interviews. I'll grunt a couple of times over the phone and say, "Sure, show up Wednesday. I'll see if we can find some bears."

So, when the folks who run Animal Planet approach me, I think it is going to be just another press op, another chance for me to get my message across on nonlethal ways to coexist with bears.

Executives and key producers hold a big meeting in a private room at the Rafters restaurant, where one of the producers warns me that the show would change my life. I laugh.

"You just don't know, Steve," one producer assures me.

"Hardly," I think to myself. This wouldn't be my first media rodeo.

Boy, am I wrong.

The Bear Whisperer runs two years on Animal Planet, and brings me the kind of attention I never wanted. As I say, I prefer to work in the shadows, the way the bears do. Suddenly, I'm working with Slee, in an arranged marriage.

"Look, do you really want to do this?" I ask Slee as we are starting out.

"I sure do," he assures me.

"Well, I don't want to see you. I don't want to see your camera. I don't want to hear you step on a stick.

"During the year, you need to learn to track me. If I turn and look and don't see you, you're doing your job," I say.

This is the potential dealbreaker. Bears are easily spooked, keen to anything that's out of the ordinary. For this to work, to get the stunning visuals that TV worships, I need to go about my work in as stealthy a manner as I always have.

Among the other terms: in return for uncommon control of the content, I will receive little compensation. I get "final cut," as film directors say. Often, a television show leads to big money—insane money—and I am willing to forgo it for the chance to tell my stories authentically. Yeah, I was an idiot, in the eyes of many. But I am proud of my work and don't want a bunch of desperate TV types cheesing it up. Truth is everywhere, as they say. Just rarely on so-called reality shows.

I also insist that they can't show street locations or film me smoking. Otherwise, they are relentless; they film everything. So, when I need a break from the closeups, I light up a cigarette, I hold up my middle finger, and the camera finally goes off.

Slee and I mostly shoot the first season ourselves. I wear a microphone and he has an earpiece. I will say, "Mike, two hundred yards to the left, behind the boulder." We become a team . . . of video snipers. After we finish the two-hour premiere, it holds and holds. I start to get antsy. Maybe they don't like it? For some reason, they don't seem to have much faith in their new show. When it finally airs, the ratings are through the roof. It beats some huge sporting event in the same time slot. We're a hit.

By the second season, they've upped the budget and what TV people call "the production values," hoping to make it even more slick and popular. Well, I'm not very slick and I don't want to be popular. I'm better at gruff and cantankerous.

We set up a makeshift production office, with a storyboard of each of the bears . . . their behavioral issues . . . their mugshots. So that we're all on the same page, they have similar set-ups at offices in New York and Hollywood. They edit the footage in L.A., and we get constant feedback from producers there and in New York. "More of this, less of that"—and off Mike and I go, running and gunning.

They delete any scenes where I swear, at least till the second season, where they bleep me out. Drives me nuts to lose good scenes over that, but that tells you who I am and who they are.

Throughout, I insist that we can't recreate situations. I refuse to embellish or overdramatize. I have a little cam that fits in my vest pocket, and since I am always closest to the action—in the bears' faces, in their dens—the producers at the remote offices see the choppy dailies I shoot and ask for a cleaner reshoot.

Nope. "Not going to happen," I say. To my mind, that's a slippery slope, and once we start staging situations, we'll lose the authenticity. So we argue a lot. That's the inside language of the entertainment world: heated debate. Producers and execs must think they can bully the bumpkin, wear me down, get me to fold. But I just get more stubborn, as I often do when cornered. In the end, not one bit of the show is scripted or ginned up. I can't overemphasize how difficult it is to remain true to the cause. I tell them: "I have to live here when you leave." I have to be real.

No big success goes unpunished. The first season is low-key and workable. In the second season, they throw more people at it. To get the juice, the good stuff, we have to keep it simple though. Bears don't like sound booms or lighting bounce boards. In a moment, they can detect when something is wrong or different.

Can I enjoy this success? You know me. Though we are a hit, the experience tests my sense of self-worth. I question everything, including this. I feel like I am giving away one of my few real gifts—my magic touch with bears and other animals. In moments of reflection, I think it will benefit me and the bears to call attention to my work, and honor Mammoth Lakes for its enlightened approach to its beloved bears. That is my rationalization, my tradeoff. I try very hard to convince myself it is worth it.

Everyone likes a little attention, maybe even a lot of attention. But this is too much. Like the bears, I prefer working in the shadows. Bears sleep in trees, often unnoticed, because that's where people will leave them alone. They are the masters of the ghostly sidestep, the deft escape. Like pickpockets, they exist on the periphery of a place.

That's the way I feel too. I want to live in the shadows, do my job, no fuss.

Seems everyone in America wants to be a rock star except maybe me. I am a quiet and contemplative man. As the universe often does, it notes what I want and gives me the opposite—the very notoriety I dread. Sure, everyone gets their fifteen minutes of fame; I am getting the whole half hour.

As the show's producer had warned, the show dramatically changes my life. Fans of the show start turning up at my doorstep. One female fan moves here from Washington state and rents a room down the street from me. She tells me the show has helped her mental health. Stuff like this happens a lot. "My boyfriend and I are huge fans of your work," writes one fan from northern Canada. "We even named our bong after you."

One couple tattoos "Don't Feed Our Bears" on their arms and sends me photos. People come to visit all the way from France, from Israel, fans who speak English, some who don't. They pull up on the side of the road and ask cops to take my picture with them. To protect my home and family, the court takes out restraining orders on some who crossed the line from fan to stalker. More than once, I tape mugshots inside the front door to alert Debs and Tyler to any who might approach. When I feel especially threatened, I leash the dogs to the ball hitch on the back of the truck to protect the house overnight.

I have to keep changing out cars because people start to follow me. Fans show up with police scanners, eavesdrop on dispatch and beat me to the scene of a bear encounter. One family drives all the way from Georgia just to meet me, take a few photos, and turn around and drive back.

Human distractions aside, we shoot tons of footage—the most uncanny stuff—and get so lucky so many times, another example of my consistent good fortune.

At that point, after years of TV segments and newspaper requests, I understand a bit about getting the money shot, where to rig cameras, and what sort of encounters excite the camera crews and producers. We often end our long days on the golf course, where we shoot B-roll of the bears lounging about. I know that at the end of a hot summer day the bears are going to be thirsty and head over to the course's plentiful ponds and streams.

I know the bears' tendencies so well that I can perform circus tricks. For example, a scared bear will always scamper up the nearest tree and stay there till the danger passes. Knowing that, I might yell "Get up that tree," realizing all along that the bear is going to do that anyway. Then I yell, "You stay up there!" I know there is no way she is coming down, whether I tell her to or not.

To a layman, it looks like the bears are following my voice commands. In fact, I am just narrating what I know they are about to do on their own.

Next time you're about to give your dog a treat, tell her to lick her lips. She'll probably do that anyway, in anticipation. The kids will think you taught her some new lip-licking trick. My chats with the bears follow that same principle.

On the golf course one day, a foursome comes along as we wait for the bears to arrive. At that point, the locals have learned to ignore the bears, to "play through," as golfers like to put it. They loft an approach shot over a bear, or leave a shot short, so as not to disturb him as he naps in the middle of a fairway. They don't call 9-1-1. They just play on. I am proud of them. Coexistence has become a reality for countless golfers.

Well, this day, a bear scampers across a putting green and starts to take off with a golf ball. I yell, "Drop that ball!" and the stunned bear drops the ball and scampers off, all of it caught on film.

In truth, he was probably going to drop the ball anyway.

And that's how I become known—around the world, for better or for worse—as the Bear Whisperer. I am a bit of a con, a bit of a vaudeville act. But all that works in the best interest of the bears. My guiding truth in a wacky business: "It's for the bears."

The show doesn't air for a year over various issues, including something I say during a segment where a bear running from a fire is ambushed by a car. The camera records me driving the dead bear up to a vista, singing a song in tribute and smudging him off with sage. On camera, I explain what we're doing and why, trying to capture for viewers the poignancy of the moment. A proper and respectful send-off is important. "Whatever god you pray to," I say. Later, execs begin to fear "Whatever god you pray to" is blasphemous. They beg me to edit it out. I stand my ground. I think I've been inclusive, respectful to everyone. Eventually, it airs, without any backlash. As it turns out, that scene—me singing in Paiute, and smudging off the bear—is the most watched scene in the show.

CHAPTER TWENTY-FIVE

MORE MEDIA MAGIC

L ike many kids in the sixties, I grow up watching *Mutual of Omaha's Wild Kingdom*, with Marlin Perkins and Jim Fowler.

Thirty years later, Jim Fowler calls me. I get tingles just hearing the familiar voice. "Hello, Steve, this is Jim Fowler." Same modulated voice that we used to hear as children on Sunday nights.

He tells me they're rebooting the classic show, and that he'd like to send up his son, who is taking film courses at USC, with hopes of becoming a wildlife cinematographer.

His son shows up with a small crew, and we go out to see Center Street, the talking bear that lives close to my house. The filmmakers' eyes are big as saucers. Within ninety seconds of arriving, they've already seen a live bear. Then we spot another bear, who has crashed in the area for a nap.

I tell them to get down low on the ground with me, because their gear is making the bear nervous. We do our interviews. One crew member won't come closer than two truck lengths, he's so spooked.

That was the start of *Affairs with Bears*, a documentary by director Jay Majer, who was the crew member who wouldn't get close.

His documentary is particularly simple, particularly effective. It begins with me addressing a bear hiding out in a corrugated-tube culvert. In voiceover,

I say, "I grew up with the same lies, the same misconceptions, the same campfire stories as everybody else." Then, as the camera looks into the eyes of the bears—soulful and a bit melancholy—I explain how I discovered the truth about their gentleness and generally peaceful demeanor.

"The biggest bear in the world will have less of a negative impact on the planet than a human," I say, in describing their carbon footprint. "Each of us will build homes, drive cars . . . generate mountains of garbage . . . [a bear] has left little footprint by the time he dies."

Debs and I attend the premiere at a theater at USC. They give me a signed poster. In the theater, my image is up on the big screen.

For another documentary project, British biologist-broadcaster David Attenborough, brother of the noted actor Richard, sends a cinematographer to collect bear footage for a BBC documentary, paying me $1,000 per day for my help. The cinematographer rents a van, tears out the seats, sandbags a tripod so it can peer out the side.

I race over to a spot. I can hear the giant camera whirl to life . . . "See that! See that?" I ask. We get the best stuff, the kinds of closeups you never see—a paw, a muscle in the jaw.

Please note that at this point in my career, I've met dozens of bear experts from all ranges of life, from wildlife control people to zookeepers to academics. I don't know anyone who has worked with bears for any extended period of time who didn't bleed, or get cuffed or slapped.

How does this work out so well for me? How am I able to go decades without injury, without even a scratch? No training whatsoever. No wise old bear mentor to tell me not to do this or that.

In the course of my career, why do the animals show me this much grace? We're talking thousands of encounters. It's not because of my novice skill set. So how? I think they understand me, because I am there from their births to the time they die. That certainly helps. They must've regarded me as an odd family doctor, in faded Levi's and puffing on my smokes, dropping f-bombs everywhere I go. I am the unlikeliest savior you ever saw. If you saw me walking down the street, you might be inclined to move to the other side. You sure wouldn't honk at me in traffic. To you, I might look like Daniel Boone, or the Boogey Man. To them, I am merely a gruff guy with some anger issues who seems to scold them a lot. I'm not warm and fuzzy. Neither am I a bully and a menace. I have learned to be consistent with them, so they know when they are crossing a line. I am their beat cop, looking for ways to keep them alive.

CHAPTER TWENTY-SIX

BLONDIE'S LUCKLESS LIFE

Blondie is a big, gorgeous, sandy-colored bear who loves Häagen-Dazs ice cream. She also has a nose for tragedy. She loses her two cubs in separate incidents. When the second one dies, Blondie flips out and goes on a bit of a rampage. A theme for her: a luckless life that starts out with tragedy and never really changes.

Of all the bears profiled on *The Bear Whisperer*, Blondie's story gets the most response. Her saga is more than the sad tale of a misbehaving bear. The segment highlights the hardships faced by females tasked with raising cubs in an often cruel environment where fathers are known to kill their own offspring. As I've said, half of California's bear cubs don't even make it to age two. Nationally, the average age of a hunted bear is three and a half years old. The world seems stacked against them.

Blondie herself is an orphan. As such, she missed out on much of what a mother would teach a bear about foraging for natural foods, how to steer clear of people and cars, and, essentially, lead a low-key and healthy life. In short, Blondie has no boundaries. Even when she is young, she is messing around in people's kitchens. People cut her all kinds of slack because she is cute. They come home, find her on the counter with her snout in the cookies, chase her off. Often, they won't even call me to report it. It is just Blondie, the beautiful little cub, the neighborhood ingenue. For her, there are fewer rules. Then she has cubs very young, an ill-prepared mother.

The Animal Planet film crew are still filming at this point. When the Blondie call comes in, we are resting and hanging out at the popular hangout called Nevado's, literally three minutes away on Lake Mary Road. The moment we get there we know something isn't right. Blondie is moaning and distraught. Her second cub, her only surviving cub, has been slammed by a car; the beautiful mother is pacing back and forth over the injured offspring, which lies dying off the downhill side on Lake Mary Road, the gateway to the area's fishing and camping.

It's dark now as we stand at the side of the road. We can barely make out her silhouette as she grieves for the cub twenty-five feet away. Mom is screaming; the baby is screaming. Eventually the moaning stops, meaning her cub has taken its last breath. "We're done here," I tell the crew. Careful not to disturb her, barely making a sound, we pack up and leave.

In the course of her life, Blondie has had a long record of break-ins, often what we call "soft entries," where she goes through an open door or window. But after her second cub dies, she goes berserk, forcing her way in, breaking into and damaging an estimated fifty-one cabins. Minus her cubs, she is on a rampage. Typically, cubs slow a mother down; moms have to adjust their pace to suit them. Crossing a street, a mother has to wait till their little three-inch legs can catch up to her. Once free of her cubs, Blondie can move freely and fast, as she works through her sorrow and loss. She can now cross a road at full steam, thirty-five miles per hour. Despite the fact that residents are all about bears by this point, despite the bears' rock-star status, the town is eventually out to kill her over the extensive property damage she causes.

All the bears in town are nocturnal except Blondie, so not only is she aggressive about entering homes, but she does it in broad daylight, when there are plenty of witnesses.

She blows through locked doors and windows, just uses her brute strength, does all the things we're afraid of yet seldom see, traits she never demonstrated before. Nose up, she just marches right into a house; you can see her determination and attitude. She leaves four inches of debris on the floor. Her specialties: Häagen-Dazs and melon. Never once do I see her eating trash.

The film crew and the producers are wowed by it all. "Steve, are you OK?" they ask. Well . . .

This is a very big deal, the talk of the town. Over a two-year period, the break-ins have spread. We have town hall meetings on Blondie's activities, which are centered in the upper Lakes Basin, where the hundred or so cabins are old, single-paned glass . . . fragile, easy pickings. All my focus is on this honey-colored bear; Blondie tests everything I know. I assure everyone that I am throwing the world at it. We arm residents with air horns to announce a bear, so no one will be surprised when they encounter her. When Blondie has a full head of steam, you hear the air horns going off from cabin to cabin.

I am on high alert. I am first to every scene. There's all this tension. I roll up on every call, in hopes of reprimanding a misbehaving bear. I'm firing nonlethal when I see her, to no effect. She is so determined, so off the rails, that she just goes barreling off, only to return later. Animal Planet is filming it all—we have more than thirty scenes of Blondie's break-ins and human encounters. There are blown-out windows, torn up kitchens . . . thousands of dollars in property damage. A sign of how desperate things are, federal wildlife officials bring in barrel traps, with doors that snap shut top to bottom. Knowing bears usually work at night, the trappers stay up all night and sleep during the day, when Blondie is actually most active. At one point, Blondie breaks into the mayor's house and eats a pound of chocolate-coated Ex-Lax. I'll spare you the details. But can you imagine the jokes?

Authorities are frustrated and fed up with the situation. The Department of Fish and Game issues a rare kill order, a "depredation permit." The department does not issue them without cause and a pre-permit investigation. The law allows the local law enforcement agency, in this case the Mammoth police, to fulfill the kill order on behalf of the property owners.

I am willing to take the kill shot at this point. Yet, they've brought in the federal trappers/hunters. To me, that's the worst decision they could have made. I am very open about it: "Just let me do it," knowing I'll do it quickly and compassionately, hitting her in a spot where death will be instant and nearly painless. On the other hand, the trappers will place the frightened bear in a cage, slide a rifle barrel through the slots, and kill her.

As the two-year case comes to a head, state and local agencies hold a meeting at the Fish and Game offices down in Bishop, forty-five minutes away. I'm not included; I'm not even aware of it. By then, maybe they've lost faith in me, or just don't respect how much I know, or don't want to defer to me. I face a lot of that from conventionally trained wildlife officers. There is also a lot of animosity from residents over how long this has gone on. They're blaming me, the Bear Whisperer guy. The sense of desperation is peaking.

Ironically, as the meeting is taking place, we get a 9-1-1 call from cabin 11, up in the Lakes Basin. I call for backup. Two officers find me; the Animal Planet cameras begin to roll.

By the time we reach her, all Blondie wants to do is nap. She's full of lunch, fat, happy, sleeping. She's curled up on the edge of a slope, unaware that the cavalry has arrived. I'm pulling on a bulletproof vest as the watch commander, Sergeant Karen Smart, pulls up. She orders her officers to put their guns in their units as she heads off to kill the bear.

Now, I am pretty reliable with a gun. I like bears, and I like Blondie. But I've said in meetings and told reporters that I'm prepared, trained, and mentally capable of putting that bear down humanely. I'm a sure shot, thanks mostly to my experience. When Mammoth Police would set up shooting range drills, I'd be relaxed and efficient, though my weapons were far less sophisticated. Through my work, I'd just had the opportunity to shoot more often in the field, in live circumstances, than any of the cops. I feel very natural shooting lethal or nonlethal.

If Blondie needs to be taken out, I just assume I will be the one to do it. Over the years, I've had Blondie in my crosshairs more times than I can count. On this day I am prepared to take her out, as sad as that would be.

Smart is determined to handle it herself. We walk over, Smart carrying a shotgun with a single-slug shell, rather than buckshot. I point out the bear snoozing on the slope. I say to her, "Karen, are you going to shoot the bear?" She answers, "I'm going to shoot it right now."

Before I know it, she braces her barrel in the fork of a small tree to take the shot from sixty yards, far too far with a shotgun. I tell her, "Wait, wait, wait. Don't shoot. Jesus Christ. Let's get closer."

She agrees, walks about five more paces, suddenly shoulders the gun and sends it, hitting Blondie in the belly. The bear, in a deep sleep and probably dreaming of more ice cream and melon, starts screaming. The stomach is the most agonizing place to shoot a bear, not on point, not lethal. Surprises everyone.

The bear bellows. Smart asks, "Should I shoot it again?" I say yes, shoot it again. She shoots again. It's not the hit we need. The bear continues to scream, still in the base of the tree, still lying down. We're walking slightly uphill, half the original distance, the TV cameras rolling. Karen is starting to melt down, I take her gun away and hand her my orange shotgun, with double-aught buckshot, urging her to use it to finish the job. She shoulders the gun without bracing it on anything, hammers the wounded bear with a spray of buckshot, chambers another round and fires again.

Now, the dying cry of a rabbit, a deer, a bear carries a haunting, nearly human anguish. And we hear these death moans with our human ears. Doesn't matter what line of work you're in, whether you're used to it or not, that sorrow goes straight to your gut. In my line of work, those sounds make my trigger finger twitch. I want to end their awful pain.

Oddly enough, a lot of the people witnessing this were the same ones who complained to town officials earlier, where they urged authorities to "Kill the bear, kill the bear." Now they're hearing Blondie's last gasps firsthand.

The screaming stops but the bear is still not dead.

With my pistol drawn, I go over to put my foot on the bear's chest to push the air out of her lungs and hasten her death—it's just more humane, if that term can even be applied at this point.

Just when the situation can't get more bizarre or unsettling, an infuriated resident charges up, cussing loudly. I see immediately that he is wearing a gun in his waistband, always a red flag that the person is an amateur. A holstered handgun is a far safer gun. For cops, it's always a quick sign that the individual is careless and probably untrained. So this angry older man is stomping toward us, continuing his tirade, and we're not sure what he's furious about: Us? The bear? He's shaking, screaming: "Motherfucker! Motherfucker!" I turn my gun on him: "Stand down! Stand down!" I can't overstate how bizarre it all is.

The resident ignores us and stomps over and starts kicking Blondie in the head. He is so angry at all the damage she caused to his cabin that apparently he needs his moment of vengeance. Multiple cameras are rolling, catching this ugly retaliation.

We finally get the angry resident to back off; we don't arrest him, though the officers could've charged him with obstructing police work.

At this point, Smart is still very distraught that she had to resort to shooting four times, rather than a single, well-placed kill shot that would've been more humane. She apologizes to me, though I have no ill will toward her. She is just fulfilling her duty. Our boss, Chief Watson, later said he considered it strong and effective leadership on her part. In the moment, though, she is suffering the same remorse and sadness I always feel when I have to shoot a bear.

We put Blondie in a body bag, zip it up. It has handles, so we can carry her down the slope and lift her into the back of my truck. At a nearby stream, we wash our bloody hands, then take her to my place, the row of garages that contains our workroom for the reality show. The camera guys and the field producer sit on the ground in silence. I pull out some white sage and smudge the bear—and the crew.

The footage goes quickly to L.A., where they have been collecting Blondie footage from when she was a cub to her death. Everybody who worked on *The Bear Whisperer* is impacted by the Blondie event, whether they were in the field with me or following along in an edit bay. These folks who work in this cutthroat industry are calling my phone for days, some in tears. The raw footage is even more powerful and unsettling than the segment that's still online today.

The Animal Planet segment on Blondie doesn't air for a year, but the reaction then is immediate. To this day, viewers write to me, offering condolences over what they saw of that day.

Blondie's death, though tragic, might have been inevitable. She had a very rough life. And in the end, she gave her life. Given her circumstances, you could almost see it coming. Here's a bear, not a very good bear, and the outcome still feels awful.

I don't know how many bears are shot in America each year, certainly thousands. We shoot bears every day for fun, for sport, we do it for enjoyment. Lots of folks find it fun to drink a beer, stomp around in the forest, and pop one.

But none of those bears got a TV deal, their moment of fame, the way Blondie did. In fact, her story probably saved more bears than I ever did. Anyone who saw her story on the Animal Planet segment learned to protect their food, to close their cabin doors, to not train and reward bears for entering homes at will.

Brings to mind the old adage: the loss of one for the whole.

CHAPTER TWENTY-SEVEN

ALL IN A DAY'S WORK

Mammoth is laced with hiking and bike paths. I take my truck down one of the bike lanes to look for an injured deer reported slightly south of town. Bushes, manzanita, no injured deer. A quarter mile in, I find a family crowded around a bench, five or six of them. I get out and they mob me as if they've been stranded for years on a desert island.

"What's going on?" I ask.

"Thank God you're here," says the oldest, about thirty.

They say they've been praying, and I can't figure out what the issue is and why they're thanking me so profusely. I see some hard candy, in a fifteen-foot circle around a bench, in this little rest area along the bike lane. I ask why the candy is sprinkled around the bench. She says, "It's to keep the bears away." The candy is an offering to the bears, they explain, a perimeter of candy they thought would keep the bears from eating them.

The leader explains that they are lost and don't have the strength to go another step.

They are desperately lost—two hundred yards from a busy industrial park on the edge of Mammoth Lakes. They insist they would've had to spend the night out here and probably died if I hadn't come along. A little dramatic, considering they are in earshot of town. They could've simply headed in the direction of the tourists honking their car horns at each other. But OK. I'm polite, I'm a pro, but half my brain is having an aneurysm over how silly it all is. Thank God I can help them out.

I pile them into the truck. I pull into their campsite, where three other groups come out to mob them. At most, the lost hikers were a mile and a half from their campground.

This is a weird and whimsical encounter, not of much consequence, but it speaks to the range of situations I face. Throughout my career, I continue to have these Forrest Gump moments, sometimes the hero, sometimes the goat. My experiences may seem unlikely, almost charming, frequently inexplicable. Though many of my big moments are delightful, keep in mind I have a gun with me at all times. I'm not Hansel and Gretel dropping breadcrumbs out in the forest. This isn't always just a Sunday walk in the woods.

Bad bears are one part of my job. Inevitably, bad people are another.

Routine day, I'm at the police station, checking in, hanging with the officers about to go on patrol. We are fully staffed, with twenty-one total officers, only a few of whom will be on duty at any given time. One off-duty cop is hanging around, playing Candy Crush. A typical snoozy day in a mostly quiet mountain town.

Suddenly, all the radios start to cackle. Armed robbery in progress, at the Bank of America a half mile away. The suspect is described as wearing a bluish-green hoodie. The cops race out. An off-duty cop gives me a stern look, warning me not to get involved. "As if I ever would," I say as I head out to my truck.

Of course I totally would. I've been responding to dangerous situations my entire career, and I love my town and its quirky inhabitants. We are one big dysfunctional family. It angers me that someone might be waving a gun around a busy bank, frightening and threatening my friends and neighbors.

As I'm driving toward the bank—I never follow sensible advice—I know that the suspect has fled with the money by now, and I don't expect to find him sauntering up Old Mammoth Road hugging a bundle of bills. But I know the lay of the land. I know the bank has a wooded area 150–200 yards to the west, about an eighth of a mile from my own house, roughly the same place I practiced my language lessons with the bear called Center Street.

On a hunch, I pull up to a spot that looks out on what is known as Diaper Forest. By a big boulder, I spot a guy forty yards away. He's holding up a bluish-green hoodie. On the boulder, a backpack. I pull out my binoculars for a better look.

On the radio, I hear "Code 33, code 33." Officers are responding to the robbery from fifty miles away, from Bishop, Crowley, and Bridgeport. All the law enforcement agencies in earshot are rolling. Code 33 means to maintain radio silence unless there is something vital to the emergency at hand. It pings every lawman in the region.

Meanwhile, I'm watching this guy holding up the hoodie. I instantly know. He sees me glassin' him and takes off sprinting with the hoodie through the forest, across Center Street toward Main Street.

What are you going to do, Searles? You a man or a mouse? I floor it down the road that runs along Main Street. I see the dude dart through the door of a gas mart/liquor store. I'm the wildlife specialist, with no legal right to be doing this, but I'm on it. I pull right up to the door, slam on the brakes, pull out my Glock, and confront the guy.

"Get on the ground, get on the fucking ground now! Don't move."

The guy keeps shouting: "Take the sweatshirt, take the sweatshirt. I'm sorry."

I grab my radio: "Mono 1, Wildlife 1."

That's my radio handle. Instantly, the other officers know it's me. *Oh man*, they must be thinking.

"Mono 1, Wildlife 1," I say again, after getting no response.

Finally, my cell rings. It's Andy Lear, one of the officers at the bank.

"Whataya got, Steve?"

"Andy, I'm at the little Shell Mart on Main. I'm going to need a unit over here."

A minute later, up drives Chief Watson, wearing jeans and a Hawaiian shirt. He pulls up to me at the gas station with the guy on the ground. At this point in my career, I've got post-traumatic Schienle syndrome from all the conflict with my last boss. I feel like I am perpetually under the spotlight and in trouble. When I see the chief, I say, "Dude, I'm not going down on this, I'm not going down on this." He says, "Steve, stop it. What do you got?"

I tell him that on a hunch I swung by the Center Street wooded area, where I found this guy with a backpack and a hoodie that matched the description of the bank suspect.

Watson tells me he'll stay with the suspect and asks me to drive back to the rock and see if the backpack is still there. When I do, I find the backpack still there. But there is no money. The backpack contains the robber's change of clothes. The guy I'd caught is just some poor idiot who wandered by, thinking he'd found a free sweatshirt.

I hear Watson over the police radio: "Respond to Steve Searles at Center Street Forest, behind the radio station." I can hear sirens from the highway three miles away.

Only fifteen minutes have passed since the robbery. I'm jumpy as a long-tailed cat at a polka party.

Other officers arrive. We search the backpack. In a side pocket is a driver's license with a Bishop address. In two seconds, they ask dispatch to run priors on anyone from that address. The son of the man who owns the driver's license matches the description of the bank robber. Now they have a DMV mugshot of the suspect. The photo is on the department's website and on Facebook in twenty minutes. Facebook immediately lights up. Even the suspect's mom weighs in, confirming that it's her son.

Small towns, huh? Facebook makes them even smaller.

Things are happening super fast. The clerk at the Motel 6 spots the mugshot online and calls police, saying the suspect checked in that morning.

Police show up and ask the clerk to call the room to tell the suspect to come down to the office for a free box lunch or something, a hoax to lure him from the room. He opens the door, spots a police car, darts back inside. Now they have a standoff.

A crazy scene. Officers start taking the other guests out of their rooms in case they end up shooting through walls. Hour or so later, the guy comes out of the room, hands over his head. Police find the gun in a heater vent but no money. They even find the note he gave the teller. A week later, a guest who rented the same room reports the toilet is clogged. After a plumber pulls the toilet, they discover that the clog was the bank loot, which the robber had tried to flush.

Long story short, the suspect goes to prison, and I get a written commendation from Watson.

Another non-bear case, even stranger. In the late sixties, Charles Manson used the Eastern Sierra as his stomping grounds, and was arrested at Barker Ranch, in Death Valley, about two hundred miles southeast of here, an area once known for gold and uranium mining, one of the hottest, most desolate places you can imagine. Due to some natural springs, the Manson family had used the abandoned ranch as its headquarters, where they held orgies and assorted other weirdness. Responding to vandalism of some nearby road equipment, authorities closed in on the ranch, expecting to find only some drugged-out squatters. The cops found Manson hiding under a sink. Fortunately, the guards Manson posted to ambush police had fallen asleep.

Cut to decades later: my friend Paul Dostie, a sergeant with the Mammoth Police Department, is doing some side work on murder victim recovery, using a cadaver dog, specially trained to sniff out and identify bodies. He drags me along on one of his adventures to the Manson ranch, where we are scheduled to meet up with Sharon Tate's sister, Debra, who has made a life of keeping Manson and his murderous disciples behind bars.

On the way, Dostie says there's something he has to tell me.

"What?"

"It's the anniversary of Charlie's arrest," he says.

Lord, how have I gotten involved in this?

Over the years, the LAPD has linked an additional twelve homicides to Manson and his followers, and Dostie is convinced that Manson buried victims at this ranch. Until his death in 2017, Manson was like the pope of the macabre. He kept in touch with followers, detectives, crime buffs, all from his state prison cell in Corcoran, California. According to guards, Manson had a Rolodex the size of an L.A. phone book. So weird, in every way. He'd make these little sculptures using his own hair. He also had his own letterhead, stationery with watermarks. My buddy Paul had hundreds of conversations with Manson. Dostie would make maps of the area, mail them to Charlie, and ask him where the bodies were.

Spooky, of course, as is anything associated with a sociopath like Manson. Once at the ranch, the three of us walk Dostie's cadaver dog around to suspected gravesites. "Find Fred! Find Fred!" Dostie says, his usual command to locate remains, regardless of the victim's name.

We take a break. On the porch, we're sitting on Charlie's couch, a wooden coffee table in front. We decide to explore the various rooms, including the reputed orgy room, the pool. On some shelves in the living room, there are trinkets and little notes left by those who came here to pay homage to Manson. A chilling shrine.

Paul gets a rolling ice chest out of the Bronco and starts spreading out sandwich stuff on the porch, where we put lunch meats and bread. "Let's put our feet up and have a sandwich." Already creeped out, we start hearing a series of gunshots hundreds of yards away but behind the next hill. Paul fires off some rounds to let them know we're here, and we go back to our lunches. Minutes later, five armed dudes show up in dune buggies, blocking our Bronco in. They get out, slip through the gate, and start to walk up the driveway toward us, shoulder to shoulder, like characters in a Western showdown. They are heavily armed. We are heavily armed. As we sit on the porch, one of them makes a comment about Tate's breasts.

"You shoulda seen me when I was younger," Tate spouts back.

I take a big breath. Holy shit. They can see our firepower—assault rifles and shotgun. Dostie, an expert marksman, whispers to me: "I'll take the three on the left, you take the two on the right."

I said, "Screw that. Take the four on the left, I'll take the one on the right."

With that, the leader says, "Hey, I think we maybe have the wrong place," as if they turned down the wrong cul-de-sac in a subdivision. There's not another house for miles. They turn, climb into their buggies, and fly off into the desert in a cloud of dust.

Who knows what they were after. All we know is that Manson's sphere of evil is still strong. In 2009, fire leveled most of the buildings on the ranch, leaving only the crude foundations.

The surreal saga is just one of the many non-bear-related adventures I have over the years, in a region that seems to attract a fair share of drama and death.

Another memorable adventure involves one of the many airplane crashes in the Sierra, a graveyard for pilots who refuse to respect the ferocious winds that roar through the region all year long.

In the Ritter Range, which separates Mammoth from Yosemite, with its jagged spires—our own Tyrolean Alps—renowned adventurer Steve Fossett landed too hard in rocky and remote country. After numerous record-setting adventures, around the world in hot-air balloons and planes, the renowned adventurer would never be seen again.

Like me, Fossett was an Orange County kid whose early love of the mountains would change his life. After a hugely successful investment career, Fossett devoted his life to setting world records by land and sea, some one hundred or so in boats, gliders, balloons, planes, and airships. Bold, even in sports he didn't know, he swam the English Channel, despite failing to make his high school swim team. He also competed in the Iditarod and the 24 Hours of Le Mans, the type of races that rewarded endurance, which had always been his forte.

Seemingly never at rest, Fossett disappeared near Mammoth Lakes on Labor Day 2007 while flying a solo aircraft, over the Great Basin Desert, from Nevada to California. Likely culprit? A heavy downdraft brought by the chutes and ladders of the canyon winds. His plane disappeared, nearly without a trace, in some of the most beautiful and treacherous backcountry of the Pacific Crest Trail, a segment thick with backpackers.

For weeks after the crash, and up until the first snows, searchers and state-of-the-art aircraft scoured the region, finding almost a dozen unknown crash sites, but no trace of Fossett or the single-engine two-seater he was flying, or the plane's transponder.

A year later, during a rigorous day hike, an employee of a Mammoth outdoors shop runs across cash and Fossett's ID. He shows it to his boss, a pal of mine, Tom Cage. We put together a small search crew that includes Mike Slee, the producer-cameraman who is up working with me on the Animal Planet show at the time.

In we go, determined to solve what, at the time, is one of the world's great mysteries: What became of Steve Fossett? Had he died on impact, or tried to hike his way out? Where exactly is the plane?

We drive to the Reds Meadows base camp, where we foot it across the San Joaquin River, down the Pacific Crest Trail, then off trail to the spot where the ID and cash were found. The traction is lousy up the slippery pumice, above the tree line—nothing. Eventually, all we come up with are a sweatshirt and a piece of the windshield that an injured Fossett might've used as a beacon/reflector to attract searchers.

But Slee's footage from our trek is used in the Discovery Channel's *Steve Fossett: What Went Wrong?* on how perhaps the world's most renowned thrill seeker finally succumbed to the unforgiving gusts of the Eastern Sierra.

In another odd side gig, I am chosen to help toughen up a bunch of corporate executives during a team-building camp held at a fly-fishing compound near Mammoth's tiny airport. A CEO taps me and my long-time sidekick Kevin Peterson to run the camp, which he hopes will be a reward—and a bit of an eye-opener—for some of his top managers.

Like many urban/suburban types, the campers don't get enough vitamin D in their daily lives, or nearly enough nature. They work in the kind of luxury high-rises where you can't open a window; otherwise everyone might jump.

The owner flies them into this beautiful little fishing camp on Hot Creek, where the water gushes out of the mountains, clear as gin and cold as Christmas Eve. Prettiest rainbow trout on the planet play in this icy white-water, with Mammoth Mountain and the famed Minarets in the distance—a series of spires atop the Ritter Range. Shaped like upside-down icicles, they are called the Minarets for their resemblance to the spires of a mosque.

The dozen or so participants gasp at all this scenery as they stow away their gear in the series of little cabins facing the creek. They don't believe in guns, so naturally we make them shoot guns, which their boss has provided. The idea is to take them out of their comfort zones, make them show some courage, stay open minded, while becoming more rounded human beings. Judge if you like. Certainly, the setting alone is a tonic for these stressed-out high-level managers.

Kevin and I do the gun range training and the safety talk. We put them into teams and have them shoot skeet, clay pigeons fired out of a machine, similar to a baseball pitching machine. We put the machine in the back of a truck and fill it with a hundred "birds," the clay targets.

They are so bad. Each time, the targets are flying out of the truck on the same plane, the same direction . . . easy. At one point, I have them put down their guns and just track the trajectory of the clay pigeons with their arms.

"It's a trip to see people out of their element and open-minded enough to learn," I assure them. "Even you dipshits."

Part of my adopted role is to heckle them. I know it's weird, but that's one of the reasons they brought me in. It's what the campers need, a bit of razzing, a bit of boot camp, though this is very mild compared to real boot camp. These corporate kings of the world need to be challenged. They also need to know what it feels like for employees when they muck around with them. At least, that's what I suppose the goal is. In any case, everyone should be humbled a little now and then.

Within hours, I'm yelling, "You suck!" They're laughing, which just makes me dig into them more. It is all in fun. Everyone is getting a chuckle out of it.

These whiz-kid corporate go-getters don't even know how to make a campfire—which is a little sad. One has his sweater tied around his neck, like a college boy—that's even sadder. Yeah, I razz him a little bit about that. It is like a big target on his back, the male equivalent of too much lipstick.

I give them a whole lecture on the crisis in masculinity, how we've forgotten how to be men. For thousands of years, we had to perform—hunt, fish, trap—or go without food. We are still programmed emotionally to fight for survival. "Now you drive your Audi and think you're hot shit," I tell them. "You couldn't survive the night out here."

I'm pretty direct, obviously. I doubt I'll be invited back, though in the end they pool their money for a big tip. Must've gotten something out of it.

When they arrive, most don't have a real connection to nature—none. But we work on that. Little by little, they get their hands dirty, they cut themselves on fish hooks. They learn guns, they learn to tie a fly on, to land a prize trout, to release it safely back into the current, to marvel as it disappears into the depths of the raging mountain creek.

Some call this spiritual rebirth Earthing or grounding, under the theory that the electrical charges of the earth help connect us in ways important to our mental health. City folks, in the course of a month, might not touch a single blade of grass. Now, they're up to their elbows in dirt and fish slime.

You can trace it back to the Native Americans. They've been "Earthing" for thousands of years.

According to their culture, if you're not feeling good, you sit on the ground. If that's not enough, you lie down. If you hear that your grandmother died, you sit down, you reconnect, you mellow out.

Now, the New Age Berkeley types think they've invented these earthly connections.

So that raises the question: What does it mean to be a man in the twenty-first century? How evolved are we? Yeah, you're good at a keyboard, writing code, playing Madden Football. So? You can't even change a flat. Is this why we need gummies to relax and Zolpidem to sleep? Is this why we watch porn? Because we have these primordial needs that modern life doesn't address?

I'm not the right guy to answer this. I'm totally aware of toxic masculinity. I've seen all the ways that can go south. At this point, in my personal life, I've given up hunting and spend my free time at Native American sweat lodges. So, I've mellowed. I hope I have some unexpected layers to me. I'm maybe a bit more enlightened than you might expect of a guy who carries an orange shotgun instead of a laptop.

Trust me, I'd witnessed the bad behavior of men from the time I was a toddler. I didn't want to perpetuate that one bit. But I also understand our connection to nature, our need to protect, the endorphin rush of physically proving ourselves. It is a delicate line.

Yes, I know the drawbacks of a sense of masculinity tied to our baser instincts. And, despite my raw and macho exterior, I am leery as hell of it.

CHAPTER TWENTY-EIGHT

LITERALLY UP A TREE

I'm hanging from a branch, six stories up a very sappy tree, pine pitch in my beard and clothes, while winching down a bear cub so I can reunite it with its runaway mom. The cub doesn't really appreciate all I am doing for him—basically saving his life. He is wailing like the baby he is. Below, the disbelieving cops are heckling me.

Is it too late to change my major?

One sticky inch at a time, I lower this poor cub, the little bear squawking like a crow, to the forest floor below. I lower him a bit more. He gets tangled in the branches. He bellows even louder. I lift him a little to unsnag him, then try to lower him again. It is like fishing for marlin with yarn and a glow stick.

Before I go up, I tell the police officers that I am taking up a 165-foot climbing rope. I explain how I am going to tie off the cub and lower him down. I need them to hold the cage for the terrified little bear, hanging upside down, swinging like a pendulum.

"We'll be golden," I tell them.

It is like a pivotal moment in a superhero movie, where against the odds, in an implausible and outlandish situation, good will triumph over evil—you just aren't sure how in the hell they will pull it off. In this case, the little bear is convinced that I am the evil one, and the cops are completely sure I've gone insane. Other than that, I have the support of nearly all the parties involved.

How'd I manage to wind up dangling from a tree? Well, bad days like this one always seem to start early. I received the distress call before my first coffee: Vons supermarket, probably the busiest public space in town.

Bears are a constant issue with the busy supermarket. In the back of the store, near the loading dock, there is a forty-foot trash container—the kind of open bin often used for construction debris, no lid. Ignoring my pleas, Vons uses their big bin to dump expired meat and veggies. Inadvertently, they've created a giant bear trap.

In this instance, they roll down the door at closing time, and Mama dashes off, leaving her cubs wallowing in all the expired food in the indoor dumpster. When workers open up the next morning, there are the two cubs. No sign of Mom; frustrated and probably grieving, she'd run off.

Now, the little bears are on the loose. The more we chase them, the more anxious and elusive they get, full of piss and vinegar, all claws and teeth. We have three officers after them now, with capture poles and gloves. A bear cub is nothing to goof around with. You see a nice picture of a cub, you just want to hug it. When you grab on to them, that changes in a second. They aren't stuffed toys. You're always stunned by how strong they are.

I finally manage to brute-force tackle one cub and ram him into the cage and set it in the back of the truck, to bait the brother, hoping that he'll be curious and join the caged bear. No such luck. The other cub does exactly what confused bears do when they sense danger: he scampers to safety up the nearest tree.

Standing at the base of the tree looking up, I immediately think of Lynn Rogers, founder of the North American Bear Center in Minnesota. Rogers once told me how he would climb trees to reach bears, dart them, and gently belay the bear to the ground, where he could study it further.

Who in their right mind would do that? I thought at the time.

In this moment, fifteen years later, it seems to make perfect sense. "You guys stand by," I tell the officers on scene, then race home to fetch an extension ladder. (Snow reaches so high on trees here that it strips the lower branches.) I also grab some carabiners, another cage, and the 165-foot rope.

Back on site, up the tree I go. *Oooooooooomph.*

My approach may seem overly aggressive. After all, left to his own devices, wouldn't a hungry cub come out of the tree eventually? Well, in this case the young cub is still suckling, and Mom is nowhere to be found. If I am unable to reunite him and his sibling with their mother, they will probably die for lack of milk.

My alternatives are zero. If I don't do anything, I'll wind up with dead or orphaned cubs, which don't stand a chance on their own, slowly starving. As I noted earlier, even with a mom around, half the cubs don't make it to age two.

So, with time running out and the little bear bellowing, my comrades in the police department chuckling, little by little, I lower this twenty-five-pound bear to the ground as he dangles upside down from his back leg, spinning like a tree ornament.

Remember, I'm six stories up. The big pine is so tall, I need the ladder to reach the first branch. Climbing trees is for kids, not middle-aged men. Your body, your legs, your hands are not suited to climbing a tree. In no time, your feet start to hurt. In this case, there are almost too many limbs. I have to duck and weave my way up through the pine branches. Very dense, not like an oak. If I slip, I die. I climb a little higher, and the cub shimmies upward as well, just out of my reach.

In a short time, we are running out of tree. As we near the top, it begins to sway with our weight. I reach up, cinch the rope on the cub's rear foot, loop it over the branch as a sort of fulcrum, peel the clingy little bastard off the tree—an accomplishment all by itself. My face is at his belly button. I have my left leg wrapped around the tree, my right leg supporting my weight. In that situation, you need a tail—you just don't have enough hands.

I begin to inch him down, the rope rasping against the branch, again fighting the jungle gym of limbs the entire way.

We're in a really busy commercial space, with hundreds of people nearby largely unaware; it's just me and the cops.

When I get the bear about ten feet from the ground, I can hear the cops yelling, "Stop! Stop!" They have a right to be concerned. If you were trying to catch a house cat like this, you'd be concerned, let alone a baby Scissorhands.

I shout at them to shut up and catch the bear with the cage. Eventually they do. They clamp the lid on; we set the cage in the back of the truck next to his sibling, put a blanket over it. I got them both.

By now, Fish and Game is onto this, as are other agencies, as well as private trappers contracted to help in these situations. Lieutenant Art Lawrence, a take-charge guy who never appreciated my unconventional tactics, shows up angry over what he is seeing.

The state wildlife officer says he's seizing my cages. "We're taking the bears. You're done." The local cops are on my side, but the state official outranks them. Art confiscates the cubs. To me, it feels like the Arthur injustice all over again. I drive home. I'm crying with frustration, knowing the probable fate of these innocent cubs. That's just me, emotional. I'll be the first to admit that I take my failures and my bears too personally.

I get home, wallowing in self-pity, angry at the world. I explain to Debs all that has happened, and the heartbreak of seeing the state wildlife official take off with my prizes. She says, "Go find the sow. Go do it now."

To me, that's impossible. Debs doesn't know the lay of the land, or how unlikely it is to find the sow, who has split, with more than a twelve-hour lead. Far as I'm concerned, what's done is done.

Coffee in hand, I go for a drive, back to where it happened. I pull into the empty lot of the satellite community college, part of a county system. The area is full of manzanita bushes, sage, dry shrubs, very thick. I'm licking my wounds, feeling bad for myself. A couple of minutes have passed when, over the top of the manzanita, I suddenly see the top three inches of a bear moving along 150 yards away.

I fly out of my truck, leaving the door open in the empty college parking lot. On a hunch—I'm not sure yet—I race for what I hope is the mama bear, leaving my radio and my gun. I must look like an idiot, because I have to hurdle these scratchy low bushes to get to her, toward this sow, hoping to tree her. It seems inconceivable that this would be the mom, and that I'd be in the right spot to find her. Finally, we go around a corner of the complex, where there are climbable trees. I bum rush her, chasing her up the first tree we come to.

Mom's not the least bit happy over this turn of events. First, she's lost her cubs, and now this bearded, ponytailed human is mad-dogging her up a tree. I stand against the trunk of the tree, and look up: Yep. I can see from the wet teats: It's her.

At first, the bear is pretty mellow. Ten minutes later, she wants to be on her way. She starts huffing at me and clacking her jaw, signs that she's mad and wants me to go away. As she starts to slide down out of the tree, I grab a four-foot branch and start whacking the trunk to keep her up there. She's not buying it and still tries to come down. At that point, I begin to directly smash her paws. It's hard to talk about, even today. It is out-of-body for me . . . bestial and primitive and disturbing. I hit her dozens of times.

"I got her, I got her," I keep saying into my near-dead cell, not knowing if my colleagues can hear me on the other end. I tell them I'm behind the college, but don't give them enough specifics to easily find me. A teacher at the college keeps trying to call for me. With my last bit of juice, I get an incoming call from Kevin Peterson. My old pal says, "I don't know what's happening, bro, but they're coming your way."

From my pleas and the teacher's calls, Paul Dostie and others have pieced together what is happening near the college. They realize I have the sow and alert the Highway Patrol to intercept the shell camper with the cubs that is zooming north on the 395, to reunite them with their mom. With the Highway Patrol in the lead, a caravan of cops and wildlife officials shows up, and pulls in near where my truck is parked.

I am spent, physically and mentally, totally drained, still covered in sap and grit from my tree climb. I smell horrible, even to me, a nervous stench. I still haven't eaten all day.

Officer Doug Hornbeck, front and center in so many of my calls, walks to where I've treed the bear. He sits with a Handycam, filming me, asks me how I'm doing. Suddenly, I hear a booming voice from the parking lot: *"Move away from the tree. Move away from the tree now!"*

Lawrence, the state officer, has jurisdiction in times like this. When he bellows at me a third time, he racks his shotgun. I'm not sure if he's worried about me or the bear, but that sure got my attention.

Game over. In frustration, I toss the branch I'd been using off to the side and go to pick up the cellphone, which I'd tossed to the side. I look down at the parking lot, where Fish and Game officers are standing with a pair of cages. They carry the cages toward us, the cages jiggling under the weight of the cubs scurrying from one end to the other. Halfway up the hill, they set the cages down, facing us, and slide open the Plexiglas doors and release the cubs, which race for their mom.

The little family is desperate. They have all gone twelve hours without nursing. The mom doesn't climb out of the tree, she jumps—highly unusual, since a bear's front legs aren't sturdy enough to cushion that much weight. But she jumps, spins on her back, and her two cubs climb aboard. Stomach to stomach with their mama, the babies start to nurse.

You wouldn't be human if you didn't have a catch in your throat. Everybody is emotional and clapping to see the bears reunited, not just me, but maybe me the most.

Yet again, another tense standoff, another ping-pong of emotions. This time the bears win. I win . . . well, sort of anyway. I'm pretty hardcore, pretty seasoned, but this incident—the juju, the juice, the spirit—still amazes me. Without those intangibles, I'm convinced that none of this comes together so cleanly. Once again, it's as if there's a hand on my shoulder.

Bear magic.

CHAPTER TWENTY-NINE

ANOTHER BLOODY BUMPER

Summery day. T-shirt weather. The kind of day where you can taste the salt on your lips. Blue skies, bright sun at Murphy's Gulch, about two miles out of town on the speedy 203, the last leg on the long journey from L.A. to Mammoth Lakes. On the way into town, just before the visitor center, a Jeep driver accidentally *ka-bams* a bear in the road with his big, aftermarket steel I-beam bumper. Just cleaned the poor bear's clock.

The driver does the right thing, calls 9-1-1. The request for help goes to dispatch in Bridgeport fifty-five miles north of here, then to me. In a small town like this, 9-1-1 responses happen much faster. There's just less congestion, and 9-1-1 calls are far fewer, so every call gets full first responder attention. I am there in an instant.

I pull up at the same time as a police cruiser. We find the Jeep, the driver waiting on scene, he's super bummed. No sign of the bear, an old friend of mine that has been living in Murphy's Gulch for a long time. Never gave me any trouble, just a good bear.

"How fast you going?" I ask the driver. Fifty, he says. Looking at the big steel bumper, I know the bear is seriously hurt.

The driver is honest and straight up about what happened. I've heard people lie to cops my whole career. Me they trust. Sometimes I know them, sometimes I don't. In any case, I'm just the wildlife officer. They think the worst I'll ever do is hand them a free T-shirt or a "Don't Feed Our Bears" sticker, which is pretty true. I leave it to the police to make arrests and issue non-animal-related citations.

Doug Hornbeck, total pro, a thirty-year officer, offers to take the report but doesn't have any interest in euthanizing the bear, assuming we can find it.

I grab my gun and gear and head off. I soon discover there are zero drops of blood to follow, not one single drop.

Up the embankment I go, to a dry streambed full of sand, where I can see his prints. Past that, nothing. Generally, this is barren landscape, compared to the greener, softer areas in town and up around the lakes. Bears are soft footed, nimble, difficult to track. Their weight is usually spread out over four legs, not two, so the depth of the tracks is different from a bird or even a deer. Following them through the hardpan is tough, though I'm a pretty experienced tracker. The bushes are waist high, with a subtle drooping of leaves that I notice, the broken twigs that trackers spot. I zig and zag through the brush, lose the trail, and notice a big tree six hundred yards in the distance. I just have a feeling that, seriously hurt, that big tree would be the refuge he needs. When bears are scared, they just climb a tree.

Sure enough, after forty minutes, I find him at the bottom of the tree. As he pulls himself up the tree, I can see his back end is broken, his back leg dislocated from the hip. He pulls himself up the tree using his front paws and jaws. Literally, he chews himself to safety. At spots where he'd normally use his back legs, he just chomps into the tree trunk, grabs hold with his jaws, then reaches further with his front legs, pulling his injured and useless rear end along, a brutal and desperate effort. Do animals display courage? Do bears have adrenaline? Sure they do. That bald eagle circling above you has adrenaline. The mouse in your kitchen does too. Their survival depends on it.

It's an old tree, must've been hit by lightning. I love trees, they're almost all uniform. The ones that are gnarled and deformed, or "forked," are still healthy, but something happened to them. Most of the time, it's from a lightning strike years before. That's the sort of prehistoric tree the injured bear has chosen.

I'm in the middle of my two-year stint with the Animal Planet show, so I set out my tripod, turn on the camera, and hit Record.

The injured bear is splayed out on a branch, about ten feet above my head. I can see he is barely hanging on, fading fast, in pain that is probably beyond measure. He is staring at me. I pray for an accurate shot. With my shotgun, I take aim behind his ear, at that spot where the skull connects to the spine. The goal is to shut off the nerve center as quickly as possible. I pull the trigger. He is dead before he can even hear the shot. Droplets of blood drift across the site, misting my clothes, my gun, my eyeglasses.

But he doesn't fall from the branch.

I set my safety, put down the gun and gear, and begin to climb. As I've said, it's dirty and sticky to climb a tree, especially if you're not a kid.

Once I reach him, I push him gently off the branch, four hundred pounds plus. He lands with a huge thump.

Consider this: You go to a friend's funeral, you know it's going to be sad. You get out your funeral clothes, you pick out the right tie. You slip on your best shoes and sunglasses—you're prepared for the emotion of the day. You set your mind for the task at hand. If you're going to a wedding, you pick out a brighter, different tie, then prepare emotionally for fun and celebration.

When a bear is hit by a car, you don't have any time for preparation. You don't have any idea of what you're going into. You just know that the magnificent animal is suffering.

Add in the emotion of carrying a loaded firearm, sometimes in the middle of a town, people everywhere. I don't take it lightly at all. You want to hurry but not rush, as team coaches like to say. You have to clinically assess the situation, take in the animal's condition, look out for the safety of the humans who are curious and often standing too close.

When I have to euthanize an animal, I step back to take in the entire scene. I look at the backdrop, consider which ammo to use, the glint of the sun, the line of fire, the direction that cars are coming. I'm being as thoughtful and considerate and professionally cool as I can, while preparing to kill a creature very high on the food chain. In this situation, I can't pull the trigger with tears in my eyes. I'm shooting a very powerful weapon in a populated area. I have to hold myself together.

Some animals that are hit could recover. I pointed a gun at many of them, then wound up not pulling the trigger. Sometimes, I'd wait, in hopes there might be some hope, a chance to recover, as they often did. Many times, I said, "Hey, I'll check on you in the morning."

If you go to a funeral, emotionally it's maybe a six or an eight. For me, these traffic calls are always a ten. When I'm taking the safety off and putting my finger gently on the trigger . . . well, that moment is a twenty.

On other calls, I get there to fix the problem; it's just a bear in a campground, or a bear in a cabin; it turns out well. With a traffic collision, it turns out lethal more than half the time. Folks don't call 9-1-1 to wish the dispatcher happy birthday. They call because the situation is desperate, and maybe life or death.

There's not one animal life that I took that I've forgotten. I can remember what time it was, the direction I was facing, the time of year. It's not the healthiest thing. I lie down in bed at eleven P.M. after a long day, exhale, try to collect my thoughts; the phone rings. In five minutes, I'm on some dark roadside, putting down a wounded deer, then lifting her—still warm, this gloriously beautiful creature—into the back of my truck to take her off into the woods, where I will leave her.

As I said earlier, Mammoth Lakes is a "sanctuary city" for all kinds of wild animals. On the soccer field, you can find probably fifteen deer grazing in the wet morning grass. Can I tell one doe from another? No. You don't know them individually; they're herd animals.

Bears are different. They are solitary, independent-thinking animals. They have an identity. You show up to a scene, and the car flashers are on, there's glass in the road. Chances are I'm going to have to kill one of them. Imagine putting a dog down every week. Vets leave their practices from the accumulated trauma of having to put pets down all the time.

On this warm day, my dreary task completed, I climb back down the tree. I have tobacco and sage with me. I want to make an offering of tobacco, then white sage to rinse his spirit.

On camera, the blood still on my specs, I explain to the Animal Planet audience: "Some days are really good and some days suck."

What I really want to give the bear is a song—an honoring song I picked up from the Paiute. But the emotions get to me. I can't seem to summon a song. I'm just drawing a blank. I call Debs. I'm sobbing. "Where are you? What's going on?" she asks. I tell her I can't catch a song. She doesn't say a word. My wife just begins to sing a haunting, thousand-year-old bear song.

Right then, it starts snowing, on this otherwise warm and clear day. Astonishing. Snow?

Eventually, I gather my gun, my camera, my gear. The bear will stay right where he fell, provide sustenance for other creatures, eventually melt back into the earth itself . . . dust to dust. I trudge the fifteen minutes back to my truck. When I get back to the highway, I look up from the last pitch and see Debs's big SUV parked right next to my truck. No Debs. Disturbed by my earlier call, she has taken off to find and help me. She also headed to the tree, where I track her.

I finally reach her, walking up to the bear. She drops to her knees and says a prayer for the bear.

To this day, one of the oddest, most spiritual progressions of events I've experienced: locating the bear in difficult circumstances, the way the bear chewed himself up the tree, having to call Debs for a song, the impossible snowfall. Then Debs showing up and being able to walk right toward the bear when she could've gone a hundred different directions.

When the Animal Planet producer sees my footage, she calls me to say it brought her to tears and that it was the "heaviest stuff we've seen."

Heavy. Heartbreaking. Haunting. Wonderful.

Hand on my shoulder. The bear spirit at work.

CHRIS WEIGHS IN ONE LAST TIME . . .

Good books change your life. Is this a good book? I'm too close. Working on it certainly changed my life though.

At first glance, the written word seems like such a wispy, ethereal thing—eyelashes on a page. But good words are bricks. You can build a life of them. The best ones outlast cities, empires, even civilizations. In a thousand years, we'll still be quoting Shakespeare. In a thousand years, we'll still be singing to the Beatles.

Will Vegas still be around? Probably not.

To my mind, lasting power is the best indication of true quality. Great cars, great architecture, great writing, great lives all have lasting power. Great works of art more than anything.

I don't know that Steve's story belongs in the British Museum. I approached his life story as if it does. Despite my rep as a wiseguy, I took his work very seriously, even as we had fun producing it. I feel privileged to witness how he changes over the course of these pages. I return to John Muir, who once said of Steve's beloved Eastern Sierra: "When one tugs at a single thing in nature, he finds it attached to the rest of the world."

I also think of the words of that old Apple Computer ad: "Here's to the crazy ones. The misfits. The rebels. The troublemakers. . . . The ones who see things differently. . . . They invent. They imagine. They heal. They explore. . . . They push the human race forward."

So please buckle up. These last few chapters aren't easy. As you know by now, Steve is tough, hearty, effusive, and literally the match of any wild bear.

But nothing survives a raging wildfire. Forest fires steal our homes, our pets, our family albums, our holiday treasures, our favorite pillows. Worst of all, they destroy any sense of security. And wildfires devastate pristine wilderness for generations to come. They seem to undermine God's best work. If there's an understated threat to America in the next fifty years, it's probably wildfires.

In Steve's case, can he survive something that no one else can?

Hint: if Steve does survive, he won't do it alone.

Do we ever?

CHAPTER THIRTY

SO LONG, DEBS

In 2017, Debs takes off for a Cuba vacation with a bunch of girlfriends. When she returns, she hands me six cigars in a plastic bag and tells me she wants a divorce. March 6. My birthday.

I quit smoking a year ago, and she brings me cigars? I guess that gives you some idea of where her head is at.

In hindsight, she probably should've left me sooner. With my life, my career, my obsessive nature, a spouse gets lots of downside. Most husbands don't deal with blood and trauma all the time. Insurance agents or high school teachers don't go around euthanizing injured bears, or smudging them with sage, or wrestling plastic canisters off cubs' heads. Most husbands don't get into standoffs with the state, or spend their off hours hanging out with Paiute bear dancers.

As I noted earlier, I'm probably not the forever type women dream about. My love is the outdoors. My passion is trucks and dogs and outdoor gear. I'm a total guy's guy. But Debs . . . she is something special.

I try my best to convince her not to pursue a divorce. I fight hard. Before she moves out, I get up every morning, pour my coffee, then sit at the table and tick off the reasons I think she should stay. I'm trying to be reasonable and realistic. I list all the positives and negatives of getting a divorce.

Ultimately, I beg her not to throw away a thirty-year relationship. Move into the guest room, I tell her. We'll figure it out, I say.

After a month of this, she moves out—into one of our rental units, two streets over, and files the paperwork for the divorce, taking Tyler and our dog, May, to live with her. Way too close; it just salts the wound. The dog would get out and sneak over, lick my face, roll over so I could rub her belly. Eventually, Debs would show up in her car, open the door, and order the dog to come with her.

"Come on, May," she'd say, and the dog would scamper into the car.

I am crushed. It folds my cards.

As everyone does, we accumulated a lot of assets and possessions over three decades together. "Take whatever you want," I tell her. She shows up with trucks. She takes the living room table, the couch, backs the moving trucks up to the garage. The paddleboards, the kayaks, the lightbulbs. Gone.

It isn't that I am in a bad place in my head, or anything like that. In this situation, reality is my bad place. I feel faint, I am lightheaded, my stomach is constantly in a knot—everything a person goes through when they lose a lifeline. I wake up one day, and my trademark baritone voice, which had served me so well with the bears and with the media, has turned to a whisper. Psychologists say the loss of my voice is all in my head. Surgeons say it is something physical. I wait, hoping for it to return on its own.

I'm relatively tame at this stage of my life. I drink but I don't drink and drive, I don't go out and cause trouble or start fights. Sometimes sitting at home in my chair, that's even worse, a sad solo act. It is the darkest of times.

Over the years, whenever I'd receive public recognition for my work—some award, some little tribute—I would make sure to thank Debs. Every time. As I've said, she is responsible for every success I've had. So, when word gets around town that we split, everyone knows how devastated I will be. In small towns, there are no secrets. Friends spot me at the end of an aisle at the Vons, pivot the shopping cart, and go the other way, just to avoid an awkward encounter. Understandable. That's just how people are.

Debs won't budge. Her decision is final. She tells me during all this that she'll be my reference when I start dating again, vouch that I am a good guy. She even gives me a list of prospective dating candidates.

Ouch.

People with my personality, we overly internalize, we dwell. I worry over things in my sleep, my brain won't turn off. Being as honest as I am is probably not natural. Is it healthy? Only time will tell. The way we live our lives always catches up to us when we're sixty or seventy. Was I too vulnerable? Too forthright? Too direct?

Instead of a monthly payment, I make a lump sum deal with the approval of Debs and the court. I give her the good stuff, the best property, all the assets that are actual assets. The stuff on the other side of my ledger list, the property that doesn't generate income, or hasn't escalated in value, I keep for myself. She notes the discrepancy. She is grateful. Am I, in some way, trying to get her to reconsider, to bribe her to come back? Perhaps. For now, I am glad to be done with it all. I've paid my ransom.

My own fault, of course, but for thirty years Debs has done all my personal chores, all the shopping, all the clothes. I don't know how to do the most basic life tasks: shop for ground beef, how to flip a flapjack. Lord have mercy, I don't even know what size jeans I wear.

My friends are there for me, but it's not doing the trick. Wish I had Shorty to lean on.

During my lowest moments, a friend recommends a high-end therapist—the therapist of therapists—and talks him into taking me on. When I read this renowned therapist a list of my personal issues—the challenges I've faced in the course of my crazy life—he starts crying. I read it to my best friend. He leaves me. I tear up the list. So much for therapy. So much for lists. As I drive home from the therapist, I actually feel worse.

In time, I come to terms with her leaving us and returning to New Zealand. Fortunately, Tyler stays behind, and we have a terrific relationship. I climb slowly out of my funk, learning to be more appreciative than angry. But angry still and struggling to understand.

Yet, if I had it to do over, I'd marry Debs again. I would. We had thirty years, some ups and downs, a fantastic son, an interesting life in a remarkable place, where we were known and respected in the community. We had a long run of friendship, affection, adventure, and self-discovery . . . of anguish and of hope.

We had a life. Can a man ask for anything more?

Little do I realize, this is just the beginning.

CHAPTER THIRTY-ONE

"I DON'T DO THAT ANYMORE"

The call comes to me at home, on the cell number I've given out to the community for decades now, 937-BEAR. A resident tells me a mother bear has been hovering over her dead cub in a yard in Old Mammoth, won't leave its side in a nice neighborhood of wide yards popular for day and evening walks. The grieving mother stalks the yard as dog owners and nannies with strollers wander by, joined by anyone else out looking for fresh air in the midst of the COVID crisis.

The mama bear is probably still breastfeeding the little bear when he dies, and all her maternal hormones, all her emotional telemetry, tell her this baby still needs her. She is confused and probably traumatized.

"Thanks for callin'," I tell the resident. "Unfortunately, I don't do that anymore."

In midsummer 2020, in a thirty-minute meeting out of nowhere, the city manager of Mammoth Lakes informs me that the town is rolling back my contract to six months a year. He says the move is not performance related. He cites the financial pinch the town is under during the pandemic.

My immediate reaction: I can't abide that, I say. To me, this would be like asking a zookeeper to work from July to December, leaving the animals on their own the rest of the year.

I think about it for a few days, in hopes of gaining insights from friends and colleagues. I consult all the people I respect, consider their input, then turn in my badge. After a quarter century as the wildlife specialist of Mammoth Lakes, after thousands of wildlife calls, I am done.

Despite my departure, residents still call me with bear issues. In the case of the dead cub, I tell the woman to call the police. She says she already has. Two days later, they haven't responded, she says. The poor mourning mother is still there, unable to leave her cub. Coyotes have now discovered the situation and are eyeing the dead cub from a distance, growing bolder by the hour.

"OK," I say with a sigh. "I'll come take a look."

I drive over to find Mama still in the yard and the dead cub nearby on the ground. Three coyotes are there too, hoping to seize the opportunity. I call a buddy down at the station, and soon the Mammoth Police Department is there in force.

They jump out of their cruisers in full cannon mode, carrying AR-15 assault rifles, too lethal by half. To me, AR-15s are the worst weapon for bears, particularly in a residential environment where errant shots can pierce car doors or cabin walls.

"What do we do now, Steve?" the police ask.

"Screw you," I say. "Not my job anymore."

"But, Steve . . . come on, man . . ."

I look at the grieving bear. I look at the dead cub, the circling coyotes, the people out walking their dogs not even realizing they are in a possible line of fire if nervous cops start blasting. This is exactly the sort of dangerous standoff I was originally hired to prevent.

Yet, I left my job after the town downsized my role. If I continue to get them out of messes like this, where will that leave me? For one thing, I'll be legally liable if something goes haywire. I'll also be in danger, from the jittery cops more than the bears. I no longer carry a badge, so technically I don't have any legal authority to do any of this.

I shrug, sigh, shake my head, kick at the pine needles in the cold, rocky dirt. The bears are important to me. This town is my home. I still want what is best.

"Please, Steve," the sergeant pleads to me privately, off to the side.

As usual, empathy gets the best of me. I bend down and pick up a two-foot-long stick. Hardly a club, it's as big around as your index finger.

I bang it against the leg of my Levi's. "Get up the tree!" I yell as I walk toward her. "Get up the tree!" I tomahawk the branch at her, don't hit her, I throw it just to let her know I mean business. The mother bear scampers up the tree, leaving her dead baby behind.

The dead baby bear is tossed in the back of a truck, as the cops point their AR-15s at the mama in the tree, expecting her to fly out of the tree and pounce on them. Bears don't fly. They climb out of trees butt first, awkwardly and a little at a time. The cops back away tactically, as they're trained, like they're dealing with a terrorist.

Look, you can buy all the rifles in the Russian army. Doesn't solve your bear problems. Lethal force accomplishes nothing. In situations like this, the smart response requires experience, finesse, and a passion for bears.

With a simple stick, I'd chased the grieving mother bear up the tree and solved the situation, no gunpowder involved.

I look at the cops. "You're welcome," I say, climb in my truck and drive home.

Fortunately, I am OK at this point financially, even after the divorce. The least impacted by my departure will be me, the wildlife officer. I vow not to be afraid. From my bear work, I've already learned the debilitating effects of fear. I also try to manage my anger and my feelings of being wronged. By now, I know that being furious is a natural reaction for me. I also realize that fury solves nothing. It's like drinking poison and expecting the other person to die.

To my knowledge, there was never a council vote on the cutback in my schedule, never a discussion of the alternatives. Chief Al Davis and town manager Daniel C. Holler hire a replacement, then add a second guy. The *New York Times* does a piece about my departure. In the article, the Mammoth police chief says that the bears and residents of Mammoth Lakes will be fine since his officers are fully trained by me to handle wildlife encounters. Not true. I trained officers in the past, but the current staff is new, and I haven't worked with most of them.

Asked later about the decision, the town manager explains that Mammoth is more in need of officers who can write traffic and camping citations than a wildlife specialist. "We have a bigger problem of people leaving dog poop in the parks than we do with bears," he says even as complaints of bear encounters grow.

Incidentally, the town reportedly made more money that year than ever before.

You know, it seems like life piles up on you like this. Tragedy seems to work in sets of three. In that period, I lose all that is precious: my wife, my career, my status in the community. Sometimes life gets so sad that it becomes funny. Sometimes, it gets so sad it's just sad.

After the divorce, I couldn't just sit around feeling bad for myself. I decide to go to Mexico to feel bad for myself. I drive down to Punta Bonda, Mexico, walk the beach, lick my wounds, feel pretty sorry for myself. Hey, don't I have a right after Debs's stunning departure?

While I'm away, Mammoth's harsh midwinter weather strikes. A copper pipe breaks on the second floor of my house, sending twenty-three thousand gallons of water gushing across the interior for five days. The house becomes an aquarium, the original linoleum floors under my carpet making the place watertight. The walls bulge with ice . . . an igloo. The heavy-duty stucco blows out along the bottom of the house. All four exterior walls are destroyed, top to bottom. By the time the massive leak is detected, it's too late. Firefighters say they've never seen anything to compare.

Water even strips the ceiling beams, and the varnish pours down into my closet, ruining my clothes. In a ballcap, I'd kept an emergency fund with $10,000 in hundred-dollar bills. When I return, a friend and I peel the bills apart to dry them. I need the cash for groceries.

Everything I have left after the divorce is ruined—my photos, my personal records, pretty much anything I own and treasure. The flood breaks the dining room table in half. The couch is so waterlogged, so leaden, that they have to saw it in half to get it out the door. Human beings are defined by their possessions. It shouldn't be that way. Possessions are not your identity. But damn, it's sure nice to have a couch.

I move next door into the guesthouse. A friend with a construction business sends a team immediately, which works 24/7 on the substantial rebuild.

At this point, I have a broken heart and a broken house. On New Year's Eve, I have no one to kiss. On Christmas, I have nothing to open. Same on my birthday . . . I especially dread my birthday. A year ago, that was the day Debs told me she wanted a divorce.

My pity party grows. When we hit our lowest spots, we think we have the worst problems in the world, don't we? My attitude doesn't help. I behave badly, don't eat well, like an angry adolescent acting out. I don't bother to comb my hair. I just really don't care. Yep, I've managed to become my own problem, or at least exacerbated it. I've drunk the poison. My pals start calling me Eeyore, after the gloomy-sad donkey.

The coping skills that Shorty and the Paiute taught me—their toughness, their mellow, their humbleness, their gratefulness, their beautiful connection to nature—are nowhere to be found. I am a weak man. When I need it most, I can't summon a song.

Through all this, I'm still receiving letters and emails from fans of the reality show telling me how much they enjoy my work, which they run across online and in reruns. They tell me the show has helped them, changed their lives, taught them to be more tolerant of the things we don't understand. Instead of taking comfort in that, the mail becomes a tangible reminder of all that I've lost.

Remember my holy trinity of mental health? How there are three vital indicators of self-worth: the way you see yourself; the way others see you; the way you actually are? When those three assessments are closely aligned, you're in pretty good shape. When they are grossly out of whack, when the discrepancies are widest, you're in trouble.

At this point, you can't give me pep talks. This isn't some teachable moment. You can't soothe my wounds with platitudes such as "tough times make you stronger." These aren't problems that some mental trickery can overcome. My struggles are real. I am in trouble. I am in the darkest place. It starts to feel like midnight all day, quiet and lonely. In addition to Debs, my true love is the outdoors—always there for me. No judgment, only beauty. Yet, even the outdoors seems to be forsaking me at this point. I want to sleep—I want to drift off and sleep so the pain goes away forever. By the time the giant wildfire strikes, I am contemplating putting a pistol to my head.

CHAPTER THIRTY-TWO

THE CREEK FIRE CLOSES IN

As high winds continue pushing the firestorm through the canyons, the mood in Mammoth Lakes is brittle as the sagebrush. Those who haven't fled are wishing they had. My usually unflappable town—so tough during blizzards, so resilient at the harshest times—is in full panic.

Normally, this is a land of flickering campfires and starlight filtering through the pines. A campfire warms the heart, repairs the mind, makes the world whole again. In contrast, a roaring wildfire pings every nerve ending, stirs every fight-or-flight instinct we own. A forest fire miles from your home is an approaching Russian army.

The massive Creek Fire starts September 4, 2020, two months after my firing, in the midst of the pandemic, most likely sparked when lightning zaps a super-crisp pine tree. The town, still reeling from the pandemic, doesn't fare well. Employees are working from home, and it seems there is no rallying point, crisis center, or up-to-date information. Everything is happening too fast. Unlike in past fires, there are no reinforcements. Just an eerie quiet and a glow inching over the ridge.

With the fire closing in, I become even more fretful and despondent. I reflect on my life with the bears, with Debs and my adult son, Tyler, knowing that my family life and career are finished. My job situation isn't unique. Everyone's career ends sometime, and in the past few decades, fewer and fewer workers have been fortunate enough to leave on their own terms. Ageism is rampant. Early termination has become the natural order. Many employees don't make it to age sixty. I'm sixty-one. Why should I be any different? I lasted longer than many devoted employees.

Yet, no gold watch, no sheet cake, no hearty slaps on the back. In fact, quite the reverse: I am shunned. Anyone who is anyone in this city seems to be avoiding me. Did I do something wrong? If so, what?

My mind is all over the place, struggling to take this all in stride. It's not the end of the world, just the end of the paychecks. Besides, haven't I earned some time to myself by this point, away from bosses and late-night calls? This is how a career is supposed to wind down. Employees work their tails off for decades, then get to kick back to ponder and reflect and play . . . to do all the things that they really like to do. Well, all I ever had in life was my family and my work. And they are in the past tense.

Now—at my lowest point—the wildfires are bearing down, and my newly rebuilt little home, my sanctuary, virtually all that I have left, is in its path. Fire teams predict that the granite topography to the west of town will be our safety moat. But nobody really knows. In a firestorm, sparks jump rivers, firebreaks, and granite. A single ember can whirligig, jump a firebreak, land hundreds of feet away. With blowtorch winds behind it, that tiny sprig can quickly grow to engulf a hillside. And that's what happens at the San Joaquin River.

Oddly, we seem to have been forgotten by outside authorities. During the Rainbow Fire ten years earlier, a vast fleet of fire trucks showed up, stationed on nearly every block as part of a massive response to save the town. Water-dropping aircraft flew their sorties dawn to dusk; the roar was constant and reassuring. Not this time. We keep looking to the sky, hoping for help, waiting for the buzzing of aircraft, praying the heroes will arrive.

This is more than just my emotions getting the best of me, of life ganging up. The toxicity of the sooty air is quantifiable. The air quality levels, AQI, are usually indexed at 0–500, with 500 being the absolute worst, and reason enough to hunker down indoors. During the fires, our AQI reaches 1,616, more than triple the most hazardous levels. We spread wet towels across the bases of the doors and windows. In the morning, when air is usually at its freshest, our homes smell like giant ashtrays.

Through my front window, I see a bear on my front porch drinking from the water bucket I put out. He's eyeing me as he drinks. The world is cloudy, uncertain. Ash is in our noses, our teeth, under our eyelids. Mine, his, every living creature in town. It feels like the Book of Revelation—apocalyptic, and almost too nightmarish to be believed. It is a horrid real-life situation getting worse by the hour, no outside help in sight, the kind of emergency I always thrived on. In this case, I have no answers, no response, I am spent. Hero to zero.

Though it started forty-two miles away, the wildfire is now closing to within five miles of Mammoth. I race around in my truck, trying to find fresh information, running up to where I might see the edge of the fires coming through the canyon. On the shores of Lake Mary, I find more bears pushed out of the forest by the fires. As I noted, a deer will run till her lungs explode, dancing herself to death. Bears, as is their way, will mosey along just ahead of the fire, expending as little energy as possible, trying to keep up the weight they will need for the coming winter. Essentially, stomachs with feet, as I've said. Even in a crisis, they are all about the next meal.

Up at Lake Mary, the bears are behaving strangely, as if happy to have the company. Bears that I have never seen are coming up to me. "OK, good to see you too," I say, a little mystified. They are silhouettes against the burning orange horizon. The fire keeps coming.

And so do the bears.

I can be a slow and deliberate learner, we certainly know that by now. Maybe someone else would've seen the symbolism sooner, had a eureka moment, a breakthrough, an enlightenment. With me, learning often takes a little longer. I get there last, but I get there, solving puzzles one piece at a time. If nothing else in life, I've proven that I keep going no matter what.

Back home, the bear is still on my porch, looking at me while slurping water out of the bucket. New bears, big and small, are wandering my yard and the surrounding neighborhood, more than I've ever seen.

In fits and bursts, it finally dawns on me: for years, I was there for the bears; now I feel the bears have come to me. At the lowest point of my life, the creatures that taught me how to connect with nature seem now to sense my distress, to answer my 9-1-1 call. For years, I'd jumped out of bed to rescue and protect them. Now, were they here to rescue me? To get me to remember?

Breathe, Steve, breathe . . .

All along, bears seemed to have had a hand on my shoulder. Now, in the smoky alpine light, this lifelong allegiance becomes clearer and clearer to me . . . a kind of karma. Or maybe a redemption. I'm finally able to piece together this parable: a renowned rescuer, down for the count, now saved by his redeemers.

Bear magic, indeed.

As we know, important stuff always seems to happen on December 24. The birth of saviors. John Muir's death. The Treaty of Ghent. And on Christmas Eve 2020, four months after it began, the Forest Service announces that the Creek Fire is contained. Little by little, the winds shift, the fire burns itself out when it reaches that church-granite alleyway between Mammoth and Yosemite. Blessedly, the huge blaze sputters out before it can level my beloved town, though it smolders for months.

Since its September start, the Forest Service reports, the blaze has burned approximately 379,895 acres, destroyed 917 structures, cost $193 million to fight, wiped out countless ecosystems and food chains. At the time, it was the largest fire in the history of California.

Despite an exhaustive investigation, the cause of the fire is officially categorized as "undetermined," though lightning still seems the likely culprit.

Given time, and softened by the snow and rain, the blackened terrain will begin to green again, as forests always do. But how much time? Whether an act of God or climate change, forest fires are often portrayed as a necessary step in the life cycle of the wilderness. In truth, the West now has such monstrous and intense fires that they moonscape these areas, they sterilize them, the fires so searing that they wipe all life out of a forest. Compared to even a decade ago, forests now take much longer to heal and rebound. I blame antiquated federal policy and bad management that shuns any proactive measures.

To the spiritual lives of you and me, these monumental fires can be devastating. Long for the way the resin smells in your favorite campground, the whisper of pine needles in the wind? Well, stand by. Be patient. Because that could now take seventy-five years.

Increasingly, we're unlikely to live long enough to see a forest fully recover from one of these monster wildfires. In this case, the only animals that survive the Creek Fire are all the bears that rallied on my porch.

Without sarcasm, without a wry aside, or a self-effacing punchline, I want to tell you that I feel lucky to be alive today. I am so embarrassed to have reached that emotional low point. Yet, I am so grateful for every shred of light . . . the breezy friendships and the genuine concern . . . the camaraderie, the laughter, and the tears. All the slaps on the back I got but never paused long enough to appreciate.

Not just from friends and family. In this case—and especially—from the bears.

Over three decades, I served as liaison between nature and civilization. I've seen people cry over bears, I've seen people scared out of their shoes, I've seen people sing lullabies to bears, and pray over bears.

Through all this, I was the luckiest, most blessed person ever. Millions of us have spiritual voids, unable to voice what is missing from our lives. I am fortunate that my office was the woods, where I could look into the eyes of a buck or a bear on an almost daily basis. As it turns out, that is exactly what I needed.

When I did that—when any of us do that—are we looking at something even more magnificent than a simple forest creature? Does it change how you treat your kids, how you deal with neighbors, the way you pet your dog? People still write to me to this day about their wildlife encounters. For that moment, they didn't think about the credit card debt, or their nasty ex, or the bum knee that's soon going to need a surgeon's knife. For a moment, they feel the magic.

In the end, did I have a bigger role than the wildlife officer in Mammoth Lakes, California? I think I did. Who wouldn't be proud to devote a life to this masterpiece of American wilderness, once the picture-perfect backyard of Ansel Adams and John Muir.

At the time of this book's publication, Mammoth Lakes swirled with small-town drama. In January, longtime police chief Al Davis was led off in handcuffs after a suspected drunk driving incident, then left the department in February. Meanwhile, many residents were still calling for the town to rehire me, as the bears struggled in the aftermath of the worst winter on record.

On a grander scale, black bears continue to thrive in America. Their ranges are expanding. In response, more and more companies are offering nonlethal ammo than ever before. When I started, none of that was available. Lots of folks had a hand in it, but it has been a huge part of my mission.

Wild bears remain important to me, for the otherworldly ways they've enriched my life and the lives of millions of others. I hope my work with them is not over. But who knows? My prayer is that this little memoir allows my hard work to carry on through the years.

Because, as we've learned, bears deserve our understanding and respect. They are spectacular, near-mythic creatures. From them, I learned perhaps the most important life lesson of all, a lesson no human managed to deliver. Bears taught me not to fear the unknown. Unjustified fears are society's barbed-wire fence. They hold us back from being our best, fullest selves.

I hate fear. We all should.

EPILOGUE

Summer 2022. Nearly two years after the fires, COVID finally fading. Two hours south of town, they are holding an annual car race on abandoned runways across from the old Manzanar internment camp, a historic landmark along the long, arid highway from L.A. to Mammoth Lakes.

I'm here in support of car number 15, a pet project that doesn't fit in with the rest: number 15 is a chopped-down Subaru Forester wagon with a hood scoop and turbo engine, an outcast among the other gleaming race cars, one topping $160,000.

As I watch, my son, Tyler, the driver-mechanic of this four-wheel beater, finishes third, covering the two-mile slalom course in one minute, twenty-six seconds—four passes of flawless driving. I ride with him on the second of the timed trials. He takes third in his class, and his time would've placed him third in more competitive classes.

As I wander the site, all the guys and gals in the pits are talking about Tyler Searles, the speedy kid in the oddball Subie wagon.

You know, when I was a kid myself, I was always trying to get someplace faster than I should. I was doing adult stuff at thirteen, driving a car before I was sixteen, and drinking before I was twenty-one. I was always trying to fill my own boots, always feeling unworthy and inadequate. I think that propelled me to grow up too fast. I was running from my troubled childhood.

And as I grew older, one of my great fears was that I would be an unfit father. My own dad's behavior, the behavior of so many surrounding adults, made me worry that I didn't have the tools or the temperament to be a decent dad.

I worried that my entire life.

Now, here is my son, all grown. At twenty-three, he's exceeded all my expectations, managed his fears far sooner than I did—yet, like me, he basks in the role of longshot underdog, accomplishing more than anyone expected.

Like his dad, he pushed the pedal to the metal.

I let out my deepest breath. We made it.

BLACK BEAR TIP SHEET

Grizzlies are apex predators. Black bears are mostly interested in your Cheetos. Understandably, the two get lumped together. Here's what you need to know about the far more common black bear, found from the subdivisions of New Jersey to the hot tubs of Southern California:

THE MYTHS

"Don't run from bears": Stupidest advice in the world. They could not care less that you're running away. They won't pursue any food source. They're all about saving calories and keeping their weight up for the long winter ahead. A grizzly may chase you. A black bear rarely will.

"Don't make eye contact": Government brochures often say, "Don't make eye contact, divert your eyes." Hey, it's not the Virgin Mary. I want you to stare at the bear. I encourage it. You're going to do it anyway—it's impossible not to. In thousands of encounters, I have never seen anyone look away. It's a bear! To my knowledge, not once has that led to an attack.

"Never walk alone in the forest": They tell us to walk in groups. And to make lots of noise, ring bells, sing songs, so that you won't surprise them.

Trust me, the bears know you're in the forest a mile before you see them. They live there. Out of all my encounters with bears, I could count on one hand the number of times I've surprised them. In fact, for our mental and physical well-being, most of us need to walk alone in the forest. It's the Church of the Mountains.

"Don't go out in the forest if you're menstruating": Absolutely insane. Black bears are not carnivores. It's misogynistic to warn women away from the woods for this reason. It's not the bears that are out to hurt you; it's the creepy two-legged humans.

"Dogs attract bears": One of the reasons that we domesticated the wolf was to keep the bears out of our stuff. Once in a while, does it go wrong? Yes. But having a dog around is much better than carrying a handgun. I'll take a barking dog anytime.

"Put small children on your shoulders": That's a fear-based reaction with no justification. Instead, embrace the moment. Put your child's face as close as possible to your face. Say, "Hey, aren't we blessed?" Or get down on your knees to be at the child's level so you can share a moment you'll never forget.

THE REALITIES

"Don't feed the bears": Most bear problems are food related. A bear's prowess develops over time. He'll start with a day-use picnic site—easy food, sloppily stored. That goes so well, he'll raid a campsite, where he'll find even more grub. By now, he realizes humans don't do a thing besides take some photos. So, at that point, the bear might be emboldened to go through the open window of a condo or cabin. Point is, it takes time to build up their bad behaviors. What can you do? Hide stuff in car trunks out of view. Never hand-feed them marshmallows or treats. And perhaps most of all . . .

"Use bear lockers": Many drive-up campsites have bear-proof lockers in which to store your food. Never leave food—even scraps—out on a picnic table when you go off for even a short hike. Your Pringles will be gone when you get back, and the bear will be back the next day for more. Put anything with an odor into the lockers—toothpaste, roll-on deodorant, flavored aspirin. Who would eat a bar of Irish Spring? A bear would.

"Use bear canisters and bags": Backpackers who don't have access to lockers should use canisters and special bear bags to store food, away from the campsite. Black bears climb, so the current thinking is that storing canisters in trees is pretty useless. Note that bears can smell soup or corned beef through a metal can, so don't assume those are safe. To get at chili or hash, they will bite right through the heavy metal can.

"Bear spray works": For peace of mind, carry a big canister of pepper spray for bears (not human spray for muggers). Give one to everyone. Best thing in the world, way better than guns. If a cloud of spray blows back at you, you'll be in agony. Just remember: milk is an antidote.

"If you catch a bear in your stuff": If a bear gets into your cabin, just open a door or window so he can get out. At that point, he just wants to avoid you and go take a nap. If you find one in your campsite, yell and throw rocks to scare it off. The bear will be intimidated enough to turn and go. Then take stock of what you have left, and take proper precautions—food lockers, etc.—because he'll probably be back, as stray cats will if you feed them once. The real secret is to keep him out of the food in the first place.

—Steve Searles

ACKNOWLEDGMENTS

To anyone who told me I wasn't good enough, and even to those who told me I was. I probably wouldn't have made it without the love and support of my godfather, the late Larry Freeman. He and his dear wife, Mickey, and their son, Craig, were my lighthouse during the darkest days of my childhood.

To Debs—we had quite a run.

To all the officers and town officials who had my back through the years, especially Dan Watson. To Kevin Peterson—my sidekick, my Huck Finn—and one of the most capable men I've ever been around.

To Mammoth Lakes and its incredible residents, the best place in the world; I hope to never leave. To Stacey Bardfield for her long friendship and help in the proofing process.

Thanks to others who have helped me privately and professionally through the years, including Ralph Foster, Miriam Phillips, Glen Thompson, John Maloy, Alan Lancaster, my grandfather Homer W. Searles RIP, Shorty Stone RIP, Carol Stone, Thomas Stone, Ambie Stone, Coco Sly, and my entire sweat family.

To Suzanne Boone, Alex Siskin, and Watson for providing keen feedback on the manuscript. To my son, Tyler, of course, to whom I've dedicated this memoir, along with Chris's two sons, Christopher and Jack.

Finally, thanks to all the bears who left us—in life and in death—so many important lessons: Half Nose, Big, Center Street, One Ear, Ace, Arthur, Hemorrhoid, Blondie, Rasta, and all the rest. You were my professors. I will be forever grateful for all that we shared.

I hope readers feel blessed by the same bear spirit that blessed me.

—Steve